HARLEQUIN

HARLEQUIN

OR

*The Rise and Fall of a
Bergamask Rogue*

IO RINASCO

THELMA NIKLAUS

New York
GEORGE BRAZILLER, INC.
1956

Preface

As a theatrical producer with catholic tastes in entertainment, I am delighted to welcome this exhaustive and entertaining study of the progress of the clown Harlequin from his clumsy beginnings to his highly developed technical adroitness in Drury Lane spectacle. There are many—we may sometimes be inclined to think far too many—books written on Theatre. Yet for the many that need never have been written, there are always a few that add to our knowledge of the long history and tradition of drama. These are invaluable, for how else can we seize upon and preserve for posterity so evanescent a form, that dies and is reborn with every performance? For me, this book is among that select few, since it secures within its covers the total history of one of the most exciting theatrical figures ever conceived. Harlequin, and the Italian comedy in which he was generated, had a turbulent history and an immense influence upon drama, and later upon cinema and ballet, an influence persisting to the present day.

As an old friend, I am delighted that the author has successfully completed a work I know to be a very real labour of love. Some few years ago, when we were working together upon our joint study of Chaplin, we found ourselves discussing Harlequin: for it is impossible to touch upon the world of great clowns and mimes without finding Harlequin and Chaplin in juxtaposition. In that sense, it may be said that our joint effort led to this book; for this biography of Harlequin sheds light upon the universal kinship and appeal of all clowns.

Harlequin's form changed with the changing years: the coarse humour and elementary slapstick of his early days became the wit and acrobatic control of a later age, until he had turned into the shining dancer of pantomime. Yet throughout he kept in touch with the common man; Italian yokel, French gallant, English pantomime hero, he was one with his audiences, as are all great clowns.

Harlequin is rarely seen in these days of mammoth music-hall panto-mimes and super-colossal ice shows. Harlequin's slim shape would flit sadly lost among these ever more lavish displays. Yet perhaps his day will come again, when the ice has melted from people's eyes and they can enjoy once more the clowns whose comedy comes from within, and is not dependent upon elaborate props and tricks. Then will Harlequin dance back into his proper place in the centre of the lime-light. Meanwhile, we can be grateful for his story, told as it is here with charm, wit, and a rare understanding.

PETER COTES.

Contents

Illustrations

Introduction

FOR ME, drama is the most exciting manifestation of the human spirit, and its history the only one I can read without boredom or despair. To be a theatre addict, a somewhat different creature from a theatre-goer, is to give oneself over to an endless enjoyment, since the ramifications of drama are multitudinous and embrace all the activities, emotions, traditions, and vital impulses of mankind. If this seems a large claim, an examination of the origins of drama throughout the world will sustain it.

From such an addiction has come the present book. No theatre-lover could avoid falling under the spell of Harlequin, one of the most magical figures ever created. The four hundred years of his life cover a personal and a dramatic history as fascinating and as entertaining as any known in the theatre, where fascination and entertainment abound. Pantomime, where he reigned for so long, is perhaps frivolous: but it has a deeper significance, expressed so vividly by Théophile Gautier: 'Pantomime is true human comedy.... With four or five characters it covers the whole range of human experience. Cassander represents the family; Leander, the foolish and monied fop approved of by parents; Columbine, the ideal; Beatrix, the haunting dream, the flower of youth and beauty; Harlequin, with the phiz of a monkey and the body of a snake, with his black mask, his motley diamond-shaped patches, and his glittering spangles, embodies love, wit, mobility, daring, all the shining qualities and all the shining vices; Pierrot, pale, slender, in ghostly dress, always hungry and always beaten, is the slave of old, the present-day proletarian, the outcast, the passive and disinherited creature who, dejected and crafty, witnesses the drunken orgies and follies of his masters.'

Yet perhaps my grandfather should be held responsible for this book. At the end of the nineteenth century he danced Harlequin at

Drury Lane; and when he was too old to leap through windows, he carefully put aside his mask, his spangled tights, his soft heelless slippers, and his magic slapstick. They were kept in a chest containing a complete set of Harlequinade costumes. I well remember how, as a child, I loved to handle Columbine's crushed tarlatan and little rose-bud wreath; Clown's scarlet and white frills, his red-hot poker made of wood, and long string of pink cotton sausages. Yet even then the greatest pleasure came with the unfolding of Harlequin's tights, that sparkled in the sunlight with myriad little fires, as once they had sparkled in the spotlight of Drury Lane. The child I was knew nothing of Harlequin's strange genesis and history, nor ever realised that in that chest, smelling of camphor and grease paint, was locked away the end of an ancient story.

The costumes, the tinsel pictures, programmes, and playbills found their way to some ragman's barrow before I was old enough to claim them for my own. All I have of that collection, whose loss I shall always mourn, is a little brass figure of Harlequin in his early *commedia dell'arte* costume, only two inches high, and worn smooth by the fingers of my grandfather, who, so I am told, invariably touched it before he went on.

The seeds were sown by my grandfather; but they might have remained quiescent, had it not been for Nijinski. In 1950, when I happened to be in Paris, I went to the Musée de l'Opéra to see an exhibition of Nijinski relics, arriving some three weeks too late. The exhibition was on its way to America. Disconsolate I wandered down the long, narrow, dark room, hardly aware of the theatrical bric-à-brac with which it was filled. Then I found myself staring, for the first time, into the pin-sized eyeholes of Arlecchino's early mask: staring in fascinated horror at the sly, brutish features, the two flamboyant warts, the animal hair of this dark leather face. It was a shock to meet, without warning, the feral ancestor of the shining Harlequin for ever associated in my mind with the little black mask, the spangles, and the white frill I had played with in my grandfather's chest.

I hung over that dark mask leering up from the glass case, and began to wonder—where did Harlequin begin? How? Why?—Why the negroid face, the costume spattered with bright colour, the perpetual bat? That same day, in the library next to the museum, I pursued a chase after Harlequin as erratic and uncontrolled as his own pursuit of

Columbine in early pantomime, growing steadily more bewildered and filled with greater curiosity.

The search was baffling, and I might have relinquished it on my return to England. But in the spring of the following year I saw Festival Ballet's charming *Harlequinade*, a Victorian theatre-print come to life: and heard an American girl ask her neighbour, 'What *is* Harlequinade?' The neighbour had no idea. That was the moment that crystallised my determination to write the book I had been looking for, that would trace Harlequin's history from beginning to end, and answer some of the questions concerning him.

My decision took me on a pilgrimage as fantastic and entertaining as Harlequin's own. It has necessitated an excursion into the ancient theatres of Greece and Rome. It has covered all Europe and four centuries in time. I have pursued my quarry in the airy library of the Opéra, the claustrophobic depths of the Bibliothèque Nationale, the small fastness of the Arsenal, all along the quayside *bouquinistes* of the Seine, across the Channel and into the farthest corners of the British Museum reading room, the Victoria and Albert, and the fabulous collection of Ray Mander and Joe Mitchenson. I have pinned him down between the heavy covers of learned works, pursued him across the cheap paper of ill-printed pamphlets, and into faded scripts of ancient pantomimes. I have accompanied him into realms of farce, burlesque, mime, improvisation, drama, satire, parody, ballet; into literature, poetry, painting, and porcelain; discovered him at the royal courts of Europe, on the halls, in the market place, at the fair, and in the marionette booths. I have read the theories and disputes of scholars; and fallen prey to the falsity of the misinformed.

I know now that there is no end to such a pilgrimage: one simply calls halt at a given stage. For me, the journey is over now that I have found answers to my most urgent questions.

Familiarity with Harlequin's past has not destroyed the fascination, nor explained the enigma. Generated from a seed of universal humour, he is, from his loutish beginnings to his decadent end, so potent a theatrical concept that he still kindles the imagination. I hope that I have been able, in some measure, to convey his magical essence: for this book is at once a testament of fascination, and a requiem.

T. N.

Acknowledgements

I WISH to express my grateful thanks to Peter Cotes, for writing the preface to this book; to Miss Eleanor Farjeon, for permission to reproduce *Harlequin in Search of His Heart*, the Harlequinade from *The Glass Slipper*; to Clifford Williams (Director of the Mime Theatre Company), for allowing me to include his comedy *The Disguises of Arlecchino*; to Raymond Mander and Joe Mitchenson, for putting the resources of their theatre collection at my disposal; to Jean Cocteau, Duncan Grant, and Pablo Picasso, for their generous permission to reproduce their work; to William D. Handcock, Kate Hutchin, John Jump, Robin Mathewson, Joan Miller, Madame L. Weill-Guillardet of the Galerie du Pont des Arts, Monsieur René Varin, of the French Embassy, London, and especially to Robert Niklaus, for their advice and information.

I should like to record my appreciation of the courtesy and kindness of Mademoiselle Henriette Boschot (Librarian at the Opéra, Paris), Miss Norah Traylen (Stills Librarian, B.F.I.); and my debt to the Christie Library, Manchester; the Roborough Library, Exeter; and the Library of the University of Reading, for the extended loan of essential works of reference not otherwise available.

Acknowledgements to photographers and holders of copyright are given with the illustrations.

T. N.

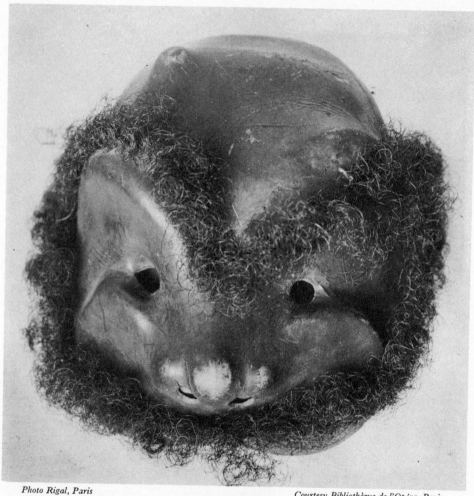

HARLEQUIN'S MASK

Eighteenth century

COMPOSITIONS
DE RHETORIQVE.

De M.' Don *ARLEQVIN,* Comicorum de ciuitatis Noualensis, Corrigidor de la bonna langua Francese & Latina, Condutier de Comediens, Connestable de Messieurs les Badaux de Paris, & Capital ennemi de tut les laquais inuenteurs desrobber chapiaux.

ARLECHIN.

IMPRIME' DELA' LE BOVT DV MONDE.

TRISTANO MARTINELLI (1553–1630)

A sixteenth-century engraving, reputed to be the earliest known representation of Arlecchino

PART ONE

---◄‹✳›►---

Arlecchino in Italy

CHAPTER ONE

The Ancestry of Arlecchino

HARLEQUIN is one of the most mysterious figures ever created, with a fascination that has endured from the Renaissance to the present day. Born in the theatre, he travelled all over the world during the four hundred years of his life, and into the realms of pottery, painting, poetry, literature, and sculpture, entering the world a rustic clown, and leaving it a poetic symbol.

It is difficult, but not impossible, to determine his ancestry; it would be foolish to be dogmatic about it, since much of it is wrapped in the mist of pre-history. It seems probable that all mimes, clowns, drolls, and mummers known to Europe were engendered by the Satyr of Greek Old Comedy, a form of entertainment derived from the phallic ritual and ceremonies of Dionysos, and existing, as far as it is possible to tell, from about 500–400 B.C.

The earliest known theatre forms show that the Greeks filled their stages with the ordinary folk of their cosmopolitan world. Characters drawn from life, from all classes of society, indigenous and foreign, were presented in popular comedy—wise men and fools, young girls and courtesans, heroes and pimps, merchants from Tyre and Phoenicia, magicians from Egypt and Persia, Chaldean priests, Scythian barbarians, African and Asiatic slaves, peasants, soldiers, doctors, magistrates, and the nobility. The slaves were always the clowns, and among them was one always known as the Young Satyr. His invariable costume was a dappled animal skin, a brown mask to suggest an African slave, and a white peasant's hat on his shaved head. He carried a small stick, and his legs and feet were bare. The Young Satyr was an acrobatic clown who leapt from heights, fell and turned cartwheels, showing unusual muscular dexterity even when drunk. He served his master with a minimum of discomfort to himself, set out to seduce every girl who came his way, ran in terror from soldiers and priests and, when he could no longer avoid it, defended himself against the onslaughts of wild beasts and his fellow-men with his ridiculous little stick.

When the Romans were developing their native drama, they came under Greek influence and borrowed largely from Greek theatre. The Young Satyr, adopted by the Romans, founded a large family of clowns—the *Sanniones, Lenones, Planipedes*, and certain *Histriones*.

Native drama in Italy sprang from the dialogue exchanged between two clowns wearing cork masks, part of the celebration of nuptials, or harvest-home, much as Dionysian ritual gave rise to Greek theatre. The clown's coarse and salacious patter, concerned wholly with fertility, propagation, and phallephoric humour, became known as Fescennine verse, a name derived either from *fascinium*, the male organ of generation, regarded as a symbol of fertility and magic in all folk-lore; or from the town of Fescennium, where harvest-home may always have been celebrated with such clowning.

To these native clowns Greek sources brought new impetus: and by about 400 B.C. Roman popular comedy was more or less established, the *histriones* having apparently mingled Fescennine verse with their own primitive shows to form the *Satura*, or *Fabulae Saturae*, simple farces of daily life.

It is impossible to be sure of the time of emergence of these early theatre forms in Greece and in Italy, since there is very little direct evidence to draw upon: and statements made at a later period by Roman or Greek writers are not necessarily infallible. Such evidence as there is shows a common pattern of evolution in those earliest beginnings and a strong Greek influence on the native Italian pattern.

Drama flourished particularly in Campania, where it would seem that rustic farces were regularly performed throughout the area to celebrate feast days and holy days, some two or three hundreds of years before Christ. These farces, as time went on, invariably contained easily recognisable stock types—the Clown, the Old Man, the Guzzler, the Ogre. They lasted well into the sixth century A.D. and were particularly well established in Atella, a little Campanian town nine miles from Capua along the road to Naples, and today known as Aversa.

Atellan comedy contained always the same traditional characters, coarse and gluttonous clowns with animal characteristics, who delighted their rural audiences with the frankest manifestations of drunkenness, greed, lechery, and cowardice. All wore masks of abnormal ugliness, with a traditional costume immediately recognised by the audience. Maccus and Bucco were the slave-clowns; Pappus the senile old man; Dossenus, a hunchback with prominent warts upon his mask, since many Campanians suffered from warts; and Manducus the Ogre with wide slavering jaws. All wore the grossly exaggerated leather phallus of the old Greek farces. The troupe improvised on a given theme, evolving as the show progressed plots of incredible complication. The basis of the comedy was the placing of each clown in an impossible situation—the cowardly Maccus in the army, the senile Pappus as a young bride—then to wring all possible humour from the incongruity.

The comedies dealt with the ordinary details of daily life, and the stage was peopled with bakers, fishermen, sailors, apprentices, and gladiators. The clowns were sometimes slaves serving masters of dubious character, sometimes tradesmen of a curious kind. The farces were essentially trivial, popular, and, like Fescennine verse, wholly given over to phallephoric comedy. As time went on, they became increasingly obscene and licentious, until the term Atellan became synonymous with scabrous.

The Atellan clowns, also known as *Planipedes* or flat feet, because they played downstage, near the audience, and did not wear the *cothurnus* or highboot assumed by tragic actors, were among those generated by the Young Satyr. There were others, the mimes, that were equally popular, and the oldest and most permanent of the actors of the Roman stage, present at the beginning of its known history, remaining until its end. Though Atellan comedy survived into the sixth century A.D., it was being supplanted by the pure mime about the beginning of the second century.

Originally the mimes played solo; later they gave dialogues with what we should now call stooges or feeds—the Fescennine clowns gave an early kind of mime show. Then came the inauguration of small companies of players, who travelled over Italy, giving simple performances in public places, on a rough platform, with a portable curtain for scenery. By about 200 B.C. these shows were regularly given at the Roman Games—*Ludi Romani*—which were being held with increasing frequency.

The social status of the mimes was, and remained, much lower than that of the Atellan comedians, who were often drawn from the gilded youth of the district, wealthy amateurs securely incogniti behind their great masks. Nor did their shows ever achieve a literary form, as the Atellan farces did in the first century B.C. But the element of indecency was common to both theatre forms; cuckoldry, sexual exhibitionism, shrewish wives, theft, and drunkenness were greatly to popular taste.

In each company the leading mime, the *Archimimus*, was almost continuously upon the stage, supported by the second lead, who played the clown, and by the rest of the company, who undertook whatever rôle the improvisation of the *Archimimus* might require. Mimes traditionally wore a patchwork jacket of several colours, padded tights or fleshings, and a gigantic phallus. Their feet were bare, their heads shaved, and their faces covered with soot.

These factors in antique drama have led many theatre historians to state that Harlequin was derived directly from the Young Satyr of Greek Old Comedy through the *Archimimus* of the Roman theatre and the clowns of Atellan farce. It is a tempting conclusion, but a little too facile. The emergence of European comedy through the mists of antiquity is, in its earliest forms, a matter of conjecture, inference, and analogy as much as of information, evidence, and fact. There are lacunæ in our knowledge of the development of the *Satura*, Atellan farce, and mime shows of pre-history, and an almost total lack of information concerning them after the Fall of the Roman Empire. In view of such uncertainty, it is impossible to be absolutely sure of Harlequin's derivation.

Yet there are haunting resemblances between Roman improvised comedy and the commedia dell'arte, into which Arlecchino was born. The shows given by the Atellan players and mimes were of the same genre as those in which he first appeared—a blending of farce and satire offered by a number of clown-types in traditional costume, interspersed with singing, dancing, and acrobatics. The Roman stage, with its three doors, each of which could represent a different house, seems to lead directly to the row of shops in the English Harlequinade many hundreds of years later, three in number, and essential to Harlequin's acrobatics until his death in the nineteenth century.

There are also strong resemblances between Arlecchino of the Italian Renaissance, and the many clowns of the Roman theatre. Bucco, from the Atellan farces, was stupid, rustic, and acrobatic. So was Arlecchino. The mimes wore a costume that comes strangely to life again in the earliest known representation of Arlecchino. Dossenus had a gigantic wart on his mask, an ill-natured comment on a Campanian ill. Arlecchino's mask was adorned with two warts. Evidence of costume is offered on vases from Herculaneum and Pompeii, as well as in literature. The Renaissance Arlecchino wore a phallus, which distinctive part of his costume had, a thousand years before, passed from the Greek *Phallophores* to the Roman mimes and the Atellan clowns. Both types of clowns traditionally wore masks or daubed their faces with soot, and shaved their heads, as their progenitor the Young Satyr had done. If Arlecchino can be derived from the latter, or his progeniture, we can reasonably explain his black and warty mask, his skull cap, and his variegated tunic, which otherwise remain mysterious.

There is, naturally, a legendary explanation of his costume. It is said that the god Mercury took Arlecchino under his special protection as, in earlier times, he had been patron of the *Sanniones*, the *Lenones*, the *Planipedes*, and all who belonged to the old family of clowns. Mercury bestowed magical power upon his protégé. Arlecchino was enabled to make himself invisible at will: to transport himself from one end of the earth to another in the twinkling of an eye: to reach the heights of Olympus, or penetrate into the depths of Pluto's dark kingdom. He was, moreover, endowed with Mercury's own winged grace, and godlike inscrutability: and so that all should know that he was under the protection of the God, he wore Mercury's own livery, as the Roman clowns had done before him. So Arlecchino acquired his multi-coloured tunic, symbol of the temperamental instability and dubious slickness of Mercury's protégés: and carried a stick as Mercury carried his caduceus.

Yet another explanation is given in the form of a naïve and enchanting French story. 'There was once a child called Arlequin who was so charming in person and in character that he was the joy and pride of his parents, and the delight of his teachers and school-fellows. His gentleness and his modesty were such that no one became jealous of his brilliance, his vivacity, and his physical powers.

'Now it was the custom of the time to bestow upon every child an entirely new outfit for Mardi Gras, when there was always merry-making throughout the district. Every child, boy and girl, enjoyed being dressed up in specially fine clothes once every year. Excitement mounted as the time grew near, and the children talked of nothing but the holiday, and the fine clothes they would wear for it. Arlequin listened to these endless discussions, but no one noticed that he took no part in them until one day his best friend said to him "What is your new suit going to be like?"

'"I shan't have one," said Arlequin. "My parents are poor, it would cost more than they can afford." Every single child was aghast at the news. Not one of them could bear to think of Arlequin, alone among them all, wearing his old clothes for Mardi Gras. They consulted together and agreed that each should give him a piece of the cloth from which their own new clothes were being made.

'The following morning each one, bursting with joy and excitement, came to Arlequin. But as they saw him standing there bewildered, clutching crimson and blue and yellow and green silks and satins and brocades, they realised how stupid they had been. Not one colour matched another, not one piece was big enough to make any part of a suit for him.

'Arlequin, seeing their sudden distress, reassured them. He told them how delighted he was with their present, particularly since every one of the many pieces represented a friend.

'The great day arrived. Arlequin put on the multi-coloured suit his mother had made him from the beautiful pieces, and since it was carnival time, he covered his face with a black mask, pinned a rabbit's scut to his everyday grey felt hat to make it more splendid, snatched up his toy wooden sword, and ran off helter-skelter through the village, leaping and twisting and dancing for joy, joking and singing and laughing, the gayest of them all, for he was entirely clothed in the love of his peers.'

From the mixture of facts, surmise, legend, and folk-lore in which Arlecchino's ancestry lies tangled, a probable but not a certain explanation can be drawn.

We have no evidence of direct derivation. We have evidence of curious resemblances. It is possible, though not verifiable, that when the fall of the Roman Empire in the fourth century A.D. dispersed the mimes and made wanderers of them, they carried with them wherever they went their traditional costume and technique, though, as time passed, they no longer knew why they wore many coloured patches or put soot upon their faces, or shaved their heads. It is known that Byzantine mimes of the Eastern Empire were faithful to the antique tradition that arose in the West. It is probable, though not verifiable, that when, with the fall of Constantinople in 1453, they left the Eastern Empire and emigrated to Italy, they brought with them a recognisable form of the old stock types in their traditional costume, whose long-forgotten origin still set the pattern.

Such continuance of tradition in scattered parts of the known world would explain the mystery, but there is no record of it.

No final decision can ever be reached concerning the ancestry of Arlecchino. Antiquity yields the prescience of his future incarnation, his germ is present in those ancient times, and was carried through the centuries, even through the thousand hibernating years between the decadence of Rome and the Renaissance.

The pattern of humour, as of human experience from which it is drawn, is repetitive. The comedy of Ancient Greece and Rome, of Mediaeval England, Renaissance Italy, or modern France, shows the same stock types, as it reveals the common origin of clowns. But Arlecchino cannot be wholly explained by this. He transcended all other clowns, as he transcended his fellow masks in *commedia dell'arte*. They all perished, to be recreated in other times, in other countries. Harlequin alone cast off his kinship with ancient tradition, and survived to become finally the enigmatic personification of the life force.

CHAPTER TWO

Background to the Birth of Arlecchino

THE downfall of the theatre of the ancient world was brought about primarily by two factors: the decadence of the Western Roman Empire, and the hostility of the increasingly powerful Christians. Christianity, after centuries of martyrdom, was now triumphant; and the dignitaries of the new Church were wholly opposed to the obscene forms of entertainment popular with the rabble. Religious opposition, together with economic instability, political unrest, and the impact of a vigorous Germanic pattern of civilisation upon a dying Roman culture, served to send drama underground. For the years of its disappearance, following the fall of Rome, and lasting until the capture of Byzantium in 1453, there is little record to show in what forms, and in what places, it survived.

Certain factors in the history of the formation of early modern Italian Theatre are relevant to the history of Harlequin. The gradual process of the breaking-up of the Roman Empire entered upon its final phase when in 1453 Byzantium fell at the hands of the Turks. The conquerors brought their Ottoman civilisation to the Eastern Roman Empire; and there were many in Byzantium who fled before this Turkish invasion. These sought sanctuary in centres well disposed to receive them—Venice, Mantua, Florence. They brought their eastern scholarship and aesthetics to the west, where already the inevitable progress of the Middle Ages, stimulated by the clash of opposing cultures, was moving towards the dawn of modernism. The advent of the refugees from Byzantium contributed to the ferment of the Renaissance, with its revival of the classic arts of Greece and Rome.

At first sight, the impact of the Renaissance upon Italian Theatre is disappointing, as though classicism in drama were as stultifying in the theatre as it was inspirational in the other arts. Hackneyed imitation of Geeek tragedy, bawdy and inferior copies of the comedies of Terence and Plautus, imitations of Menander's plays abounded, none with any originality of technique or dialogue, most much lewder than their prototypes.

Yet, almost hidden under the avalanche of imitative plays, there were signs of the establishment of a literary comedy that lifted the drama emerging from its long years underground to a higher level of construction and presentation, if not content. In 1508 Bernardo Dovizio, generally known as Bibbiena, after the little town near Arezzo where he was born, presented his play *Calandria* at Urbino. The play was classical in construction, but it was not an adaptation or imitation from Greek or Roman comedy. The humour depended upon an extraordinary resemblance between a brother and sister, and their adventures and misadventures in male and female dress.

In the same, or possibly the following year, Ariosto's *Cassaria* was also presented, in the author's native town of Ferrara. Ariosto followed closely the Latin pattern of play construction, and his play depended for the working of its plot upon pairs of valets, girls, lovers, and upon the wiliness of the servants and the amours of their masters.

A third member of the small group that contributed vitally to the evolution of erudite comedy was Aretino of Arezzo. His plays were inevitably based upon the accepted classical pattern; only he added a study of the characters of people to the presentation of their actions, and so prepared, in a minor way, for a national drama different from the Greek or Roman.

The greatest of the founders of this literary comedy was Machiavelli, whose play *La Mandragora* was shown in 1520, and printed in Rome four years later. *La Mandragora*, which immediately achieved a great reputation for its obscenity and immorality, is in fact a careful social study of the customs, morals, and thought of the period. Since Machiavelli not only accepted but practised all the vices of his age, he offers in the play a witty and unbiassed chronical of the more scabrous aspects of daily life. It is a comedy of corruption, the more powerful for its scholarship and classicism.

Erudite comedy carried within it the seeds of quick decay. It began as imitation, and remained a sterile form, in spite of the intellectual brilliance of its major exponents.

The vitality necessary to the formation of national drama came from another source. Out of the ferment of the Renaissance in Italy grew a form of popular theatre bearing, in its earliest days, strong resemblances to Atellan farce and the mime shows of ancient Rome. It had its own family of masked clowns, wearing traditional costume, who improvised comic sketches on a given theme—the deception of a master, the cuckolding of a husband, the courtship of a serving wench, the theft of a barrel of wine. Jugglers, dancers, singers, and acrobats performed between sketches, and the show given must have been very like a primitive form of modern variety.

The origins of this native comedy are obscure. A living tradition of popular comedy, driven underground in the fifth century, may well have persisted into the sixteenth century; for though there is little direct evidence either to support or refute the idea of persistence, the resemblances between this early native drama and that of the ancient world are undeniable. It is possible that these are due to the Byzantine mimes, known to have remained faithful to antique tradition, who fled before the Turks to the welcoming shores of Italy, and brought back a form of theatre long since forgotten. Maybe, as erudite comedy was based upon classical imitation, so popular comedy was an imitation of Greek and Roman mime, brought about by the revival of classical learning. Since mime was unscripted, and its technique transmitted from player to player, such imitation could only be achieved by means of accurate and extensive documentation, surviving the cataclysms of the fifth century. There may have been such documentation: if so, it has since disappeared and left no trace.

Given such obscurity as to its source, it is impossible to determine the exact date of the emergence of this comedy: but since it was flourishing early in the sixteenth century, it may well have arisen in the preceding one, and possibly be linked with the fall of Byzantium. It received many names as it grew in popularity, and was carried all over Italy by the troupes of strolling players that sprang into being with astonishing rapidity, being known as *Commedia Improvvisa* (improvised comedy), *Commedia non Scritta* (unscripted comedy), *Commedia a Maschera* (masked comedy), or *Commedia dell'arte all'improvviso* (professional improvised comedy), which last form, shortened to *Commedia dell'arte*, ousted all the others.

By the middle of the sixteenth century, commedia dell'arte was known throughout Italy. It was a strong, vital form of national drama without any literary or artistic pretensions, enjoyed at a low level of entertainment. Erudite comedy, by that date, was already finished. There had been no successors to Machiavelli and his fellow scholars able to carry the genre another step or bring to it enough creative fire to overcome its barrenness. It seemed that the literary impulse of Renaissance drama was already expended, with nothing to take its place.

It was then that scholarly playwrights, influenced perhaps by the crude vivacity of commedia dell'arte, and by its conquest of the people, turned away from the classical pattern, abandoned erudite comedy, and began to seek both theme and character in realistic aspects of rural and provincial life, an extension of Aretino's earlier insistence on the development of character in his own erudite comedies. Such choice of background and character brought literary comedy nearer the people, and offered fecund inspiration to its writers.

It was left to Angelo Beolco, known as *Ruzzante* (the Joker) and once described as 'a sort of Italian Shakespeare', to bring about a fusion of the two forms of comedy, and so in time to found one of the most original forms of native drama ever known. By birth, talent, and type of intellect Beolco, a man of culture and distinction, belonged to the small group of *littérateurs* who had written and presented the erudite comedies: by inclination and temperament, he belonged to the troupes of strolling players who gave their improvised sketches in the market squares or the courtyards of inns. He was in his own person the incarnation of the fusion of national genius with antique tradition.

Improvised comedy necessarily depends for its style and artistry upon the type of actor engaged in it. Actors of little wit, less culture, and poor technique dragged it down to the lowest levels of threadbare entertainment, and the form would rapidly have died out had it been left in inferior hands. By 1528, Beolco had gathered round him a band of dilettanti passionately interested, as he himself was, in the theatre. For the first time the mind and spirit of men of culture were brought to bear upon popular comedy. Beolco was the first of the long line of distinguished men who set their mark upon commedia dell'arte, and transformed it from crude charade into one of the subtlest and wittiest forms of theatre ever known; vital enough to endure for three hundred years, entertaining enough to appeal to all classes of society in all European countries.

He and his circle polished native crudity with scholarship, and gave dramatic shape and impact to the unwieldy sketches. Philosopher, actor, writer and man of letters, enkindled by the Renaissance, he was peculiarly qualified to understand the implications of this most original form of comedy struggling for expression, and to seize upon and develop its potentialities.

At an early stage of its emergence, commedia dell'arte had derived part of its humour from the caricature of regional characteristics, in much the same way that Harry Lauder and Will Fyffe delighted their audiences with their canny Scotsmen: or George Formby with his Lancashire Lad, and Issy Bonn with his volatile Yid. Beolco developed this original factor. The stock characters in his troupe grew in number and in kind, until every region in Italy was represented in commedia dell'arte by a type who, based upon reality, soared to ridiculous heights of fantasy and caricature. Each type spoke the dialect, wore a theatrical version of the costume, and assumed the outstanding characteristics of the region that gave him birth. Audiences had the double amusement of seeing themselves as others saw them; and of mocking their neighbours.

Beolco's literary and classical background enabled him to apply balance and harmony to the unkempt improvisation, to build the sketches to a climax and to preserve an artistic balance between their component parts, in such a way that his rustic and fantastical types entered naturally into their classical setting. The comedy was still improvised: but improvised with artistry, and awareness of dramatic values, with such success that Beolco's treatment was imitated, and put to good use among the better troupes of his time. His comedies were simpler in theme and broader in treatment than those of con-temporary writers of erudite comedy or the literary forms of rustic farce: and the characters were wholly native. By 1560 commedia dell'arte was established in all its essentials, shaped by time and Angelo Beolco into a theatre form worthy to take place beside literary comedy. For the next fifteen years it was acclaimed through-out the whole of Italy. The people flocked to the shows, the troupes enjoyed the patronage of wealthy nobles, and even of the Church, while that patronage, and the distinction of many of the actors playing in commedia dell'arte, conferred upon them a special prestige never before granted to strolling players.

Among the first created clowns, or masks, of commedia dell'arte was Arlecchino. We shall never know how he acquired his name, phonetically so descriptive of his person. It was maybe a dialect form of *al lecchino*, gourmand or greedy guts, for the primitive Arlecchino was a glutton. There is in it perhaps a trace of the *harle*, a little darting bird with bright plumage, and more than a trace of *Alichino*, legendary demon who rose from the infernal regions at the head of a diabolic throng, to haunt and ravage the countryside, riding the night wind and striking terror in the hearts of those who saw or heard him. If Arlecchino were indeed originally Alichino, then the name was satirically applied to the simple yokel of early commedia dell'arte, in whom was the very antithesis of diabolism. His name may have some or all or none of these connotations: it may be the corrupted form of some term long since fallen into disuse. We can, if we choose, fall back upon Arlecchino's own explanation in an early farce:

> *Cinthio (to his new valet)* By the way—what is your name?
> *Arl.* Arlecchino Sbrufadelli
>
> > *Cinthio bursts out laughing.*
>
> There's nothing to laugh at! My ancestors were
> very respectable. The first Sbrufadelli made
> such excellent sausages that Nero would
> eat no others. His son Fricolola married the
> beautiful Castagna, such a vivacious girl that
> she was brought to bed with child only two
> days after her marriage. I was that child, and
> my father worshipped my beauty, my grace, and
> my wit. Or would have done, had he not been
> compelled into a moonlight flit when I was four
> days old—over a little disagreement with a
> bailiff, a tailor and a notary. He saddled his
> donkey, threw me into one saddlebag, his worldly
> goods in another, and set off at as brisk
> a pace as the donkey would allow. He was
> a sensitive man, an artist, and every tree
> and bush concealed an enemy, waiting to
> leap upon him. Or so he thought. And in
> his terror he called out, all the way along—

'Ar! lé chin! Ar! lé chin!' (Get on! He's crouching to
spring!). In the morning he
laughed at his terror, fished me out of the
saddlebag, put me right way up and with
his last bottle and his last breath christened
me Arlecchino. Hence my unique and distinguished
appellation, Arlecchino Sbrufadelli, at your service.

Whatever the source of his name, Arlecchino was born a citizen of
Bergama, a little town nestling among the hills of the Brentano
valley. The town falls naturally into two parts, Upper and Lower
Bergama. It was said that folk from Lower Bergama were always
fools, while Upper Bergama produced the wise boys. Each part of
the town produced a clown for commedia dell'arte, and both were
valets—Arlecchino from Lower and Brighella from Upper, Bergama.

Arlecchino then was born a fool: yet, from the very beginning of
his career, he showed signs of having been born in the wrong place.
The dullness of his wit, the stupidity of his repartee, the ease with
which he was gulled, the difficulty of making him understand the
simplest demand, his gluttony and his cowardice, were exactly what
everyone expected from a son of Lower Bergama in the fifteenth
and sixteenth centuries. Only his doltishness was shot through with
divine folly: and though his mind was static and clumsy, his body was
agile and dexterous, as witty as his brain was dull.

His birth was attended by ghosts. It was as if he stepped straight into
a rôle and a costume that had been waiting centuries for him. The
controlled exuberance of his movement, the violence, coarseness, and
horseplay of the scenes in which he took part, the outrageous lengths
to which he would go to raise a laugh or point an obscene jest, are
inevitably reminiscent of his putative ancestors, the *Planipedes* and
mimes of ancient Rome.

From the beginning he was a fully developed personality. Beneath
his half-witted gropings to understand the wily schemes of his half-
brother Brighella or his other sharper companions, beneath his evident
terror of almost everyone and everything, beneath his greed, his
lewdness, and his animal humour, there lurked an insolent and
mocking spirit, so far held in check, but waiting for release.

His rôle was that of the stupid and clumsy valet, faithful to his
master and his master's schemes, provided faithfulness cost him nothing

nor brought him into danger. Gluttonous, cowardly, amoral, ready to stick a finger in any pie, run from any danger, compound any felony, undertake any imposture, and lie with any woman who would let him, he was not a likeable fellow: yet one drawn to an eternal and universal pattern, and thereby rousing echoes in the minds of average men. There are other echoes. Arlecchino the valet in the feral black mask is very like the Young Satyr in character, costume, and even the type of rôle he played, for the Young Satyr was a slave who gave dubious service to his master.

Arlecchino was immediately one of the most popular of the clowns, and in a very short time became the leading player, round whom the sketches were built. In spite of his many doubtful qualities, there was something in his simplicity, his willingness to be duped, his lack of success in any of his undertakings, his frequent discomfiture, that was endearing enough for the public to forgive him his sins, sympathise with his sorrows, and enjoy to the full his lewdness. Moreover, even when his vices were most apparent, they were amply compensated for by his dancing, his acrobatics, and his delightful clowning. His body was as civilised as his mind was primitive, and it illumined his shoddiest dealings with his master, his fellow valets, or his current light o' love. That was already part of his enigma.

The earliest known illustration of Arlecchino is to be found in a curious little book published early in the seventeenth century: *Les Compositions de Rhétorique de M. Don Arlequin*, by Tristano Martinelli, the Harlequin of a troupe that was brought to Paris by Henri IV in 1600. On the title page he appears wearing a long, loose tunic and tight trousers covered here and there with large irregular patches. His jacket is untidily laced in front, and caught in at the thighs with a belt holding his purse and his wooden sword. His head is shaved, and he is wearing a cap of the time of Francis I or Henri II, with a rabbit's scut in front, while his whole face is masked in black. The effect is dual: of jaunty poverty, combined with dramatic strangeness.

Perhaps the most mysterious part of the young Arlecchino was his mask, without which he was a clown like any other. There is something undeniably sinister and terrifying about his mask, even as it lies quiescent under the glass of a museum table. Nearly everyone who describes it, having seen and handled it, describes it differently:

Agnan.	La Laictiere.	Harlequin.

Verrier traiſtre & larron, puis q̃ tu ne veux rẽdre,
Mon alleſne qu'as priſe ainſi que bien ie ſçay,
Ie te feray le ſon de ceſte flute entendre,
Et dancer à ton dan pour premier coup d'eſſay.

Dancerai-je touſiours, que veut dire ceci?
Mes œufs ſõt tous caſſez, & mõ lait eſt par terre
Maudit ſoit le Berger cauſe d'vn tel ſouci,
Et de ſa flute auſſi le ſon qui me fait guerre. ij.

Ne ſone plus (Berger) humbleſṁẽt ie t'en prie,
Ie re ren ton alleſne & me delaiſſe en paix,
Mes verres ſont rompus, dõt par grãd faſcherie
Me faudra demeurer pauure pour tout iamais.

ARLEQUIN UN PEU GRISÉ
Recueil Fossard. Sixteenth century

Harlequin. Zany Cornetto.

Non, non, n'estime pas en courant en barbet,
En clabaut ou mastin, me rauit Fracisquine,
Ie veux estre pendu maintenant au gibet,
Si plus viste que toy sur les mains ne chemine.

Ie fay l'arbre fourchu, portant les pieds en l'ær,
Pour (dispost) triompher en si haulte conqueste
Et toy plus l'ourd qu'vn Ours, ne sçaurois reculler,
Ny aller en auant, tant tu és grosse beste.

Dy ce que tu voudras, ie seray des premiers
Au cõbat amoureux, que sur tout ie pourchasse,
Il n'est chasse en tout tëps õ de bõs vieux limiers,
Qui sçauët des cõnils le terroir & la trace.   iiij.

ARLEQUIN ACROBATE
Recueil Fossard. Sixteenth century

every drawing or engraving shows fundamental differences: almost as though, in spite of its rigid detail, it called to different things in different men. Brutish, negroid, cunning, sly, atavistic, sardonic, feline, are among the varied terms employed to qualify it. All of them apply, and none convey the effect, at once sub-human and superhuman, of the black half-mask with its warts and pin-head eyeholes and chinstrap of coarse black hair.

Arlecchino's complete presentation is one of the most perfect costumes ever conceived for the theatre, conveying immediately the mystery of his generation, the enigma of his personality, the haunting resemblances to ancient tradition, and his own prosaic, rustic reality. If his mask is not to be derived from the sooty faces or African masks of the phallophores and mimes, then it is terrifying in its implications, with its thick coarse brows over deep eye-sockets, with the heavy furrows along the narrow forehead outlining the astonished brow, the heavy pouches under the minute eyeholes, the vivid impression of sensuality and cunning, of diabolism and bestiality. It is repulsive and attractive. It takes us far beyond the Satyrs and the African slaves, into the darkness of mankind's primal imagination, back to the primitive emergence of man from beast, reminding us that the beast still lurks within the man.

Closely linked with Arlecchino was his brother and complement, Brighella of Upper Bergama, who was destined to play a vital part in the shaping of Arlecchino's character and fortunes. He also was a valet, and wore a livery of white banded with green, a short cloak, a green and white cap, carried a well-filled purse and had a sharp dagger in his belt, a symbol of the roistering, truculent clown he was. His costume was as straightforward as Arlecchino's was mysterious: his mask, of a dingy yellowish-green, gave him the cynical expression of a man for whom life holds no more surprises. His slanting eyes, great hooked nose, thick and sensual lips, ferocious beard and upturned moustaches made a fearsome, if raffish, figure of him, powerful and unpleasant.

His brazen assurance carried him victoriously through his career of confidence trickster and hired bully. He was the interloper, the braggart, the eavesdropper, stealthy and sinister in his comings and goings, boding no good for anyone who came in contact with him, and always ready to sell his honour, his master, or his mother's coffin for the price of a drink. Originally Bergamask, he emigrated to Naples, where his countless ill-gotten progeny followed in their father's footsteps.

Both Arlecchino and Brighella were dancers and acrobats, the first with the suppleness of a cat, the latter with the antics of a monkey. Both were always ready to scheme, lie, trick, cheat, and seduce. The difference between them was in their intentions. Arlecchino was too simple to know what he did, too stupid to realise where his action would lead him. Brighella always knew exactly what he was doing, and what the result of his action would be. He took a savage delight in scoring off a friend or an enemy, in making trouble, in committing crimes. While Arlecchino was always amazed at the consequences of his own blunders, Brighella's villainy was conscious and purposeful.

Together they enlivened the earliest improvisations of commedia dell'arte, bad servants of doubtful masters, and as entertaining in their roguery as they were with their dancing. From the beginning, Arlecchino was the pivot of each sketch given: and though Brighella worked closely with him, he never shared Arlecchino's universal popularity. When the number of clowns became legion, Arlecchino still held first place, while his brother was all but lost among the many valet-types that had been created.

CHAPTER THREE

The Masks

THROUGHOUT the world, drama was born with religion, from the awareness of the mystery of creation, and its symbolisation and worship in ritual. The sources of life were unknown to primitive man, and all manifestations of vital force—the upthrusting of the young plant, the coming of night and day, the radiance of the sun, the flame of fire—were magical. The Dionysian revels, the Fescennine festivals, were examples of the way in which he strove to express the mystery, propitiate the magic, and secure his own preservation. Phallic worship, fertility rites, fire and sun worship were all part of a reaching towards the idea of divinity as a means of explaining the unknown. Offerings were brought to representations of the phallus: blood was sprinkled over the fields: the coming of rain was mimed in times of drought: and the sun incarnated and worshipped. Good harvests, good hunting were essential to the continuance of life: the fertility of the soil was linked with the fertility of man, and those who took part in the ritual called upon symbolic magic to secure and protect them.

The primitive man who clothed himself in an animal skin, and placed the carved head of a beast upon his own, had no other intention than that of gaining power over the beast by assuming its likeness and so bring about a good day's hunting. Yet the putting on of the carved head was deeply significant apart from that intention. The first mask had been assumed, and because of its primary association with magic and ritual, it remained enigmatic.

The mask of all primitive rites was potent in three ways. It gave the wearer magical powers over the creature whose likeness he assumed: it released his own personality, by concealing it beneath another that was different: and it was a symbol of the universal

awareness of godhead: of creative power, understood first in its phallic
term, and then to cover the mystery of the universe.

With its extended use in antique drama, it assumed other functions
but never lost its divinity. The mask of ancient tragedy not only concealed the ordinary features of the actor, and obliterated his own
personality by that of the character he represented, but gave him an
objective reality greater than himself or any man. It forced his audience
into a conception of beings upon whom the passions and emotions of
humanity seized with more force than in ordinary life.

With this specialised use in the theatre went the assumption of
masks at religious festivals, as when men covered their faces with
vine leaves to honour the great god Pan. Of equal significance was the
presence of the *archimimus* at funerals, wearing the recognisable mask
of the dead person, and enacting the major deeds, both good and bad,
of the life now brought to its close: a form of dramatic obituary.
Throughout these early times the wearing of the mask, outside the
theatre, was linked with the cult of life and, in the case of the funerary
mime, with its obverse, the cult of death.

As well as the religious connotation of the mask, there is its influence
upon the release of personality, whether in the dramatic sense or in
ordinary life. It was soon realised that the assumption of a mask implied
concealment of identity: and that such concealment offered liberation
from oneself. A man in a mask was anonymous, and since he was not
himself, had no obligation to respect the limitations of his own
character. Masks came to be worn for discretion's sake in the conduct
of amorous or political intrigue. Human nature being what it is, the
freedom thus conferred soon degenerated into licence, and masks were
found useful to the concealment of crimes, scandals, and disorders of
all kind. Their wearers were protected by the inviolability conferred
by the association of the mask with religion and with the concealment
of personality. Any extravagance of speech or behaviour could be
forgiven a man who wore one, since it came, not from him, but from
the unknown. To lay hands upon a mask was a grave social offence:
to unmask a woman against her will an infamy. The privilege of
anonymity became sacrosanct, since men are free only when they have
lost their identity: and there were many petty criminals ever ready
to take advantage of the fact, with no knowledge of the reason for it.

These considerations are all relevant to any study of commedia dell'arte, since it is the only form of masked theatre known to modern Europe. Its originality was largely due to that one factor: for though its characters were drawn from all the ordinary sources of mirth, were real and human persons in whom normal characteristics had developed abnormal proportions, wearing a dramatised version of ordinary dress, their mask added a special quality that made each one unique.

There was, for example, Pantalone, one of the four primary characters, and based on one of the figures of fun of all time—the old man driven to unbelievable indiscretion by the last flickerings of senile passion, a creature fit to be scorned and derided, cheated and deceived, a very easy prey to any rogue through his greed and his concupiscence. Pantalone represented the middle-class Venetian merchant of his time. He was sometimes wealthy, sometimes poor, but always avaricious. If he were married, he was cuckolded; a widower, he pursued young girls who invariably married younger and more personable men. His valet deceived him, and so did his mistress: his friends plotted among themselves to destroy his hopes or his fortunes: and he always saw the ruin of all his plans, amorous, matrimonial, and monetary. He shuffled across the stage in his Turkish slippers, his withered shank cruelly exposed in scarlet tights, his black or purple gabardine flowing out behind his lean anxious body. He wore the tall, red woollen cap of the Venetian merchant: and, in his earlier days, a dangling leather phallus, the subject of much pertinent joking among his fellows. So far, he was a commonplace clown derived from a specific town.

His mask took him into another category. It was aquiline, brown in colour, with long drooping moustaches and a thin pointed beard that gave him a lean and hungry look. It was enough to see him flap across the stage to receive the vivid impression of a bird of prey, for ever seeking carrion, restless and alert. Basically, Pantalone was the carica-ture of a typical elderly Venetian. As such, he was immediately recognised by his audience, who were as amused by his exaggeration of regional characteristics as they were by his presentation of a silly old man with one foot in the grave and one eye on a pretty wench. With the assumption of his mask, everything in him that was ordinary and familiar became strange and unknown. His costume, in con-junction with the lean and stylised brown face, ceased to be commonplace and became fantastic. It was as if a fusion of elements had taken place, resulting in his emergence as a fixed figure—ageless, timeless, and extraordinary. Once this fusion was achieved through the wearing of the mask, the more he maintained his normal human qualities in his rôle, the more inhuman and fantastic he appeared. To the familiar humour of his character was added the mysterious humour of his unique personality, grafted on him with his mask.

And so it was with all the other clowns of commedia dell'arte, whether they played leading or minor rôles. Pantalone, Arlecchino, and Brighella were already present in the earliest known forms of the comedy, with Il Dottore making the fourth. The Doctor, born in the shadow of the University of Bologna, if not upon its doorstep, was another elderly type, wearing his black academic dress with the same sinister effect as Pantalone, two old crows in a flock of parrots. He was a member of all the learned societies of his native city, a doctor of law originally, although later in the seventeenth century he became one of medicine. He is the pompous bore, the hollow pedant who lays claim to learning he does not possess. His Latin, in which tongue he often expressed himself, was excruciatingly bad: his knowledge of medicine, extremely dangerous to his patients, while his earlier acquaintance with the Law was so misguided that his clients invariably lost their cases even if they did not find themselves in jail, following his advice. When he was not showing off his Latin tags, inanities couched in terms of great scholarship rolled from his tongue in a rich Bolognese accent. Like his friend Pantalone, he was miserly and amorous: and as his public speeches sent his audience to sleep, so his amorous advances were received with yawns and giggles, and met with no success. He was in essence an incarnation of the popular desire to laugh at the intellectual, in the person of this pretentious don with his dubious learning.

His mask had a black nose and forehead, and vinous pouched cheeks, an indication perhaps of his addiction to the bottle: or as some would have it, due to the fact that a well-known judge of the day had a great birth-mark disfiguring his cheeks.

These four, two masters and two servants, Pantalone and Arlecchino, Il Dottore and Brighella, were those from whom other masked characters sprang. As commedia dell'arte grew in popularity

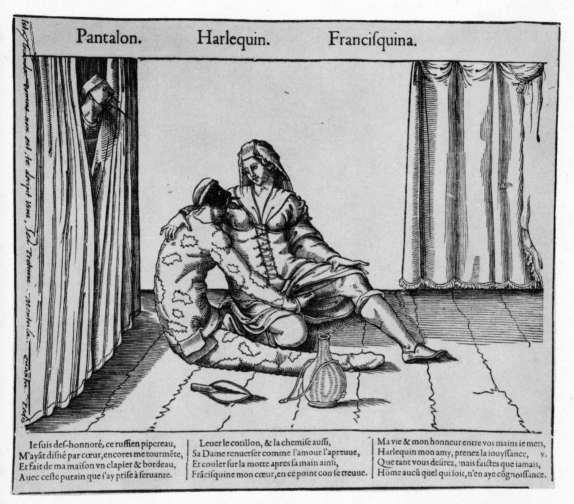

ARLEQUIN FAIT L'AMOUR À FRANCISQUINA

Recueil Fossard. Sixteenth century

ARLEQUIN VOLE UN BAISER À LA DONA

Recueil Fossard. Sixteenth Century

and spread throughout Italy, these primary characters were increasingly represented under regional names, sometimes with slight costume changes to suit a local dress, but always with the original mask. Pantalone and the Dottore, so alike in character and in type, finally merged. Pantalone continued, the Dottore disappeared, but was to some extent replaced by Bisegliese, Pasquariello, and Ciccombimbo in Naples, Cassandrino in Rome, Il Barone in Sicily: and elsewhere Facanappa or Gaultier-Gargouille, variations that provided a Pantalone with certain Doctor characteristics—pedantry, or an interest in medicine. Pantalone reaches across the centuries into present time, surviving to the nineteenth century as Pantaloon in English Harlequinade: and as the bad Baron in modern pantomime.

Among the more interesting variations on the valet type were the Neapolitan trio, Pulcinella, Il Capitano, and Scaramuccia, all of whom played an active part in the plots engendered by Pantalone and fostered by his valet Arlecchino. Of this trio, Pulcinella is perhaps the most enduring, and certainly a most troublesome character.

He was the supreme egotist, determined to secure for himself riches, fame, women, and fat living, at whatever cost to others. Beneath an apparent good humour lurked a cynical depravity and the smouldering volcano of his brutal personality. His megalomania was wonderfully exposed in his song: 'When I march along the whole earth trembles. I am master of the sun.' He delighted in sowing seeds of dissension among his fellows, fomenting discord, provoking violence. His dearest possession was his stout cudgel, put to frequent use, and always to his own profit—the destruction of an enemy, the waylaying of a traveller to be robbed, the threatening of a rival in love. He wore in his earliest days a costume very like that worn by the Acerran peasants, a district said to have known his birth. His wide white jacket, loose white trousers, and ragged cloak gave him the appearance of a ghostly scarecrow. His black mask with its ferocious moustaches and great, hooked fleshy nose was sinister: and his body deformed with its sagging paunch, pigeon chest, and humped back. He wore a white skull-cap, and a large grey hat with upturned sides. His mask and his deformities are strangely like those of the Maccus of Atellan farce and, after a world-wide career under the names Mea Patacca or Marco-Pepe in Rome, Il Sitonno, Birrichino elsewhere in

Italy, Polichinelle in France and Hanswurst in Germany, he is with us today in marionette form in the guise of Punch, still brutal, still attached to his cudgel but not to his wife: and sadly dwindled in size and personality.

The second Neapolitan was Il Capitano, believed by some to have descended from Plautus' *Miles Gloriosus*, the braggart soldier who flees in terror from battle. He was full of bombast: beneath the roaring appearance of a lion lurked the heart of a mouse; and though he growled incessantly of massacre and assassination, of the power of his strong right arm and the edge of his trusty blade, he shook and quavered at the sight of any weapon levelled in his direction, and dropped his growl to a squeak whenever anyone called his bluff. He always came on to the stage with a mighty battle cry, and his sword drawn. He always left it limping, after the thorough beating he endured from the rest of the troupe without ever lifting a finger to defend himself. Most often his rank was a military one, and his costume was that of a Spanish soldier of the time, a sly satire on the conquering heroes from Spain who had overcome Italy. The Italians might be under the heel of Spain, and politically in her power: that did not prevent them from creating a Capitano so absurdly like the real thing that when commedia dell'arte reached Spain he was one of the most popular clowns. His mask was flesh-coloured, with a great ruddy nose and long, upturned black moustaches. Under the various names Spezzafer, Gianguilo, Il Vappo, Rogantino, he often represented an officer of the law, who cared nothing for law and order, but very much for his own enrichment. Should his guilty prisoner escape, he was capable of bringing any innocent passer-by to execution for the sake of the blood money. He was always closely associated with Pulcinella, whom he aided and abetted in all his violence and brutality. He is still with Punch, sometimes as Jack Ketch the hangman, sometimes the Policeman. In the latter rôle he entered English Harlequinade with Arlecchino and Pantalone: while under the name Matamore he played a major rôle in French dramatic literature of the seventeenth century.

Scaramuccia, the third Neapolitan, was closely related to both Pulcinella and Il Capitano in character. He was cowardly and quarrelsome, and, according to his own story, of noble birth—a prince or a marquis or lord of some castle in Spain. According to the celebrated Riccoboni, he was another attempt of the Neapolitans to mock the Spaniards, this time in civilian form. Scaramuccia was dressed entirely in black, after the Spanish fashion. His mask gave him enormous moustaches under a monumental nose, and a vast mouth stretching from ear to ear. It seemed probable that he was born and reared in jail, and he certainly spent his early years in the galleys, however he tried to disguise these sordid details. His rôle was nearly always that of valet to a minor lordling, or to a mere bourgeois. He was the very worst of all the dubious valets of commedia dell'arte, and linked in conspiracy with Pulcinella, who always subdued his accomplice by beating him. The recurrent scene in their association is a drinking bout culminating in a violent quarrel. Scaramuccia scrambles under the table just in time to avoid the swipe of Pulcinella's cudgel. When Pulcinella is safely drunk, Scaramuccia bobs up and begins recounting his amorous success, with much boastful detail. Suddenly Pulcinella, who was apparently in a drunken stupor, loses all patience and with mighty whacks of his cudgel sends tables, chairs, bottles, and glasses flying. Scaramuccia crawls under what is left of the table, and is driven howling from the stage under the well-directed blows of his accomplice.

Between them, the trio demonstrated all facets of Neapolitan character, including their mockery of their Spanish overlords. In the theatre they played the violent and disruptive element that interfered with, and often defeated, the intrigues of Pantalone or the Dottore, or the machinations of Arlecchino and Brighella. They also satirised civil and military law: and the very worst can be deduced from their enormous fleshy noses.

One of the most interesting of the valets is of later creation, only appearing towards the end of the sixteenth century. This was Pagliaccio, an Italian peasant, known as Pepe-Nappa in Sicily, as Pedrolino and Bertoldo: in France as Gros-Guillaume, Pierrot, or Gilles: and in England as Clown and Pierrot. He was the best valet Pantalone ever came by, with all the naïve honesty of the peasant, and the frankness of an ingenuous soul. When he played valet to the young lover, he brought a certain charm to the part that was entirely lacking in his fellows. He was a great coward, driven always by fear: but in spite of his terror he took childish delight in practical jokes, even when they brought swift retribution upon his head. His costume was borrowed from Pulcinella, but it was better fitting, and looked quite different without Pulcinella's sagging belly, and hump. He wore a frill round his neck, a black skull-cap, and a round white hat with a large brim. Pagliaccio was originally a chubby, greedy, anxious, mischievous child. His development was due to French influences of a dual kind. In the eighteenth century, Watteau had painted many canvases showing a pale and wistful Pierrot; in the early nineteenth century Gaston Deburau transformed him from a naughty child into a sinister villain, capable of all vices and all crimes, sardonic, solitary, and silent. Pierrot had neither wife nor mistress: his white mask showed no emotion: it became the terrifying outward symbol of an inner corruption. Deburau's Pierrot was a terrible figure, far removed from Pagliaccio.

A little later in the same century, the Goncourt brothers published their study and interpretation of the melancholy of Watteau, until then imperfectly realised, and cited the portraits of Pierrot to prove their case. This, together with Leoncavallo's short opera *I Pagliacci*, the title rôle magnificently sung by Caruso, destroyed the terrible Pierrot of Deburau and set in its place the sad, romantic, dreaming Pierrot of modern times. This last Pierrot is no longer a person: he is the haunting and poetic symbol of man's perpetual frustration. The pallor of his wistful face, the drooping shoulders under the loose white jacket, express an unbearable sorrow. He is the seeker of dreams. The old chubby Pagliaccio only survives by the seaside, in Pierrot troupes on the pier. His descendant found a subtler ambience, and entered into music, painting, poetry, and literature, to remain permanently in the imagination.

These were the clowns that were always represented whether under their original names or variations of those names. Towns and villages added their own clowns. Milan added Beltramo and Scapino to Brighella: and among the colourful throng of knavish valets were also to be found Fenocchino, Flautino, Gradelino, Mezzetino, Turlupino, and Narcisino, this last, like the Doctor, from Bologna. There were others cut to Arlecchino's doltish pattern—Trivelino, Truffaldino, Guazeto, Zaccagnino, Bagatino, among others. Venice gave the valet Zacometo to their own Pantalone, while Naples added Tartaglia, a talkative servant with a pronounced stammer who in his time generated all the functionaries of the commedia dell'arte—the lawyer, the judge, the apothecary, the notary, who each assumed their proper dress, but kept the stammer.

The eighteenth century marked another development, for then the *caratterista* were born. Here was testimony indeed to the enthusiasm with which commedia dell'arte was received throughout Italy, and the exuberance it aroused in its audience. For the *caratterista* existed simply to please the audience by making entrances and exits that had nothing whatever to do with the plot, and no purpose of any theatrical kind whatever: their sole *raison d'être* was that they were indigenous to the part of the country in which the show was given. In Tuscany it was Stentarello who appeared in the costume of the region, in Milan it was Meneghino, in Piedmont, Gianduna. Every region had its special *caratterista*, and among them only one played a special rôle. This was Coviello, who in different shows bore the name Fritellino or Tabarino. Occasionally, the players dried up, their improvisation suddenly failed, with such paralysing effect that a lengthy pause might ensue; or the troupe involved themselves in dialogue so complicated that it could not be continued. Whenever this happened, it was as though Coviello had received his cue. He would come downstage and begin to talk intimately with the audience, diverting attention from the embarrassed players, and forcing it upon himself. His act was very much like that of a good music-hall comedian sensitive to the pulse of the audience, and able to control them absolutely while keeping them hilariously entertained with his comic patter. Then, the players having enjoyed a breathing space while the audience were being soothed, delighted and boisterously amused by Coviello, the show would go on, and he would slip back into his rôle, of ordinary *caratterista*. His relation with the audience and the type of comedy he put over in his solo turn was, in modern terms, that of Danny Kaye or Gracie Fields.

All these clowns—merchants, doctors of law and medicine, soldiers, lawyers, apothecaries, notaries and valets were masked. So significant was this part of their costume that the characters were known as Masks. Players soon discovered that, since their faces were covered and a new personality assumed that had nothing to do with their own, they must make their whole body expressive. Their limbs must convey the emotions their hidden faces could not tell, and their bodies must seem to belong to the mask. The best of the players in commedia dell'arte were such fabulous mimes that the history of their genre is uplifted by the whole-hearted admiration of the *cognoscenti* : no doubt the worst of them were as bad as any schoolboy playing charades against his will.

These then were the Masks of commedia dell'arte, who set forth to conquer Europe, and enjoyed a triumphant career some three hundred years long. Very few of the variations ever left Italy: but a gallant band consisting of Arlecchino, Brighella, Pantalone and Il Dottore, Pulcinella, Scaramuccia, Il Capitano, and Pagliaccio, together with some others we shall discuss in the next chapter, were responsible for the great invasion.

CHAPTER FOUR

The Lover and His Lass

COMMEDIA dell'arte had, of course, its *jeune premier*—the Lover, with unmasked face, richly dressed in the most fashionable garb of his time. Even in the poorer companies, every effort was made to present the Lover as beautifully as possible: so that if finances were at a low ebb, as they so often were among the strolling players, Arlecchino's patches could be real ones, and Pulcinella's cloak truly rags, provided that the Lover looked like a young nobleman of fashion. He was very often called Lelio, in honour of Luigi Riccoboni, one of the most celebrated players of the rôle; and appeared also under the romantic names Flavio, Orazio, Silvio, or Leandrino. He was the young gallant, handsome, elegant, and well born; he spoke with an aristocratic drawl, and had enough talent to write a sonnet to his mistress's eyebrow. In manner and in dress, he was always a little larger than life. It was he who wooed and won Pantalone's daughter or ward or paramour. Lelio's rôle was less grotesquely comic than that of the clowns. When he appeared most sincere in his perfervid declarations and deeply moving protestations of undying love, he nevertheless managed to be just a little ridiculous. The excesses of his adoration made him faintly comic, in spite of his romantic air.

It is evident that so lusty a company as the Masks were not disposed to live in monastic seclusion. There was not one of them who did not have an eye for a pretty face, provocative swing of the hip, and a trim ankle. A day without all the excitements of amorous dalliance —pursuit, elopement, liaison, or at least a promise for the morrow— was a day lost. Nor could Lelio take part in the comedies without an Inamorata. His approach was romantic and tender, leading in most cases to a permanent and honourable establishment: but those of Brighella, Pantalone, and Scaramuccia were best glossed over. Among those whose intentions were unmistakable and dishonourable, Arlecchino was the leading amorist. Like most Latins, he responded immediately to the titillation of a shapely leg, a demure but promising smile or a half-veiled bosom, and pursued with unconcealed ardour the object of his excitement.

The Masks, who shared his leisure occupation, were fortunate in living among a galaxy of incomparable women, as bewildering in their variety of charm and temperament as they were scintillating in their beauty and their talent. Moreover, their company was enjoyed at a time when Christianity had driven women from the theatre throughout Europe. One of the major attractions of commedia dell'arte in the sixteenth century was that the feminine rôles were played by women, and not by youths, as was the custom in all other forms of theatre.

The veto against actresses, in force for many hundreds of years, gave to the women of the commedia their special character. They were not characters with haunting resemblances to those of an older tradition; nor were they regional types, as were all the male characters, with the exception of Lelio. They were simply women, part of the normal pattern of human relationship: and to stress the simplicity of their presence, they wore the costume of their time, and their faces were unmasked.

It is just possible that two of the female rôles arose in the mists of antiquity. These were *La Cantarina* and *La Ballerina*, one member of a company often taking the two rôles.

La Cantarina would appear to have survived the ban of centuries. As in ancient Roman theatre, she was a melodious singer, a talented dancer, and a musician able to play several instruments. She served sometimes as narrator when plots were unduly complex: she entertained the audience during *entr'actes* and took part in the comedy, or supplied music or sound effects for it, as required. The rôle of the *Ballerina* was almost identical, except that hers contained more dancing and less singing. They were both necessary to a company performing on a curtainless stage without a proscenium arch. Since no curtain could be lowered, any gap in the programme was immediately filled by the singers, dancers, and musicians who surged on and gave a musical or acrobatic show whenever the Masks left the stage at the end of a comedy. These *entr'acte* entertainments were entirely independent of the rest of the show. The singer and the dancer both wore a stylised form of contemporary dress, with sometimes a pseudo-classical effect to represent a pagan divinity—Melpomene or Minerva or Artemis.

Within the framework of the commedia itself, and easily accessible to the priapic Masks, was the vivacious and wholly enchanting race of serving wenches, born maybe from the corrupt and wanton slave girls of Roman tradition. With her renaissance as the Servetta or Fantesca of the comedy, she was given a series of delightful names— Gitta, Nina, Betta—as staccato as her pert wit, as fresh and charming as her person, as light as her morals. She was first a peasant wench, comely in a rustic manner: then with passing years, and travel abroad, she acquired sophistication under the names of Olivetta, Nespolia, Spinetta, Franceschina, Diamantine, and Colombina—names increasingly suggestive of the sparkling light o' love she represented. All that remained in her of the debaucheries and corruption of her putative ancestry was an infinite capacity to take love lightly, a joyous wantonness that found a ready response in Arlecchino, whose boon companion she was, friend, lover, co-plotter, goad and tormentor. They grew together. When Arlecchino was a rustic clod, Colombina was a buxom dairymaid: like many a similar pair before them, they kicked off the rural dust from their feet and went to town, with what success we shall see in future chapters.

Arlecchino was a fortunate amorist. Colombina, even if she occasionally left him for Brighella or Scaramuccia or Il Capitano, always returned to him, and offered him all the satisfactions of the flesh. La Cantarina, remote from his orbit, outside his particular destiny, represented the ideal woman. And there was, among the women of the commedia, another still—the woman always out of reach—Colombina's mistress, Pantalone's daughter or ward, Lelio's beloved or betrothed or aspiration.

Where Colombina is iridescent, a bubble light as air, her mistress is opalescent, clouded with untouched reserves. Colombina is a frank, a pagan amoralist. Her mistress is hidden and secret. She first appears under rustic names—Beatrice, Valeria, Isotta, Ginevra: and runs the whole gamut of womanhood in her rôles, from the pure and compassionate woman made for love in its noblest forms through all the gradations to the born courtesan, able through the accident of being well-born to conceal her true nature. In a few comedies she was in fact a practising courtesan, whose adventures led her finally to prison.

Through the centuries those who played her added wit and refinement and grace to the original rustic heroine. Her name became genteel—Lavinia, Lucrezia, Isabella—and then indicated her new status of great lady—Lucia, Pandolfina, Flaminia, Ortensia— with Isabella becoming her generic name, as her maid's became Colombina. Under her later names she had shed all her dubious characteristics, which were embodied in another character, Fiorinetta, the type of great courtesan who so often stands near a throne. From the moment Fiorinetta pursued her separate existence Isabella, released from her carnal self, becomes increasingly the tender and delicate lover, whose purity is as absolute as it is unassailable, whose love is gently and irrevocably bestowed upon Lelio or Leander, and helped to its consummation by Arlecchino and Colombina, or hindered by Pantalone and the Dottore.

Both Isabella and Colombina were created not by tradition but by the women who played them, talented women who were required to be agreeable to look upon, graceful and charming in movement, with a pretty voice, and an ability to sing and dance and play upon musical instruments, whenever their rôles demanded such embellishment.

Their costume was not, as in the case of the Masks, traditional or mysterious. There was no special costume for Colombina or Isabella, little to indicate the mistress, the courtesan, the *entremetteuse*, or the serving maid. They normally wore a slightly stylised form of the dress of the period: fortunately the Renaissance had had tremendous impact upon dress, as upon art and literature. Ordinary clothes showed such bejewelled splendour, were made in such gorgeous stuffs, with such superb line, that they were theatrical enough to be immediately put to dramatic use.

The only differences between the costume of the mistress, the courtesan, and the serving maid were those of degree, not of kind. Colombina's dress was fashionable and attractive, but made of fairly sober cloth, not overtrimmed. Her hair was simply dressed, and everything about her suggested the girl who liked to look neat and pretty, and who modelled herself, in a humble way, upon her mistress.

Isabella wore beautiful dresses of silk and satin and brocade,

DOMENICO LOCATELLI (1613–1671) AS TRIVELINO,
the Harlequin variant he created

Photo Rigal, Paris

Courtesy Comédie Français

THE ITALIAN PLAYERS

With Molière and members of his Company, on stage at the *Théâtre Royal* in 1670

sparkling with jewelled embroidery. She dressed her hair in the latest mode, wore suitable jewels, and conveyed an impression of elegance and dignity.

The courtesan was overdressed. She wore too many jewels, her *coiffure* was too elaborate, her dress too modish in cut, and covered with too much trimming, flowers, feathers, and ribbons. She was attractive, but flashy.

Whenever the comedy included, as it frequently did, an interlude in which the gods and goddesses of ancient mythology came down to earth in a chariot of clouds to unravel the intrigues and misfortunes of Arlecchino and his fellows, the women wore special costumes in the 'antique tradition', fantastic and lovely dresses that bore no relation whatever to the tunics and robes of ancient Greece and Rome, and very little to the dress of the period. These costumes for divinities allowed free rein to the highest flights of imagination, and were wildly applauded as the goddesses descended slowly backstage.

Traditional costume for the women players never developed. When, in the seventeenth century, Colombina appeared in France as Arlequina or Pierrette, the costume she then wore was simply a feminine version of the costume of Arlecchino or Pagliaccio (Pierrot), with no new invention: nor were any masks ever developed. When Isabella concealed her face beneath a *loup*, she was simply doing what any fashionable lady of her time would do when she wished to escape recognition.

Colombina, in her rôle of a faithful maid and faithless lover, was often led by the necessity of her many intrigues to assume disguises, nearly always designed to hide the fact that she was a woman. When she appeared as a doctor, a poor scholar, a lawyer, or once as Arlecchino, she wore the recognisable dress of the character she was impersonating. Her costume as Arlecchina, which underlined her close relationship with Arlecchino, was basically in the fashion of the seventeenth century, but was covered with patches of different colours. Her bodice was fastened with ribbons, and she wore a frill round its low-cut neck. Her hat was the twin of Arlecchino's: but when she appeared in this guise, she was still unmasked. The Arlequina variation was first seen in France in 1695, on the occasion of the reopening of the *Foire de Bezons*. In the late nineteenth century, in unknowing repetition of a long-forgotten tradition, she appeared again in English pantomime, where Harlequin was sometimes accompanied by Harlequina, and sometimes played by a woman.

Among the factors contributing to the dramatic originality of commedia dell'arte was surely the juxtaposition of the masked clowns and the unmasked *innamorate*. The Lovers, the Mistress, and the Maid represented the romantic element in humanity. They were young and fair, they were elegant and in love, touched with the magic that stays for ever with Cinderella and her Prince Charming. In their handsome contemporary dress they looked like the poetic vision of the youth and beauty of their age. The fantastic costumes and stylised mask of the clowns, on the other hand, created a strange race of ageless and timeless beings remote from humanity, representing nothing but themselves. And what were they? A paradox, in appearance remote from the contemporary scene, in fact and in action steeped in its social and political implications: not human in presentation, but recognisably human in personality. Among them, the unmasked characters shone like jewels in curious settings. We can vividly imagine the dramatic impact of Diamantine's fresh young face framed in a circle of inhuman masks, upraised to flirt with Pulcinella, smiling upon the black aviz'd Arlecchino, making pert reference to Scaramuccia's monumental nose. The calm beauty of Isabella must have glowed beside the black brow and purple-veined cheeks of the doctor, and taken new values from the proximity of her guardian's vulturine profile. Those young laughing faces, glimpsed amid the brown, black, white, and olive-green masks with their grotesque features, brought fresh assurance of the eternal beauty of women and the inevitability of the pursuit of love.

There could not have been a man in the audience who did not share the concupiscence of the clowns, even to the point of finding himself in secret sympathy with Pantalone's senile desires.

There was only one female character who lacked the power to charm; the Neapolitan *La Ruffiania*, based on a well-known type of garrulous old peasant wife, obstinate, limited, narrow, primitive in all her reactions, yet withal good-hearted and generous in spirit if not in purse. In other parts of Italy she appeared as *La Guarassa*, and in France as *L'Entremetteuse* or *La Commère*. She wore Neapolitan peasant costume, and her rôle was generally that of the mother of *Fiorinetta*, the courtesan type of Isabella.

Arlecchino, the born amorist, was fortunate in that, throughout his long career, he lived among a multitude of enchanting women, brilliant and beautiful, exacting and rewarding, filled with the zest of loving and living, offering between them every facet of feminine temperament, character, and charm. He could worship an ideal, in the person of *La Cantarina*; pursue, in Isabella, the all but unattainable; and console himself with Colombina, the charmingly accessible. No man could ask for more: few men enjoy as much.

CHAPTER FIVE

The Show Goes On

Now that the players are assembled—not in the wings, for there were no wings: but beneath the pageant cart in the market place, or behind the back-curtain of the inn-yard trestles—the moment has come to examine the shows they put on.

Enthusiasm for commedia dell'arte and its implications in the worlds of theatre, tradition, and legend should not lead us into the error of confusing its crude beginnings with the impeccable comedy achieved some hundred or so years later. In the early years of the Renaissance, any mountebank out of a job gathered round him a few of his kind, and launched yet another of the small companies of wandering players bent upon meeting the popular demand for improvised comedy, without having any special gift or training for this most exacting form of drama. They could, at best, offer boisterous charades in which the clowns endeared themselves to their audiences by chaffing local bigwigs, guying local customs, assuming local accents, and dragging local skeletons into hilarious prominence.

Among these numerous small companies, however, were a few directed by men of intelligence, and containing trained actors and dancers who were able, through their sense of the theatre, and their technical skill, to develop the potentialities of unwritten comedy.

The play to be created spontaneously by the company at each performance was built upon a skeleton plot or *scenario* giving the outline of the action, the locale in which it took place, the order in which the characters appeared, and the part each was to play in the development of the action.

This brief scenario was read to the assembled company by the director, *il guido maestro*, who was very often the originator of the theme, and the leading player of the group. There followed a discussion in which the exact position of each house was fixed, the exact name of each character—so that no lover shall call today's Isabella by the name of yesterday's Olivia, nor she mistake Leander for Lelio: and the relation each bore to the others. Exits and entrances were fixed, and players given the timing for their soliloquies and mime, so that neither should be either too brief, or unduly protracted. Finally, the *lazzi* were assigned to those Masks who were customarily called upon to watch the pace and development of the comedy: and the brief preparation for the coming performance was over.

Since the *lazzi* played an increasingly important part in the rôle of Arlecchino, and finally became symbolic of his excellence in mime, it would be wise to unveil their mystery here.

The curious term was derived, according to many authorities, from a Lombard mispronunciation of the Tuscan word *lacci*, ribbon; and was applied to the solo acts of brief duration, acrobatic, comic, or musical, that served many useful purposes within the play.

The pauses in the comedy comparable to our intermission or interval were, in the absence of a curtain, filled by singers, dancers, or tumblers. But there were sometimes other, more sinister pauses due to the improvised nature of the performance. They might occur through the drying-up of a player before his allotted time, or an unforeseen complication in the plot which would need some thought to disentangle. Since the impact of the comedy would be destroyed, were it to be held up by any such contretemps, Arlecchino and his fellow Masks were always prepared to fill the breach, as they were ready to interrupt a scene in progress when it was flagging and sometimes, it must be confessed, even when it wasn't. Arlecchino would sit cross-legged eating imaginary cherries from his hat, throwing the invisible stones, each one of which reached its mark, at his fellow players. Sometimes he would catch a fly, tear off its wings with all the heedless cruelty of a child, and then munch the deprived corpse with evident enjoyment. Or if he were startled or annoyed, he would turn a series of somersaults and backsprings, bouncing among and recoiling from the other Masks, all of whom were seriously incommoded by this human projectile. Another, more complicated *lazzi*, came about through Arlecchino's determination to climb a wall by means of a ladder, and Brighella's determination that he should never reach the top: while another gave Arlecchino the appearance of consuming himself, beginning with his heels, until finally the crown of his own head disappeared into his insatiable maw. One which found great favour with his earlier audiences, and was practised for years, was a scene in which he received so violent a blow upon the head from Scaramuccia that his brain spurted out. Slowly and pensively, he, the gourmand, sat down and feasted upon this unexpected delicacy: and when he had finished, was discovered to be more stupid than ever, since he had no brain to speak of left. This comic cannibalism is little to our modern taste, but it was one of Arlecchino's most famous *lazzi* for nearly two hundred years.

These and similar tricks not only served to fill pauses, cover hesitation, and revive interest; they were also used to tie up disconnected parts of the plot—hence the term ribbon—or to turn an unwieldy sequence back into the mainstream of the action. Later, by extension, the term was applied to any special acrobatic or comic trick of Arlecchino.

The scenari fundamentally were all the same, based largely on amorous intrigue, in which young lovers were continually frustrated by parent or guardian, and aided and abetted by a throng of servants and valets. Sometimes the story began with a secret marriage between two lovers, who, after much persecution, were put to flight, pursued, and finally escaped into marital bliss. Sometimes the beautiful young heroine was to be forced into marriage with an elderly and wealthy admirer, and was only enabled to escape from this fate worse than death through the devotion and cunning of her maid and her fiancé's valet. Whatever the story, the lovers were always opposed to cantankerous and eccentric old men, and served by comic or greedy valets. As the genre developed, Pantalone and the Dottore invariably played the deceived and frustrated parent or guardian, or elderly cuckolded husband: while Arlecchino and Colombina together brought disaster to the aged and love and joy to Isabella and her Lelio.

At an early stage, these simple plots were complicated by the machinations of the subsidiary characters; with Scaramuccia and Pagliaccino also pursuing Isabella, while Brighella and Punchinello offered plot and counterplot for and against Arlecchino or Pantalone, according to where the most profit was to be found.

A curious bias was given to the locale of many of the early scenari by the revival of humanism and the classics at the time of the Renaissance. It was inevitable that popular comedy should turn to its own account the literate and cultured enthusiasm for, and imitation of, the classical tradition. Arlecchino and his fellow Masks found themselves very often scaling the heights of Olympus and fraternising with the gods and goddesses of Ancient Greece and Rome: or penetrating into Pluto's dark and frightening kingdom, or Vulcan's caverns, or Poseidon's watery depths. And since their comedy had no written forms, but was handed down from father to son, from company to company, the classical flavour, strangely distorted, was carried by them through the years into the twentieth century. Among scenari still extant are those bearing the titles—*Arlecchino, Gallant Mercury*: *The Matron of Ephesus*: *Arlecchino Proteus*: *Arlecchino Jason and the Comic Golden Fleece*: *The Descent of Mezzetin to the Infernal Regions*.

It needs a highly imaginative reconstruction to revitalise the brief scenari, and gain from them any impression at all of the shows which so delighted the rustic mobs of Italy and the cultured men and women of all the courts of Europe.

The genre depended entirely upon the wit and skill of its players. Every actor of experience had, tucked away in his prodigious memory, his *repertorio*, a vast collection of phrases and speeches that could be drawn upon to fit any occasion. According to the type of rôle he normally played, his *repertorio* would consist of reproaches, boasting, obscene jokes, angry tirades, declarations of love, challenges to mortal combat, protestations of despair, delight, or delirium, streams of wild oaths, soliloquies that were rhetorical, impassioned, or gibberish, all ready to spring to mind when required. Each player held this store, each part of it capable of being lengthened or shortened according to the time allotted or unforeseen emergencies. Good entrance and exit lines were essential to draw forth due meeds of applause from the audience: and certain general aspects of dramatic conversation must be held in readiness, as well as the specialised rhetoric of each part.

The actors were clearly called upon to be alert the whole time, since not only were they required to develop the plot within the framework of their own *repertorio* and mime but also to produce the right speech in character for each occasion, the right sort of mime as needed, and, in addition, to watch each other and the scene closely in order to perform one of the essential *lazzi* whenever a danger point was reached.

The humour of improvised comedy embraced all known popular sources. The Masks filled their cheeks with water so that when their faces were slapped, fountains drenched the aggressor. In *Arlequin Lingère du Palais*, the *lingère* is described as 'Providing layettes for all the children of the eunuchs of the *Grand Seraglio*.'

Transvestism is another fecund source of humour, and all the primary Masks appear from time to time in women's clothing. Indeed, in *Arlequin Lingère*, Arlecchino appears in comic hermaphroditic form, dressed one half as a man, the other as a woman, much to the confusion of his customers. He often appeared disguised as a widow, a goddess, a courtesan, a vestal virgin, or a lady of fashion. In one comedy, Mezzetino was accosted by a young courtesan who asked him the way to the *Place de Grève* (where executions took place). Mezzetino bowed to her with great courtesy, saying, 'You have only to continue, Madame, in the direction in which you are going, to be sure of getting there in the end.' Since the young courtesan was Arlecchino in disguise, a great battle ensued, which gave full scope to the sword play of Mezzetino and the acrobatic suppleness of Arlecchino.

In a comedy based upon the Don Juan theme from which Mozart took his opera, Arlecchino toasted a woman in the presence of the Statue, upon which the Statue bowed to him. In his terror, Arlecchino turned a complete somersault with the glass of wine in his hand, without spilling a drop—a *lazzi* made famous by Thomassin, a celebrated eighteenth-century Arlecchino.

In yet another, Isabella, alone in a garden, is soliloquising on the anguish of love when a piece of statuary sneezes. She pauses, dismayed, then sees each statue descend from its pedestal, and realises that she has been surrounded by eavesdroppers of dubious character when she had believed herself to be alone.

To these examples of broad and effective humour, much of which is still with us on the halls, in the circuses, and in contemporary farce, must be added the crudities of a less inhibited age. There were, throughout the comedies, frequent indecencies and obscenities, both verbal and visual, in which Arlecchino's stick, the Captain's sword, and the dangling phallus worn by Pantalone played their shameless part, to the wholehearted delight of the audience. As always, sex and all bodily functions provided ready cause for mirth, and were exploited to the utmost, as were comment and insinuation concerning all

DOMENICO BIANCOLLELI, KNOWN AS DOMINIQUE

1640–1688

BRIGHELLA
Seventeenth century

ARLEQUIN DISGUISED AS DIANA
Seventeenth century

known vices, and inquiry into those that are esoteric. The sight of Arlecchino trying to hide beneath a woman's skirt was enough to provoke punning innuendo of a most scabrous kind from the other Masks. The earliest commedia dell'arte was full-blooded comedy given to an age coarser and less canting than ours, which draws popular comedy from the same sources, but veils them.

By the late sixteenth century, it had passed through distinguished hands, come under the patronage of Kings and Cardinals, and revealed its fundamental originality. Of all dramatic forms, this was the only creative one. Here alone a group of players wove between them the whole structure and content of a comedy spontaneously created at each performance. These players brought immeasurable riches to their art, and showed the way to a deeper penetration of its possibilities. It is one of the tragedies of the history of Theatre that the way was too hard, so that when the giants among the Italian players died, commedia dell'arte went back to the easier path of reliance on a written scenario, and gradually became interpretative.

Creative work such as theirs at its best could only be achieved by actors of outstanding ability and intelligence, working together in a type of group theatre never known since. Evaristo Gherardi, a brilliant Arlecchino of the seventeenth century, defined a good Italian player in the foreword to his *Théâtre Italien*, a valuable collection of scenari dating from 1582 to 1697. He says, 'Qui dit "bon Comédien Italien" dit un homme qui a du fond, qui joue plus d'imagination que de mémoire; qui compose, en jouant, tout ce qu'il dit; qui sait seconder celui avec qui il se trouve sur le Théâtre; c'est-à-dire, qu'il marie si bien ses paroles et ses actions avec celles de son camarade, qu'il entre sur le champ dans tout le jeu et dans tous les mouvements que l'autre lui demande, d'une manière à faire croire qu'ils étaient déjà concertés.' Elsewhere he stated that it would be easier to train ten actors for ordinary comedy than to train one for commedia dell'arte.

The best players were so essentially creative that the same thread-bare theme was freshly presented each time they played it, with new detail and different climaxes. So expert was their technique that their improvised dialogue sparkled with wit and malice, with delicate and subtle satire: their *lazzi*, solos, soliloquies, and dancing blended one with another to sustain the pace of the comedy and ensure the development of its action. There is no record left of these brilliant performances, save in the faded skeleton feuilletons of the old scenari, and in the wholly appreciative comment, to be found in essays, diaries, memoirs, and critical reviews, of their more literate and experienced audiences. It seems evident that not only did the players offer the stylised presentation of the characters they were playing, according to tradition, but that they added depth and realism to those characters by adding to the scope of the *repertorio*, and expressing in mime not only the follies, vices, and stupidities of the Masks but also their pathos, their dignity, their humanity.

It is a remarkable thing, at this top level, that personalities strong enough, with intelligence and technique great enough to create character and situation spontaneously with all the necessary adjuncts of comedy, immediately arousing the mirth of the people, without script or rehearsal, were at the same time able to work in such intimate harmony with fellow players, as the nature of their work demanded. There were no doubt explosions of temper and temperament: there were surely jealousies and pettiness and the terror of being superseded; there must have been clashes of personality in the groups where so many outstanding men and women were gathered together. Yet their work demanded, and received, a rare degree of fusion of effort. Each player, for the fullest success of the show, had to subordinate himself and his rôle to the demand of those of the other actors, while at the same time the character he played must be fully presented, and take his exact part in the development of the plot. He must blend and merge his own part of the dialogue, drawn from his special *repertorio*, with that of his fellows, as his gestures and acrobatics were to be part of one harmonious whole. Each contribution he made, of whatever kind, must be exactly timed, in such a manner that the characters were presented, the action made clear, and the climax reached by a concerted effort enlivened with mime, dancing, singing and clowning, each in his appointed time and place, never encroaching on another. Anyone who has ever played or watched unrehearsed charades will begin to understand just how much theatrical skill and understanding were required from the Italian players. Their teamwork was necessarily of a most subtle kind, and each actor needed intimate knowledge of his fellow artists, as players, and as persons.

Time added to that close-linked intimacy. Marriages took place among the players, children were born who from infancy absorbed the traditions of their parents and close relations, all of whom were engaged in commedia dell'arte. The technique evolved through the years was handed down from father to son, from mother to daughter. Private and public life was so inextricably merged that an unseen thread of consanguinity linked the players on the stage, so that each could foretell the action or gesture of the other in any situation, could recognise instinctively the inflection of a voice that heralded a drying-up, or the natural ending of a peroration, could abandon a *lazzi* upon an intuitive feeling that someone else was about to begin on another. Arlecchino generated many of his kind, each one adding new *lazzi* to his store, each one learning how to become the pivot of the comedy, to be responsible for the guiding of the action, and to take the leading part without robbing the other Masks.

The creative nature of commedia dell'arte, the excellence of its group-work, gave it an excitement to which many who saw it have testified, and a slickness of production unusual at that time, when actors were individualists who knew no master in the theatre. By its very nature, it must be quick and polished to succeed. Yet it would be foolish to stress the perfection of the genre as practised by its most notable players, without reference to its disasters.

Out of their very speed and spontaneity must have come catastrophic moments; there is the statement of a contemporary that bears witness to the sort of accidents that could and did happen, even in the best companies: 'There are in fact two pitfalls that must be avoided—too little ardour, or too much. Some players, who are very conscientious but sadly inhibited, keep to the letter of their part, and throw themselves into it so little that they freeze their protagonist. Others are so impulsive and so uncontrolled that they come onto the stage in a sort of frenzy, and while as soloists they are superlative and often extremely original, they are the despair of their fellow players. For example, they throw the inkwell that is needed in the following scene through the window and off the stage in a transport of folly: they carry off the armchair into which the heroine must shortly sink in a swoon; they drink with great gusto the potion that was to be swallowed as a poison by another character, while the unhappy actor who was working up to a wonderful death scene looks everywhere for it with increasing anxiety, and sees himself reduced to cracking his skull against the wall, if he doesn't happen to be wearing a dagger in that scene. The perfect player is he who can give himself up to the excitement of his rôle without forgetting the least detail, and without ceasing to remain aware of what the others are doing or saying, in order to provoke the cue he needs. He must at one and the same time be the ecstatic character of the comedy and the tranquil actor who watches and guides him.'

Arlecchino was shaped by the men who played him: and here luck was with him. His part was invariably taken by the best player in the group, since it made the greatest demands. He who played Arlecchino must be a mime, a dancer, an acrobat, a wit, and a linguist: he must be so technically skilled that he could hold the play together single-handed in any emergency, delight his audience with a brilliant solo whenever the occasion presented itself, play the leading rôle spontaneously while he kept a firm hand on all the other players and all the ramifications of the plot, perform many different *lazzi* in the course of a single play: and never fail to keep the audience aware of the greedy dolt with the patched dress and strange black face. No ordinary actor would ever do for Arlecchino: and that was a factor that helped to make him extraordinary.

CHAPTER SIX

Early Adventures

IT is not easy to trace the members or follow the travels of the early companies, since many left no record, and concerning others information is scant, and dubious. A few contracts, some property lists, an account book showing payment to actors, receipts for sums received from royal or local patrons, mostly inscribed by ignorant or careless people with little regard for spelling or accuracy, are all that remain to us. Further confusion is added by the fact that leading actors soon became known by the name of the rôles they habitually played, as well as by their baptismal name, and yet a third derived from their birthplace.

Until the end of the sixteenth century the players led a nomadic life of considerable hardship, in spite of their popular success. Certain rowdy companies, with little if any dramatic quality save in the way of provoking quarrels and starting riots, earned the hostility of magistrates and municipal authorities. Others, by the extreme licentiousness of their comedy and the undisguised obscenity of their mime, drew down upon themselves the wrath and thunder of the Church. The reputation rightly acquired by a few scurrilous companies spread to them all, and the better companies struggled against the opposition of both Church and State. A paradoxical situation grew up, in which eminent cardinals of the Church and great noblemen of the State delighted in commedia dell'arte, encouraged the players, took them under their valuable patronage, and invited them to State functions: while others of equal dignity and renown put the severest punishments upon them. The Church kept strict watch upon them when they were given permission to perform, insisting on the rigorous observance of religious duties, and frequent confession. In those cities where the power of the Church was greatest, actors could be clapped into jail at the first signs of obscenity, and were on a few occasions sentenced to death because their productions offended the papal authorities. Should the players be fortunate enough to escape from the Scylla of the Church, they were sure to founder upon the Charybdis of the State. The secular arm watched them closely. A disturbance in the audience, a quarrel before a performance, too large a crowd assembled to watch, and the players were run out of town.

It was never considered wise, in view of these many pitfalls, to stay long in any locality. Their traps packed into the cart that served as stage, wrapped in the curtains that masked their exits and entrances, they went from one city to the other, sometimes impelled by the stout boot of authority, sometimes by the need for attendance at a nearby fair or carnival, where they might make a fortune, or be waylaid and robbed of the little they already possessed. They travelled not only throughout Italy but also in France, England, Austria, Bavaria, Portugal, and Spain. Their sojourn abroad added to their technique and sometimes to their companies, which became increasingly cosmopolitan. The earliest contract surviving in France is one dated 1530, which would tend to show that Arlecchino's conquest of foreign parts began in the early days of commedia dell'arte.

The first recorded troupe is that of Maffeo dei Re of Padua, whose membership list for 1545 is extant. By 1551 there is evidence of a rival company in Rome directed by one Marcantonio. After that date, there is fleeting trace of several companies established in different towns in Italy, some of them already under royal patronage. Antonio Maria of Venice, and Soldini of Florence both directed companies which from 1572 were under the patronage of Charles IX of France, passing at his death into that of Henri III, who succeeded him. Maria's company contained nine actors, Soldini's eleven, and both gave shows consisting of comedies, acrobatic or musical intermissions with dancing, in the traditional manner. Under Henri III, they produced joint shows at Paris and at Blois for the delight of the Court, both being present on the occasion of the festivities to celebrate the engagement of Catherine de Medici's daughter, Marguerite, with Henri le Béarnais. These royal experiences brought honour and wealth to the players, who later in the century merged into one company, and returned to Italy, where no more is heard of them; though doubtless they were able to exploit their dazzling successes abroad.

The leading companies were beginning to give themselves special names, and of these one of the most renowned was *I Comici Confidenti*, which made an early visit to the French provinces after a highly successful tour of Italy. It is not quite certain whether Alberto Ganassa, the earliest recorded Arlecchino, was a member of this company from the beginning, or of another of similar status travelling in Italy and France at the same time. His name first appears in Spain in 1565. He was celebrated enough to be asked, with his company, to take part in the festival celebrating the marriage of Lucrezia d'Este at Ferrara in 1570, while the following year saw him invited to attend the marriage of the young King Charles IX.

On that occasion he fell foul of the French *Parlement*, because he had not been authorised to stay on in France and give public performances, and also because his admission charges were too high—five and six sols per person as against the usual two. Ganassa, a leading player in Italy, under the King's patronage in France, was deeply affronted, and after furious protest shook the dust of France from his heels and returned to honour and glory in his own country. As it was with the nomadic players at the hands of the magistrates, so it was with Ganassa at the hands of the Parlement. The whole history of Arlecchino is marked with skirmishes of this kind, at whatever level, in whatever country he finds himself.

Clearly time brought balm to Ganassa's wounds, for in 1572 he came with his company, at the royal invitation, to celebrate the nuptials of Henri de Navarre and Marguerite de Valois. Upon this occasion, perhaps to solace his wounded dignity, he received from the King 'la Somme de soixante-quinze livres tournois en testons à douze sols par livre dont le dict seigneur luy a faict don tant a luy que à ses compagnons, en considération du plaisir qu'ils ont donné à Sa Majesté durant le mariage.'[1]

There is no record of the sort of Arlecchino played by Ganassa except that it was upon traditional lines, and brought him great wealth and success, at home and abroad. His last years are wrapped in sinister mystery. His career ended in Spain, where he achieved equal renown at the court of Philip II, up to the year 1577. There is then a

[1] Archives Nationales Xl^{ème} 1633.   Quoted by Duchartre.

silence concerning him, broken in 1582 by a record of his imprisonment on an unspecified charge. After December 1583 there is no
record of him anywhere. The first known Arlecchino came from
nowhere, danced across the stage, and vanished into darkness.

When Ganassa went to Spain, some of his company preferred to
remain in Italy, and these came to Venice to enter a company directed
by Flaminio Scala. He is perhaps the first of the striking personalities
destined to lift commedia dell'arte from the ranks of rustic farce into
those of exquisite comedy. Like Angelo Beolco, he was a cultured man
of good family. He became the director of one of the most brilliant
companies of the greatest period of commedia dell'arte, in which he
himself played the rôle of Flavio, the young lover. His company—*I
Comici Gelosi*—played throughout Italy, in all the big centres—
Venice, Rome, Milan, Mantua, Naples, Turin, Ferrara, and Bologna.
They played on well-defined scenari, of which sixty were published
in 1611, and offer invaluable evidence of the type of comedy given by
the leading company of the day. It is clear from the scenari that the
Gelosi worked on traditional themes, to which they added a certain
element of drama not usually to be found in improvised comedy.
There is evidence too of innumerable *lazzi*, some traditional, some
invented by members of the company. Unfortunately, many of them
bear such cryptic description—the *lazzi* take this and leave that—the
lazzi of he who knows—the *lazzi* of the eagle with two heads, of
Brother I know you not—that they are for ever lost to us. Contemporary records show that the performances of the Gelosi were
polished, witty, and entertaining; that the company had a flair for
unexpected endings, and had gathered together the most experienced
players of the day. Simone of Bologna was the Arlecchino, Pasquati
played Pantalone; and among the younger players, a certain Francesco
Andreini was winning great success as Il Capitano Spavento.

In 1574, Henri III, who had always been interested in the Italian
players, invited them to appear before him in Venice, through which
he was passing on his return from Poland to France, to succeed to the
throne of Charles IX. Later in the same year, the company merged
with the *Confidenti* under the title *I Comici Uniti*, and for the next two
years continued a triumphal progress through Italy, where they now
had no serious rivals. After that period, whether through internal
dissension, or because the company had grown too large, it divided

ARLEQUIN DANCING WITH ARLEQUINA

Nuremberg Book 1716

EVARISTO GHERARDI, 1666–1700

again into two parts. When, in 1576, Henri III, who had not forgotten the enchanting entertainment he had watched two years before in Venice, summoned the players to Blois for the opening of the States General in the spring of 1577, it was the *Gelosi*, still under the direction of Scala, who responded to his invitation, and suffered dire misfortune en route.

They left for France early in December, but near Lyons fell into the hands of the Huguenots, who were politically hostile, and were held prisoner in most uncomfortable surroundings until Henri III, in due course, paid a heavy ransom for them. The terrors and hardship of imprisonment, for reasons in which they had no interest, did not break their spirit. While they were held, they practised the tricks of their trade, refurbished their costumes, and thought out new scenari, and fresh *lazzi*. They arrived at Blois, shaken, but ready to entertain the King on January 25th, 1577, and scored an overnight success with *The Princess who lost her Wits*, a comedy with music, ballets, machines to achieve magical effects, and a naval battle of great extent and ferocity. Their success was due partly to the impact of their original theatre, partly to the actresses in the troupe, since in France, as in England, no woman had ever appeared upon the stage.

Their capture by Huguenots was not to be their only adventure on that visit to France. Their success at Blois and in Paris was such that they called down upon themselves the attentions of the *Confrérie de la Passion*, a body destined to enjoy many a skirmish with Arlecchino and his fellows. Originally, the *Confrérie* was a special company composed of both amateurs and professionals founded in early mediæval times to undertake the presentation of mystery and miracle plays when drama left the Church and was handed over to the secular arm in France. The company was established in Paris by letters patent of Charles VI, on December 4th, 1404. In 1548 they converted the long rectangular hall of the Hôtel de Bourgogne into a theatre, and one with which Arlecchino was to be associated over many years. There they played up to 1598, and were firmly entrenched when the Italian players began to invade France. By the time the *Gelosi* arrived, the *Confrérie* had, by a decree of 1548 forbidding religious performances, been granted a renewed monopoly on performances to be given in Paris or its vicinity. Any company therefore wishing to play in the capital must obtain permission from the

Confrérie, and needed adequate funds to pay the high rental fees demanded by the brotherhood for the use of the Hôtel de Bourgogne, the only place in which they would be allowed to present their plays. Their original privilege, of prohibiting all theatrical performances from which they did not reap profits, was confirmed by all successive Kings until 1677, much to the continual discomfiture of Arlecchino.

The immediate and overwhelming success of the *Gelosi*, who had begun to draw large crowds at every show, was at the instigation of the *Confrérie* terminated by Parlement on the well-known censorial grounds that 'the immorality of the performances served only as a school of debauchery to the flower of Parisian youth of both sexes'. It is interesting to record that the flower of Parisian youth, of both sexes, had flocked to the performances.

The *Gelosi* then presented the King's letters, which were overruled: and it was only when their plans for a return to Italy were irrevocably made that Henri III drew up an order in their favour and against the *Confrérie* and Parlement. In spite of this, Scala, no doubt as affronted as Ganassa had been before him, returned to Italy with his company. For the next five years there is no record of Italian players on French soil. Part of the hostility of Parlement was due, of course, to its deep disapproval of the royal alliances with the Medici family. Players from other foreign countries were welcomed: only the Italian companies were harried. They suffered also from the jealousy of French actors, who resented the royal favours bestowed upon them, and feared the serious rivalry of such unusual and excellent players, who everywhere attracted large crowds. When, finally, the Italians were forced to charge admission fees smaller than their travelling expenses and those of costume and scenery warranted, while at the same time they were openly accused of exploiting the public, the last insult had been administered.

By the beginning of the seventeenth century, commedia dell'arte, in spite of state and ecclesiastical opposition at home, persecution and insult abroad, and jealousy and malice to contend with in the profession, was nevertheless entrenched in the affections of the people and the patronage of the court. It was to some extent the crystallisation of the wit and comic genius of Italy, arising at the time when the brilliance of the Renaissance was shed upon the Middle Ages. As such, it answered a deep popular need, and was bound to catch the enthusiasm of the people at home and abroad. It had become a very complex and specialised form of theatre, demanding the utmost from its players. There is in existence a long correspondence between Marie de Medici in Paris and the Duke of Mantua, who was the greatest patron of commedia dell'arte in Italy, concerning the enormous difficulties arising because the famous Arlecchino Martinelli had left Italy, and was no longer available to accompany the Duke's players on a visit to Paris. His replacement was a task of overwhelming difficulty, since his absence threw out the delicate interplay of the company, and the introduction of a new Arlecchino, however skilled, necessitated weeks of work, so that subtle bonds could be established between him and the other highly competent players. It was no longer possible to gather a group of actors together, and set them to work. Intricate relations must first be established between them, since the death or absence abroad of any member of a company threw out the intimate balance and spelled great difficulty, if not disaster, for the company itself.

Commedia dell'arte, while remaining true to its original, had acquired balance and polish, wit and subtlety, at the hands of the distinguished men and women who guided its fortunes. There were changes to be noted too in Arlecchino himself by the time he was roughly a hundred years old. The clod from Lower Bergama had acquired bodily grace and wit; so that his stupidity was accepted, but not believed in. He was amoral, guided only by the principle of satisfaction of the flesh; a great greedy cowardly child, only lovable because he was without malice, and because his appetites, though coarse, were simple and honest. If he saw a pie, he wanted it; a pretty girl, he coveted her; a shining trinket, he stretched out his hands for it. If he were beaten, he cried; if he managed to overcome an enemy, he danced for joy; if he tripped up a friend by accident, he roared with laughter. He was deeply Italian, with his passion for a dramatic gesture, and his love of a sonorous phrase; and most human in all his small failings and misadventures.

He was no longer a yokel. The great individualists who had played him left their mark upon him. He was a stylised yokel. His gestures, movements, tumbling and dancing were exquisitely controlled and presented. His doltishness was very nearly witty, his patter—dialogue in several tongues—brilliant under its cloak of incomprehension. His grossness had charm, his childish mischief glowed with primeval energy, his clumsy intrigue forshadowed the expert rogue. As he played, his mind suggested the slave, his body the master, while in his enigmatic spirit he was already a god, filled with strangeness, but without terror, at once accessible and remote.

PART TWO

Arlequin in France

CHAPTER ONE

Arlecchino in France

THE adventures of Arlecchino in France, where he became naturalised as Arlequin, were not lacking in excitement. Over the years he found himself involved in a life and death struggle with ecclesiastical and civil authorities, as with the great French professional acting companies. His first visits to France, his first brush with the *Confrérie* and Parlement, were symptomatic of his future struggles, which led Duchartre, in his excellent history of commedia dell'arte to comment 'En France l'histoire de la Comédie Italienne fait penser à Arlequin chassé par une porte et revenant par une fenêtre.'

While Arlecchino had been roaming all over Italy, developing his native gifts, and gaining in technical skill, his entry into France was being prepared by forces beyond his control and understanding. When Henri II brought his Italian wife Catherine de Medici to share his French throne, he paved the way for a rapid infiltration of Italian culture at one of its most splendid periods. Through Catherine, a strong if not pleasant personality, three Kings with Italian blood and Italian sympathies were given to France. Later, Henri IV married Marie de Medici, so continuing the italo-franco line, and introducing Cardinal Mazarin into French culture and politics. In court circles, the Italian language, dress, and customs became fashionable. The fashion spread to those who would ape their betters, and, gradually, in part at least, spread over the urban centres.

These factors prepared the entry of the Italian players into France. Others help to explain the hostility of Parlement when they arrived. It was believed that Charles IX, at the instigation of his stern mother Catherine, invited Ganassa to make his first appearance in France at the time they were plotting the Massacre of St. Bartholomew, so that the Italian players might at once serve to cover their activities and distract the attention of any who might otherwise have been suspicious. If this was indeed true, the distrust and anger of the Huguenots, the insistence of Parlement that the Italian players should leave the country is understandable, but unjust to the players.

Charles's brother, Henri III, recalled the players for his own amusement, without any darker purpose, for he always enjoyed theatricals, masques, pageants, or any splendid distraction from the cares of state. Henri IV also encouraged performances, partly because he was aware that the people enjoyed commedia dell'arte, partly because it helped to console his Italian wife for her exile from her own land.

This gracious patronage excited the opposition of all who resented the royal alliance with Italy, to such a point that after the departure of Scala's troupe there was an absence of Italian comedy in France.

In 1583, however, one Battista Lazzaro rented the Hôtel de Bourgogne from the *Confrérie* and installed his troupe there. Unfortunately for him, the memory of the work of Scala's company was fresh enough to reveal the inferior standard of his own. He failed to pay his way, lost his lease of the Hôtel, and with it all the effects of his company. The year following, a worthier company, the *Confidenti*, revisited Paris and remained for a year under the partial protection of Mazarin. However, at the end of that year, and in spite of Mazarin, the *Confrérie*, after much hard labour, were able to expel them. The *Confrérie* would tolerate no cuckoo in the theatrical nest, unless the cuckoo were able to pay very heavily for the privilege of making itself at home.

Meanwhile, in Italy, changes had come to the *Gelosi*. In 1578, Francesco Andreini, the dashing Capitano Spavento, had taken over the directorship of the company from Scala, and rapidly proved himself to be a worthy successor. Shortly after this, he married the beautiful sixteen-year-old Isabella, who had already acquired a reputation for wit and learning.

She and Francesco are among the outstanding people who shaped the destiny of commedia dell'arte. Isabella would have been unusual in any age. In the sixteenth century, she was a phenomenon—a musician who played upon several instruments; a linguist who spoke fluently Italian, French, Greek, and Turkish; a poetess whose published work was appreciated by the *littérateurs* of her time; an outstanding mime, a member of several academies, a Latin scholar, and one of the most expert of the *innamorate* of Italian comedy. As if that were not enough, and to remove the suspicion that she was a prodigious blue-stocking and no more, there is ample witness to the fact that she was an unusually charming and attractive young woman, a happy wife, and mother of several children.

As she flashes all too quickly through the dusty pages of theatrical history, there is about her an enchantment that explains Tasso's desire to compose a sonnet in her honour, and illumines her portrait hanging in the Carnavalet in Paris.

Francesco, her husband, whose reputation for scholarship equalled her own—he also was a linguist, poet, musician, and member of distinguished academies—added to the reputation of the *Gelosi*. He created *Il Dottore Siciliano*, a witty variant of the original Mask; and *Falcirone* the Magician, a risible hybrid born of the Doctor crossed with Scaramuccia. He played Il Capitano Spavento with a verve and *braggadocio* that set the pattern for all future players of the part.

In 1579, the *Gelosi* began a tour of Italy that went into the following year. They were enthusiastically received in all the courts of northern Italy, and established such cordial relations with the Duke of Mantua that in 1586 he did Isabella the signal honour of standing as godfather to her daughter Lavinia.

Two years later, they paid their first visit to France since Francesco had taken over the directorship, and though their performances brought them success, they also brought calamity of the kind the players had grown to expect; and they made a hasty retreat, partly because of a decree of Parlement against them, partly due to a fear of being involved in the troubles following upon the assassination of the Duc de Guise.

It was not until 1599 that the company once more played in Paris, this time under the patronage of Henri IV, so that no other authority was able to prevent performances at court. The *Confrérie*, ever-watchful, refused to allow public performances. Andreini, having previously learnt his lesson, bought a permit from them, so satisfying the profit-making scruples of his adamant opponents, and enabling him to instal his company in the Hôtel de Bourgogne, of not very happy memory.

In spite of their struggles with civil and ecclesiastical authorities, the Italian players found themselves at home in France. Their receptive audiences stimulated them, and inspired their best work. The Italian bias of the court, and the prevalence of Italian speech and dress in Paris offered a social security not often enjoyed by foreign players: and at this time their opponents could be disarmed by the clink of gold, or a decree of the reigning monarch. Most leading companies arranged a French tour as part of the normal year's work, and the best were invariably invited to Paris at royal or ducal command to attend the outstanding festivities of the year.

Among those companies that left an honourable record were *I Comici Accesi*, the troupe of the Duke of Mantua, directed by Tristano Martinelli, the greatest of the earlier Arlecchinos known to France. He first came to Paris at the beginning of the seventeenth century, giving both private performances at the court, and public ones at the Hôtel de Bourgogne. Two of the children of Francesco and Isabella Andreini were members of his troupe in 1613.

Martinelli, an enigmatic personality in private as in public life, called himself Arlecchinus, and, at the height of his career, signed himself *Dominus Arlecchinorum*. To him we owe the first representation of Arlecchino, an engraving showing detail of the costume of the time. For Martinelli was the author of a curious work, seventy quarto pages long, with the grandiloquent title: *Compositions de Rhétorique de M. Don Arlechin, Comicorum de ciuitatis Noualensis, Corrigidor de la bonna langua Francese & Latina, Condutier de Comediens, Connestable de Messieurs les Badaux de Paris, & Capital ennemi de tut les laquais inuenteurs defrobber chapiaux*. This opus is dedicated to Henri IV and his wife Marie de Medici, and is in effect an impertinent address from one majesty to another. The seventy pages are divided into three books, each book containing more blank than written pages, and the whole gives evidence of wit, and a relation between patron and artiste resembling that of master and jester. It is clear that the considerable impudence of M. Don Arlequin is privileged.

The title pages of the books show an engraving of *Arlechin*, in the costume elsewhere described verbally in records of the time—the long, loose jacket held together with untidy ribbons; the narrow trousers; the irregularly shaped patches in various colours sewn carelessly here and there, the belt worn low upon the hips; the round cap with rabbit's scut; the general air of ragged insouciance are all present, together with the mysterious black face and the small feral eyes. The Martinelli engraving, in preserving these details, shows clearly how the Arlecchino of Henri IV was sartorially that of an earlier age. There is one significant change. This Arlecchino wears no phallus, but carries instead at his belt a crude dagger of lath. The phallus, ancient symbol of magic and power, object both of veneration and humour, has become for Arlecchino a little wooden sword, that will in turn become the bat, Harlequin's symbol of magic and power in slapstick form.

The beginning of the seventeenth century saw the brief and final appearance of the *Gelosi*, recalled to France by Henri IV, after his marriage. The company was disrupted by the tragically sudden death in 1604 of the brilliant Isabella Andreini. At Lyons, on her way home to Italy for the birth of a child, she had a serious miscarriage, and died unexpectedly a few days afterwards. Francesco, stricken by the sudden catastrophe, disbanded the company and returned to Italy, where he devoted the rest of his life to the collection and publication of his wife's writings.

Four years later, their son Giambattista or Giovanni re-established the company under the title *I Comici Fedeli*. Giovanni inherited part of the talent of his parents: he was a fine actor, a poet, and, curiously, the author of several pornographic plays. The *Fedeli* acquired all the scenari, *lazzi*, and effects of the disbanded *Gelosi*, through Giovanni; and because of their intimate connection, both private and public, with the much-loved Isabella, Marie de Medici took the *Fedeli* under her full patronage, and they were able to give performances at court and in public.

Giovanni sometimes played Arlecchino, sometimes Lelio. His writing shows the influence of the commedia dell'arte with which he had been associated since childhood. As well as his pornographic scripts, based upon the more licentious side of Italian comedy, he wrote five plays in which Bergamasque, Venetian, Bolognese and other dialects were oddly blended with Spanish, French, and German. It is obvious that he must have inherited the linguistic powers of both parents.

In the course of the seventeenth century several companies visited Paris at the same time and put on shows in different places, so that the

French public became increasingly familiar with the technique and the Masks of Italian comedy, and began to give French forms to their Italian names, a sign of affection and approval.

A factor of importance to the prestige of Italian comedy in France was the zealous interest of Mazarin, the power behind the French throne. Among the several major artists of whom he was patron was Locatelli, who invented an Arlecchino variant called Trivelino, by which name Locatelli himself was afterwards known.

Trivelino was the early rustic Arlecchino, to whom was added a soupçon of Brighella's wit and bravura. His mask and costume closely resembled Arlecchino's; but his hat was of a different shape, and without the rabbit's scut. His patches were circular, sometimes in the likeness of suns and moons. He carried neither stick nor sword. Locatelli, through his creation of Trivelino, added greatly to the development of Arlecchino. For when, after his death, Trivelino degenerated into one of the many valet-types, Arlecchino of Lower Bergama was found to have acquired some of the characteristics of Brighella of Upper Bergama. After Locatelli, Arlecchino was no longer stupid.

Encouraged by the success of Locatelli's company, Mazarin summoned other companies from Italy, among them the best players of the century. In 1660 Locatelli's company, implemented by Mazarin's players, moved into the Palais Royal Theatre, which they shared with Molière's company, taking alternate days for their performances.

In that theatre, the rustic Arlecchino, who had already shed so many of his provincial airs under the dual influence of his many travels, and the culture of the men who had played him, became Arlequin the wit in the hands of Domenico Biancolelli.

Upon the death of Locatelli in 1671, Domenico, who for twelve years had played second Arlecchino in the company, and who had watched the creation of Trivelino, became himself the Arlecchino of the company at the Palais Royal.

Biancolelli was a player in whose veins flowed the blood of generations of Italian actors. He was born in Bologna, of parents who were both members of a company established in that town. His long and fruitful apprenticeship began in his childhood, when experienced eyes noted such promise in the wit and agility of the youngster that he was from the beginning trained for the difficult rôle of Arlecchino.

When he first joined Mazarin's troupe in 1659, at the age of nineteen, he was already a Mask of exceptional technique, with a fine stage presence. In the company to which he now belonged, he was able to watch Locatelli playing Arlecchino in the conventional manner, and gradually polishing the cunning variant Trivelino. When finally he took over, the Arlecchino he played was a re-creation, the last of the Arlecchinos, the first Arlequin.

Biancolelli's Arlequin was a subtle compound, yet based upon the traditional Mask of early commedia dell'arte. Where Locatelli had created a variant in which was more of Brighella than of Arlecchino, Biancolelli achieved the fusion of the two Bergamasque clowns. His Arlequin looked like Arlecchino, practised all the traditional *lazzi*, played the same rôle: but he behaved with the bold cunning of Brighella. Brighella's mind entered Arlecchino's body. Then Biancolelli enriched that mind with his own wit and wisdom, his own culture, and shaded it with a little of his own sadness.

The Arlequin emerging from this act of creation changed rapidly from the stupid rustic glutton he had been into an impudent and cynical master crook, whose mordant wit was expressed verbally, in mime, and in supple acrobatics. This Arlequin was a wit and a philosopher, a mighty rogue with curious moments of dejection that drew his audience closely to him.

Before Biancolelli, Arlequin, true to his origins, belonged to the real life of the Italian peasantry. With Biancolelli, Arlequin entered into the realm of legend and fantasy. Until now the audience had known that beneath the mask and trappings of Arlecchino there lurked one of those wooden-headed fools from Lower Bergama. Biancolelli swept that certainty away. No one knew any more who it was or what it was concealed beneath that animal face, or whether in fact there was anything there at all but the remote fantastic in jaunty patches.

Biancolelli's innovations reached the traditional costume. He lengthened the jacket, widened the trousers, sometimes filled the ragged open neck with a small frill, and replaced the haphazard patches with symmetrical shapes of different colour arranged in an orderly manner. He left untouched the mask, belt, stick, and hat. The effect of these small but masterly changes was that Arlequin no longer looked like an untidy ruffian, but acquired a dress that was more in keeping with his new power and polish, without losing any of its traditional symbolism.

One other addition made to the playing of Arlequin was an involuntary one. Biancolelli had a laryngeal defect that made him speak in a throaty, croaking voice exactly like a parrot. His exploitation of this defect added new humour to the rôle, and after him all Arlequins spoke with a parrot's voice. Biancolelli died in 1688: yet the lingering echoes of his natural voice are still with us, whenever the Punch and Judy man slips his false larynx into his mouth to speak with Punch's voice, which is Biancolelli's voice, handed on to Punch by Arlequin.

There are many stories extant illustrating the ready wit and intelligence of Biancolelli, who in private life was a sober, introspective man, given to periods of deep gloom. A favourite story is that of the royal banquet, to which he had been invited for the entertainment of the guests of Louis XIV. Partridge was served upon a magnificent gold dish, upon which Biancolelli looked so longingly that Louis XIV, knowing him to be fond of partridge, said to the footman, 'Give that dish to Arlequin.'

'Your Majesty!' cried Biancolelli, deeply moved. 'And the partridges as well?' The King was so amused that Biancolelli received both dish and bird.

Another shows a still greater degree of subtlety. Open hostility had flared up once more between Italian and French players, and the latter were making full use of their rights of monopoly to oust the former. Biancolelli appealed to Louis XIV, who called the antagonists before him to state their case; Baron[1] to speak for the French, and Biancolelli for the Italian players. Baron spoke first, with fluency and sincerity, with impassioned rhetoric and all the certainty of a just cause. He spoke at considerable length. When he had finished, Biancolelli lifted a gloomy face to the King. 'Your Majesty,' he said. 'How shall I plead my cause?'

'In whatever manner you choose,' replied Louis XIV.

'Then, Sire, I choose the successful manner, and I have gained my case.'

Not all Baron's violent indignation could prevent the King from declaring in Biancolelli's favour. The decree went forth that henceforward the Italian players might perform without let or hindrance.

---

[1] Actor and author, member of Molière's Company.

Biancolelli's death, at the early age of forty-eight, brought great loss to the theatre. He had attended one of the King's private parties, where he engaged upon a demonstration of the most exacting acrobatics of Arlequin. Some say he became overheated and then caught a chill, others that he had some sort of seizure while he was performing. In a few days he had died of pneumonia. He was universally mourned, and his theatre was closed for a month in homage and sorrow.

CHAPTER TWO

Arlequin Learns to Speak French

ARLEQUIN had travelled and played in France for more than a hundred and fifty years before he began to speak French. There had originally been no need for him to learn the language of his adoptive country. Italian was the fashionable language at court. The mime of the Italian players, their *lazzi* and acrobatics, made their comedy accessible to the people, who were not able to understand their dialogue.

No one can remain so unusually long in a foreign land without acquiring at least a smattering of its idiom. Arlequin began to acquire a second tongue under the tutelage of Evaristo Gherardi, Biancolelli's successor at the Palais Royal.

Gherardi was the son of an actor who throughout his career played the valet Flautino, a Brighella variant. He was brought to Paris in childhood, no doubt because his father's company was playing there: and the way prepared for his future influence on the development of commedia dell'arte. For his father placed him in one of the leading seminaries in France, where he received the sound classical education of his time. The boy, quick and intelligent, was shaped by the French, not the Italian pattern of education, and, by the time his schooldays were ended, was completely bilingual. It is possible that his father hoped, by sending him away to school, to wean him from a hazardous career on the stage and to establish him in due course in some secure and respectable profession. The son, however, chose to follow in his father's footsteps. Gherardi made his first appearance, as Arlequin, in *Le Divorce Forcé*, under the direction of an old friend of his father, Tiberio Fiorelli. Fiorelli played Scaramouche (*Scaramuccia*), and was reported to have been the greatest of them all. In 1695 Angelo Constantini, who played the valet Mezzetino in Fiorelli's troupe, published a biography, *La Vie de Scaramouche*, in which Fiorelli is described as being deaf in one ear, shortsighted, and possessing a withered arm. 'As for his character,' continues the author, 'he was extremely mistrustful, covetous, and with a passionate temper. He had a lively imagination, spoke but little and had much difficulty in the delivery of his words: but in recompense, nature had endowed him with a wonderful talent of expressing, by the postures of his body and the grimaces of his face, whatever he had a mind to say.' He enjoyed royal patronage: and had the dubious honour of having his clothes ruined by the infant Dauphin, while he was nursing him in an otherwise successful attempt to turn his furious squalls into chuckles of delight. Gherardi then was sponsored by one of the most celebrated players of his age, and began his career in the company where first Locatelli and then Biancolelli had transformed the dolt Arlecchino into the witty Arlequin. Gherardi rapidly achieved a reputation equal to that of his much-loved predecessor when he took over the rôle after Biancolelli's death in 1688.

It is interesting to note that all the greatest players of Arlequin established themselves in the rôle with miraculous speed, no doubt because of their long apprenticeship, their theatrical background, and their own exceptional talent.

By birth and training, Gherardi was a player in the traditional manner. Culturally and intellectually, he belonged to the new line that was developing through the repeated and lengthening sojourns of the players in France.

When his public career was interrupted in 1697 by the closure of his theatre, he devoted himself to preparing the scenari used by his company for publication. He was able to collect fifty-six of them, eventually published in six volumes under the title *Théâtre Italien de Gherardi*, so leaving for posterity a valuable source of information concerning commedia dell'arte at a time when it was subject to major changes, among them the introduction of the French tongue into dialogue which hitherto had been wholly Italian. The earliest scenario given is dated 1682, the last 1697.[1] Gherardi collected the skeleton forms upon which the players constructed their performances, and added to them enough remembered dialogue to give as much of the content of the comedies as possible: some are the written texts of

1 For text see Appendix B, pp. 194–199.

SCENE FROM A SEVENTEENTH-CENTURY CANEVAS 'LES CHINOIS'

La Réveranse d'Arlequin

A PARIS
Chez Duchange Graveur du Roy, ruë St. Jacques près les Mathurins.
Chez Gautrot, et Jouillain, quay de la Mégisserie, à la Ville de Rome.
Avec privilège du Roy.

ENGRAVING BY CLAUDE GILLOT, 1695

miscellaneous authors who wrote them for the company. They reveal the contemporary blending of the old Italian tradition of the Renaissance companies with the new French dialogue and wit. Over the years, the repertoire of Gherardi's company was enriched by the addition to its parodies and farces in the Italian manner, of satiric comedies with a distinctly Gallic flavour.

Since, by its nature, commedia dell'arte is as evanescent as ballet, the importance of Gherardi's collected scenari cannot be overestimated. Together with the earlier ones of Flaminio Scala and J. B. Biancolelli, and the later collection of the Sacchi, they form a valuable basis to any study of commedia dell'arte.

Gherardi died untimely at the age of thirty-four, three years after the closure of his theatre, and on the very day he was to have presented a copy of his *Théâtre Italien* to his patron. At a private performance he fell heavily upon his head, and expired within a few hours from the injury received.

His future successor, then just seventeen, had already begun his theatrical career, and was about to assume the dancing shoes and motley dress of Arlequin.

Thomasso Antonio Vicentini, afterwards known as Thomassin, was born at Vicenza, a little town west of Venice, in 1683. He joined a travelling company of actors in Italy when he was in his early 'teens, where he played female rôles, and specialised in tragic parts. It is recorded of him that in Rome he enjoyed a remarkable success as a love-lorn young Princess. By chance, on a day when he was not acting, he went to watch a rival company playing improvised comedy, which he was seeing for the first time. The players immediately won him by their skill and their originality. He left the company where he had so successfully played girls and young women, and threw in his fortunes with the commedia dell'arte players. The boy sped swiftly through the successive stages of his apprenticeship; and by the time of Gherardi's death, he was already a notable young Arlecchino, and had played the rôle in most major Italian towns.

He had a physical dexterity and muscular control that were remarkable even in an age that had seen astonishing prowess. In his playing of Arlecchino he followed the traditional lines, into which Biancolelli's innovations had merged; and then, like his great predecessors, he added his original contribution to the rôle. With

6

Thomassin, an element of pathos crept into Arlequin's increasingly complex personality. Before him, Arlequin invariably aroused mirth, no matter what difficulties beset him, or what catastrophe overcame him. The Arlequin of Thomassin was able, at the height of a scene of uproarious clowning, to reduce his audience to silence and tears by the sudden desolation of his drooping head and dragging feet, by his own grief in the midst of farce. He played upon the emotions of his audience with a master hand, turning them from laughter to tears as he willed.

When in 1716 he came to Paris, he made full use in his dialogue of the infiltration of French words and phrases that was becoming increasingly common. Audiences found it hilariously funny to recognise in a spate of half-familiar foreign gibberish a homespun phrase that reached them with heightened impact. Thomassin pointed his dialogue with Gallic idiom as witty as it was obscene, and his audience rose to this comic polyglot. One of his most appreciated *lazzi* was his recital of La Fontaine's fable *The Miller, His Son, and the Ass*, in polyglot, and embellished with mime and acrobatics. He came downstage to address the audience, saying, 'Messieurs, je veux vous dire *una picciola* fable que j'ai lue ce matin. Car il me prend quelquefois envie de *diventar* savant; mais *la diro* en italien, et ceux *l'entenderanno l'explicheranno* à ceux qui ne l'entendent pas.' There followed the comic recital with its superb mime, his jargon became wilder and funnier as the story went along. At the end, he explained, first in Italian, then in French, then in polyglot, that since when he spoke Italian the ladies could not understand him, and when he spoke French the gentlemen complained that he was no longer Arlequin, he had decided to speak both at once, and so satisfy everyone—which was more than the Miller and his Son had been able to do.

It was due to Thomassin's blending of the two languages in his spontaneous dialogue that even after whole scenes in French were interpolated in the plays towards the end of the eighteenth century, Arlequin continued to talk in his Italo-Franco jargon, a *lingua franca* that was in itself an instrument of comedy and a fertile source of satire and innuendo.

Thomassin's entry upon the French scene was, however, considerably delayed by events that were taking place while he was a child in Italy, and that reached their climax when he was only fourteen, and had just begun to tread the boards.

THE ARRIVAL OF THE ITALIAN COMEDY

Duncan Grant, 1951

Photo Rigal, Paris

Frontispiece of '*Les Recueils des Parades de Corbie*'

ARLEQUIN AT THE FAIR OF ST. LAURENT, 1786

It must not be supposed that Arlequin was ever left in peace to perfect his gift and develop his comedy. The civil and ecclesiastical authorities never ceased their harrying of the Italian players. Towards the end of the seventeenth century, they were being heavily censured for indecency. It is difficult to decide, in the absence of unbiassed evidence, whether the century had grown more refined, the players more out of hand, or whether the introduction of French into the dialogue had made clearer the obscenities formerly expressed in mime and in Italian. There was certainly more than a touch of hypocrisy in this censure, since the French comedians of the time were not lacking in scabrous use of the same sources of humour.

Whatever the case, hostility against the Italian players grew to alarming proportions, until they brought their own doom upon themselves. Towards the end of the century, the company of the Duke of Modena was established at the Hôtel de Bourgogne, under the grandiloquent title of the King's Company of Italian Players. Gherardi had been invited to join the company, and was playing Arlequin with a success that brought all Paris flocking to the doors of the Hôtel. Then came the catastrophic affair of *La Fausse Prude*, in which the players themselves were largely to blame. There is an official letter, dated 1696, advising them that their performances are too unbridled now that French dialogue makes everything clear, and warning them to censor their words and gestures so that they shall not give displeasure to their audiences and to the civic authorities. They had been warned: and in the following year they blundered badly.

A romance entitled *La Fausse Prude*, recently published in Holland, purported to disclose scandals relating to Madame de Maintenon, the favourite of Louis XIV. Importation of the book into France was therefore forbidden, and nothing else was discussed in the salons and on the street. At the time of the ban, the King's Players were putting into rehearsal a comedy called *La Belle-Mère Supposée*, formerly given under the Italian title *La Finta Matrigna*. Some misguided member of the company, with an eye to the box-office, thought that in view of the recent excitements over the banned book, the gross receipts might be considerably increased if *La Belle-Mère Supposée* became *La Fausse Prude*. Theatre folk are notoriously single-minded, but the incredible stupidity of this flash of genius is breathtaking. The directors and the company, having no doubt complimented their colleague, announced the forthcoming presentation of *La Fausse Prude*, and so delivered themselves into the waiting hands of their enemies.

Before ever the play was given, and in spite of a declaration of innocent intentions (which, in the absence of a written text, could not be proved) on the part of the directors, the King closed the Hôtel de Bourgogne, and expelled the players by an immediate mandate to the Chief of Police :—*The King has dismissed his Italian Players, and his Majesty commands me to write to you that you shall tomorrow, May 13th, 1697, close their theatre for ever.* Before the bewildered company, among whom were Gherardi, and also Catharina Biancolelli, daughter of Domenico, and a famous Colombina, could draw breath, they were homeless and in exile. They knew, none better, that their play, based upon one of the earliest Renaissance scenari handed down through the generations, had nothing whatever to do with Madame de Maintenon, and contained not even a single reference to that scurrilous romance, *La Fausse Prude*. Unhappily for them, the very nature of their work left them without proof, without defence : and, because of a silly change of title, without a roof or a future. That blunder robbed the public of Gherardi's Arlequin for the last three years of his life, but gave us the valuable collection of the best scenari of his company, a curious profit and loss account.

For nearly two hundred years the Italian players had enjoyed royal patronage and delighted French audiences. For over a hundred of them, and in spite of the High Court, the Church, and the *Confrérie de la Passion*, Arlequin and his fellow Masks had roamed in and out of the Hôtel de Bourgogne and made it the centre of commedia dell'arte in France. Now they were banished, ironically enough, because of a play as old as their improvised comedy itself, and which, on this occasion, was never even shown.

For over a century the flickering lights held in brackets along the backstage passages of the Hôtel de Bourgogne had cast strange shadows over the fantastic masks of Pantalone, Il Capitano, Pagliaccio, Scaramuccia, Brighella, and Arlecchino. For over a century players belonging by birth, tradition, and technique to the most original theatre in Europe had elbowed each other away from the small fluttering scenario pinned to a board, upon whose brief directions they would in a few moments begin to build a dazzling superstructure. Along those echoing corridors Arlecchino had practised his

THE EXPULSION OF THE ITALIAN PLAYERS FROM THE HÔTEL DE BOURGOGNE
IN 1697

Engraving by Jacob of a painting by Watteau

ARLEQUIN ET COLOMBINE

From the painting by Watteau

leaps and pirouettes, flirted with Colombina, or leaned pensive against a wall, thinking out new *lazzi*, or another impudence.

Within that place the Masks had earned the affection of Paris, become known as Pantalon, Pierrot, Scaramouche, and Arlequin. The Hôtel de Bourgogne was alive with the grumbles and jealousies, the loves and hates, the fatigue and excitement, the delights and disappoint-ments of generations of Italian players offstage: and with the haunting memory of their skilled team work on stage. Now magic and memory were stripped with a ruthless hand, the doors were closed and sealed, the players dismissed, and their expulsion made known throughout Paris by the King's mandate and the official notice upon the sealed doors. In all their difficult career, the players had never known a disaster like this.

It was nineteen years before the Italian Comedians returned. In those years Gherardi, Madame de Maintenon, Louis XIV died. The old scandals were forgotten: and Arlequin pursued his adventures in odd places.

CHAPTER THREE

Arlequin Goes to the Fair

THE expulsion of the Italian Comedians from the Hôtel de Bourgogne was a bitter blow to Arlequin. At the peak of his maturity, and of his career, he was suddenly brought low. Now nearly two hundred years old, and destined to live as long again, he was very different from the Bergamasque lout he had been in his early years. He had grown accustomed to the company of kings and nobles, scholars and poets: to the plaudits of a cultured court as well as to the unrestrained enthusiasm of the mob. He was familiar with fine manners, sophisticated wit, and elegant women. He accepted as his due clean linen, exquisite food, and comfortable living. His talent had grown into a poetic genius that made him first among the Masks, and promised much for the future.

Overnight his kingdom tumbled into dust. All that he had won was snatched from him for ever, or so it seemed in that dark moment when he with his fellows stood outside the Hôtel de Bourgogne. Yet the years and the men that had shaped Arlequin had given him an unconquerable spirit. He was not destroyed by the disaster that had overtaken him: it simply forced him into a curious retrogression. His triumphal march suddenly halted, and he went briskly back the way he had come.

After the King's mandate, the leading players of the company returned to Italy, where they were certain of being invited to join one or other of the ducal troupes. The rest decided to divide into two small companies, and return to the nomadic life of their forebears. It would be impossible to cover the travelling expenses of a large company, and difficult to secure each member his living wage. Two small companies, travelling in different directions, were likely to achieve better financial results, even if the standard of performances fell because of lack of choice in casting. Loyalty to his mistress had compelled Louis XIV to drive his comedians away from Paris, yet it would seem that he was unwilling to drive them from France. Both companies were granted a royal sanction to give performances in the provinces, provided that they did not appear within thirty miles of Paris.

The Italian players in France went back to an earlier day, reverting to the portable trestle stages and lustier repertoire of their ancestors, travelling through the country at a discreet distance from the capital, and experiencing hardship of a kind they had never imagined. These were hardy spirits, who rapidly adapted themselves to new conditions, and kept the tradition of commedia dell'arte alive in France at a time when it seemed it must perish there.

Yet Arlequin did not leave Paris with the players, even though there was no theatre open to him, and he could not remain at court. He went back to the home of some of his ancestors, and found congenial shelter in the great fairs of Paris.

European drama owes its origins equally to the Church and the fair. Arlequin's relations with the Church had always been somewhat strained; but generations of Italian comedians had been born and bred in the fairgrounds of their own country. Arlequin had practised all his tricks there before he became skilful enough to play at the ducal courts. There were some among the theatre folk of the fairs who saw in Arlequin's dismissal from the Hôtel de Bourgogne a magnificent opportunity for themselves. They knew how popular Italian comedy was, and realised that the departure of the players from Paris had left a void in the entertainment world. It seemed foolish not to exploit the possibility of introducing Arlequin himself into the vaudeville booths of the annual fairs, where he had been comfortably installed for years in marionette form.

Each year Paris at this time held two outstanding fairs, that of St. Germain, on a site belonging to the Abbey of St. Germain des Prés: and that of St. Laurent, on the site today filled by the Gare de l'Est, near the park of St. Lazare.

Each year a miniature universe arose in these two places. Here were to be found all the tragedies, comedies, emotions, vices, and virtues; every possible type of entertainment, every form of amusement. Here

everything imaginable and unimaginable was bought and sold—
Italian wine, French comfits, Spanish leatherwork, nightshirts, cream
tarts, cheap crockery, bonnets and mantles and laces and feathers,
eggs and cheese and live poultry, leggings and smocks and musical
instruments, sweetmeats, candied fruit, sugar hearts, spice men,
ribbons, ruffles, kid slippers, syllabub and frumenty, love and virtue.
Here teeth were pulled, hair was cut, corns doctored, remedies sold
for every ill; and love potions, wishing stones, and the elixir of life
offered every two hundred yards or so.

Nor was other entertainment lacking. The curious could gaze upon
all the deformities careless Nature brings to birth from time to time—
the dog-headed boy, the two-headed calf, the five-legged donkey,
the giant and the midget, the fat lady and the skeleton man—as well
as those encouraged by man—a singing monkey, a white rat that
could dance a saraband, performing dogs and bears and fleas. There
were cabarets and brothels and dance-halls; acrobats, puppets, wild
beasts, tight-rope walkers, waxworks, sword swallowers, fire-eaters,
marionettes, singers and musicians. From dawn till dusk and into the
night, all the fun of the fair, joyous and blaring with the cries of the
hucksters, the cacophony of rival musicians fighting for attention, lit
by blazing sun or by flaring torches, extinguished but not daunted by
sudden rain, attracted a vast mob out for any and every form of
entertainment. All the world and his wife or mistress turned out to
see the Fair of St. Germain or St. Laurent, bringing with them
country cousins to gasp at the bloodthirsty melodramas, roar at the
scabrous comedies, and weep at the poignant tragedies given by
strolling players who put up their stage at strategic points in the throng.

It was a noisy, merry crowd, given to sudden quarrels and much
horse-play, forgetful of the hierarchies of class or trade that separated
them on other days. Nobles and their equerries rubbed shoulders with
tipsy pages, and lackeys out for a girl. Wealthy merchants, penurious
clerics, shop-girls and masked ladies, soldiers, housewives, beggars,
pickpockets, cut-throats and charlatans, respected members of learned
societies, street walkers and country lasses streamed endlessly through
the fairground, shouting and laughing and singing, getting drunk and
making love, marvelling with open mouths, shuddering in happy
revulsion, each enjoying himself according to his kind, and some
afterwards amazed at themselves.

Here Arlequin was completely at home. Beneath the fine witty gentleman born of French culture there lurked still the old Arlecchino; a country clod with simple tastes whose nearest relations had always lived on fairgrounds. The stench and noise of the crowd, the lusty good humour and sudden brawls, the excitement and the fatigue, quickened his heartbeats and reminded him of his youth. If he had lost one home, he had found another, and provided the show went on, who cared where it was given? The fairs were under the patronage of the Church, whose protection extended even to the fairground theatres, who paid handsomely for the privilege. Arlequin felt safe.

Lulled by this security, he temporarily forgot the eagle eye of Parlement, alert to every infringement of the incredible number of bye-laws, privileges, and royal patents. He also forgot the relentless strength of the Comédie Française, France's national theatre, jealous of its monopolies, and ever ready to destroy any serious rival. Yet not for long was he able to ignore these factors. Almost before he had recovered from the closure of the Hôtel de Bourgogne, he found himself involved in a hundred years war, in which it seemed that he stood alone, with every man's hand against him. It was a battle fit for Arlequin, a ridiculous and tragic contest, as relentless as it was preposterous. Arlequin, who enjoyed life, never enjoyed it so much as during those tumultuous years.

The war began slowly and gathered momentum as the years went by. The suppression of the Italian players had offered an irresistible opportunity to certain fairground showmen. They helped themselves to the repertoire of the exiled players, and without demanding or being granted permission, they built real theatres, more lasting than trestle stages or booths. They covered the theft of the repertoire by explaining, to any who were interested, that since their marionettes already bore the names, Arlequin, Colombine, Scaramouche, and the like, they were entitled to make use of the repertoire for which the Italian players could have no further use. This dubious reasoning does not alter the fact that their smart showmanship helped to preserve the best of the commedia dell'arte scenari at a crucial time. They were saved from retributive action on the part of the homeless Italian players by the fact that the remaining members of the company were away from Paris, and preoccupied with their own difficulties. In 1698, only one year after the catastrophe, rival troupes had been formed that were already giving excellent shows in their new theatres at the fairs.

The two major companies were those run by the Alard brothers, and by Bertrand, Dolet, and De la Place, all previously owners of marionette shows. Their newly formed companies of live actors were heterogeneous, including experienced artistes brought from the provinces, and amateurs drawn from the artisan class, willing to work in the theatre for twenty sols a day, and a nightly bowl of soup after the last show. As far as is known, very few members of either company had ever played in commedia dell'arte.

Their performances, however, attracted such crowds that their success was their undoing. Before the end of the century, the Comédie Française, seriously concerned by this diversion of good money into other hands, had complained to the Chief of Police. They stood upon their privilege of monopoly, demanded the immediate destruction of the theatres erected without a licence, and payment of heavy damages. The fairground theatre-owners, certain of losing their case, since their position was legally untenable, but equally certain of popular support, formed a defensive alliance, and went into a battle destined to last over a century, bringing them mighty reverses, and ultimate victory.

The first ten years of the war were as fantastic as any of Arlequin's own capers, and he himself played a leading part in them. The fairground people, legally insecure, set out to circumvent the *Grands Comédiens* of the Comédie Française by whatever means their native wit and ingenuity could devise. Henceforward, Arlequin dubbed the *Grand Comédiens* the Romans—probably because of their penchant for stern duty, however painful: and for classical tragedy. Until the opening skirmish of 1709, Arlequin employed delaying tactics. Whenever the *Grand Comédiens* brought a lawsuit against the theatre-owners of the fairs, the latter hindered the law to the best of their considerable ability, showing a stupidity and an ignorance of the ways of the law so ingenious and so successful as to touch upon genius. Arlequin continued to give performances while his case was pending, whatever embargo was put upon him, announcing with bland idiocy that he was just filling in time while he was waiting for the verdict. These delaying tactics secured a breathing space of ten years before the campaign opened decisively in 1709.

The entry into battle was worthy of Arlequin. Bertrand, Dolet, and

De la Place, joint owners of one of the theatres that had earned the displeasure of the *Grand Comédiens*, pretended to sell their theatre to one Holtz, a worthy member of the Swiss Guard of Monseigneur the Duke of Orleans. By so doing they became, in their own estimation, wage earners in the employ of Monseigneur, and so ceased to be theatre-owners. Following this coup, they announced future presentations with enormous posters bearing the arms of the Cardinal d'Este, and even of the King.

The *Grands Comédiens*, who had been harassed and hindered for ten years by Arlequin and his band, found this latest effrontery intolerable, and decided that it could only be answered by violence. On Saturday February 20th, 1709, at eight o'clock in the evening, a brisk and sinister company set out for Holtz Theatre. At the head marched representatives of the *Grands Comédiens*; then came a platoon of armed members of the watch, one contingent mounted, another on foot, followed by two Sheriff's officers and a rabble of carpenters and joiners armed with hatchets and saws, who, upon arrival at the theatre, were let loose upon it, and used their arms to such good effect that before they retired, a considerable part of the auditorium and the stage was destroyed.

The following day an enormous crowd, agog with interest, and probably hoping for further excitement, filled the theatre, which had been repaired by the owners, the players, and every single member of the company working all through the night. The players had only just time to change before the show, and then to go straight on the boards after their night of hard labour. They received a rapturous welcome, and their gross receipts reached a total hitherto only dreamed of, while the *Grands Comédiens* sat moodily beside their deserted box-office. That was Sunday, February 21st, 1709.

On Monday, February 22nd, the *Comédiens*, complete as before with armed guards, Sheriff's officers, mobsters, and a holy zeal, returned to the Holtz Theatre, and this time literally razed it to the ground. All night a mighty bonfire of seats, scenery, curtains, costumes and properties of all kinds, fed by the *Comédiens*, sent its baleful message out.

This devastation was on such a scale that in due course both parties appeared before the *Grand Conseil*, the *Comédiens* joyfully awaiting the moment when Arlequin and his band would be put down with a firm hand by the law. Their consternation can be imagined when they discovered that since the sack of the Holtz Theatre had taken place at night, it was criminal in law. They heard with stupefaction that they must pay the heavy damages of 6,000 francs to the injured party. With this sum, the Holtz company built a new and handsome theatre, improving upon the old, and continued to give their shows. Arlequin developed a wicked gift for parodying the *Comédiens* in his own rôle.

The latter were, however, by no means defeated. When they had recovered from the shock of the decision against them, and the financial loss that resulted from it, they appealed directly to the King, calling upon him to honour the privilege he had granted. Their triumph then seemed absolute. They first obtained restitution of the damages they had paid, which the Holtz company were fortunately able to restore to them following a most successful season. Their next move was to secure an absolute veto in law on all performances of plays with speech, dialogue, or monologue, by the theatre people of the fairground. The jugglers, the acrobats, the mimes were untouched by the veto: Arlequin's way was blocked, or so it seemed. The *Comédiens* had yet to learn that one of Arlequin's most popular *lazzi* was his getting through a brick wall.

There was the wall, solid, impenetrable; Arlequin on one side, a dish of cherries, a bottle of wine, a pretty serving wench on the other. Arlequin never waited to climb the obstacle that kept him from his heart's desire. A bound, a leap, and he was through it, the wall behind him, solid, impenetrable. The *Comédiens* would not perhaps have been so certain that Arlequin was securely imprisoned in the silence put upon him by the embargo on speech, if they had remembered that particular *lazzi*.

CHAPTER FOUR

Guerilla Warfare

THE *Grands Comédiens* had won the first campaign, since even Arlequin dared not disobey the King's veto. But by this time, the fairground folk were determined to fight and, if they could, turn defeat into victory. The next eight years were given to guerilla warfare, aimed at hindering and irritating the *Comédiens* in every conceivable way, while the fairground theatres consolidated their forces and grew powerful enough to wage an open war. Never for a moment in those eight years did the *Comédiens* enjoy peace or Arlequin security.

His first action was to circumvent the veto on speech. The fairground theatre-owners met to discuss the problem, and decided to interpret the embargo in their own manner. Clearly, since the *Comédiens* were concerned in this, the plays Arlequin was forbidden to put on must be those on the classical pattern of the Comédie Française where unity of time, place, and action was strictly observed. No other type of play could be any concern of the *Comédiens*, nor recognised by them, and were therefore beyond the scope of the veto. Convinced by their own plausibility, they opened the campaign. *The Rape of Helen, with the Siege and Sack of Troy* was presented at the new Holtz Theatre. This remarkable scenario set out to obey none of the unities, so as to avoid being classified as a play. It covered ten years in time, ranged from Troy to Priam's Palace, through Ulysses' tent to the ramparts, and back again. It had not so much a plot as a confusion of plots. This was followed by others on a similar pattern, until the *Comédiens* managed to put an end to them by securing a veto on dialogue, regardless of the type of entertainment offered.

Arlequin then ostentatiously presented plays in which, among a throng of characters, only one spoke at a time, while the others reverted to mime. Since no Mask ever addressed another in speech, or replied to another, the plays were without dialogue, in obedience to the veto. On one happy occasion, Arlequin gave the whole show by himself. He played in turn the old man, the young girl, the lover, the braggart soldier, the valet, and the ingénue, changing from Pantalon to Scaramouche, from Scaramouche to Colombine, from Colombine to himself, as the plot demanded, changing voice and gesture as required by each Mask, and performing all the *lazzi* alone. There were six characters in that particular comedy, but since Arlequin played them all, there was no dialogue, but only a series of monologues given by one actor. In another attempt to circumvent the veto, he composed a ridiculous play entirely of short monologues, each Mask retiring abruptly at the end of his speech, to reappear as abruptly when it was again his turn to speak. This show was so well timed that, although there was never more than one character on the stage at any time, and no player directly addressed another, the plot was developed and brought to its conclusion as it would have been had the players been allowed to proceed normally. At the end each character solemnly took in turn a lonely farewell of the audience. This *tour de force* was appreciated as much as the earlier ones, and the theatre was crowded by many who came simply to see what Arlequin would do next.

The *Comédiens*, annoyed but not routed, and determined to bring to a halt the continued success of the fairground theatres, were able to enforce a veto on monologue, leaving Arlequin speechless once more.

There followed some of the oddest shows that have ever been given in the history of drama, and some of the cruellest parodies. Bringing all his natural malice to the task, Arlequin put together scenari that bore curious resemblances to the classical repertoire of the Comédie Française. He and the other Masks, all expert and practised mimes, in presenting these scenari imitated the well-known and stylised technique of the *Grands Comédiens*. With solemn virtuosity, and wearing their own motley, they reproduced the work of the Comédie Française. Gesture, movement, style, business, timing, pace, and intonation were all closely imitated. The only thing lacking were the majestic hexameters habitually spoken by the *Grands Comédiens*. For, since Arlequin was forbidden dialogue or monologue, his parody, so exact in every other detail, was given in unintelligible gibberish, drawn from no language, containing no words, yet managing to sound ridiculously like the sonorous alexandrines of classical tragedy, and voiced with all the stylised fire and passion of the *Comédiens*. The result was irresistibly comic, particularly to a public familiar with the repertoire and technique of the national theatre.

The novelty of these impudent parodies attracted a new public to the fairground theatres, while the old one enjoyed the continual skirmishing for place between the established and the fairground drama. Arlequin himself enriched his rôle in pouring ridicule upon his opponents, and learned with delight that he had so discredited their repertoire that giggles and guffaws were heard in the august reaches of the Comédie Française, as the serious work performed there from time to time reminded audiences of the incredibly funny parodies they had seen at the fair.

Arlequin, a theatre man to the core, was always aware of the public pulse. Before ever the fickle crowd began to tire of the absurdities he was presenting, the quicksilver Mask was seeking other ways in which he could circumvent prohibition, and attract the public. His next ingenuity, as lightheartedly launched as all the rest, had a lasting effect on French drama, and created a new genre.

He remembered that in his early nomadic days in Italy there had always been a *cantatrice* in commedia dell'arte, to provide musical interludes. It occurred to him that a development of the musical side of his shows might well lead to his victory over the veto on dialogue, since song was not dialogue. He discussed this inspiration with his good friend Fuzelier, who was enjoying this guerilla warfare as much as Arlequin himself. It was Fuzelier who had provided the company with *The Rape of Helen*: and who now, working upon this novel idea of turning dialogue into song, produced *Les Amours de Tremblotin et de Marinette*. This was a musical play of a kind previously unknown, a rudimentary light opera, which immediately captured the heart of Paris. Arlequin, already a dancer, acrobat, mime, and actor, became a singer. In a very short space of time he had enlarged his company to include an orchestra and a corps de ballet, and was enjoying a major triumph in a new genre.

For once luck was with him. At the time *Les Amours* was presented, Guyenet, director of the Opéra in Paris, was in serious financial difficulties. The fairground theatre folk were therefore able to buy themselves the right to employ singers and dancers, and to make use of décor and scene changes. If Guyenet had been less embarrassed for money, he would have certainly prohibited Arlequin from entering into potential rivalry with the Opéra, in the same manner that the *Comédiens* were jealously guarding their own rights and privileges. Fortunately, Guyenet was not in a position to refuse the handsome sum offered, so that for once Arlequin stood on the sunny side of the law, secure in his rights.

The *Comédiens*, however, did not leave him long to enjoy them. The administration of the Opéra was under their jurisdiction, and they forbade Guyenet 'to allow the fairground theatre-owners of Paris to employ singers, give opera or ballet in any form or use machines, scenery, or musicians'. The sum of money Arlequin had paid for the rights that were now taken from him was not returned to him.

Everything having now been prohibited, Arlequin reverted to the use of mime only in his shows. Yet he did not simply return to his earliest form of expression. He was determined to use it as a means of continuing the castigation of his oppressors. To this end he filled the right-hand pockets of his characters with large scrolls, sticking his own through his belt on the right side. His players came on the stage in silence, and greeted the expectant audience in the same manner. Then Arlequin, leaping downstage, spoke voicelessly to his public, and bowed low at the conclusion of his unheard speech. Just as his mystified audience was about to murmur, he solemnly unrolled his first scroll, and presented it to them so that they could read upon it:

> *I'm sorry you can't hear my discourse*
> *It's not that I'm tongue tied*
> *But just that my tongue's tied*
> *For Rome[1] really finds me too coarse*
> *You do understand? I thought that you would,*
> *So now I'll continue to do what I should . . .[2]*

The play then continued in mime, while at salient points each character in turn unrolled a scroll bearing an ironic comment, presented it to the audience, then put it into his left pocket. At the end of the play all the scrolls had gone from right to left, and the

[1] Rome = Comédie Française
[2] *Je n'ai pu que tout bas*
Vous faire ma harangue ;
On m'a lié la langue,
Et Rome ne veut pas . . .
Ne m'entendez-vous pas?

Dans les Ris comme dans les pleurs,
Imitateur de la Nature,
Il sçut charmer les Spectateurs,
Et leur plait encore en peinture.

ANTONIO VICENTINI THOMASSO, KNOWN AS THOMASSIN
1683–1739

NICOLET'S THEATRE
At the Foire du Temple, Place Vendôme. Eighteenth century

audience were chuckling at Arlequin's continued impudence. The device has something in common with the subtitles of silent film.

Arlequin dared not rest, however successful his sallies. He knew exactly how quickly the public tired of innovation, and he extended the original idea of the scrolls before their novelty began to wear off. He secretly placed a few singers among the audience. As soon as a Mask unrolled and presented his scroll, the claque of singers scattered among the public began to chant the satiric verses on it to the tune of some well-known song. Inevitably, sooner or later, the audience joined in, and, as the idea caught on, Arlequin and his fellow Masks mimed the whole play, while the audience obligingly sang the whole of their dialogue for them. The *Comédiens* were powerless, since the audience, not the actors, were singing, and Arlequin had managed to provide himself with dialogue without breaking the veto.

This early form of audience participation was one of Arlequin's most riotous successes, in all but the literal meaning of the term. His inspiration crossed the years, and reached modern pantomime in England, where the leading comedian, in an interlude, often encourages the audience to join in singing a song printed on an enormous scroll suspended from the flies.

The players had clearly found it difficult to manipulate the scrolls at the right time and in the right order, in addition to their usual mime and acrobatics: it says much for their expertise that they were able to manage them at all. Indeed, on one occasion Pantalon, knocked over in mock fisticuffs between Arlequin and Scaramouche, as the comedy required, discovered that all his scrolls had been scattered far and wide over the stage, from both left- and right-hand pockets. The three Masks had to interpolate a sudden *lazzi* in which Arlequin and Scaramouche, apparently helping the old man to collect his property, knocked him down each time they brought a scroll to him, whereupon Pantalon, his head bowed in his hands, mimed his senile grief at being so treated. The audience, enjoying the slapstick farce, never realised that all three players were desperately collecting and sorting Pantalon's scrolls. Every time he was knocked flat and rolled over the stage, he was giving a quick glance at the scroll just handed to him, and putting it in the right place in the right pocket. To overcome these physical difficulties, and relieve the added strain, Arlequin in 1712 introduced a different system. The pocket scrolls were

7

replaced by large placards, printed with rhymed couplets and the name of the character to whom they belonged, the whole forming a gigantic play script. These were let down from above, and supported by two children, dressed as Cupids, and suspended in the air by means of counterweights, which gave them all the appearance of flying. One of the most popular, and perhaps the masterpiece of the kind, was *Arlequin, Roi de Serendib*, produced by Lesage at St. Germain in 1713.

Arlequin's apparent defeat in 1710 at the hands of the *Grands Comédiens* was in fact yielding excellent results. Inevitably he was forced to eschew the old traditions of true commedia dell'arte. It was left to the provincial touring companies of original players in France to maintain the genre outside Paris. Within the town, Arlequin was impelled, by the implacable hostility and opposition of the Comédie Française, into developing a new type of fairground theatre if he wished to survive. One subsidiary result of these exigencies was that shows of a much higher order of wit, satire, and stagecraft than was formerly the case were now presented at the fairs.

At this stage in his fairground fortunes he received unexpectedly a helping hand from the Opéra. The director Guyenet died, having failed to retrieve the fortunes of the administration. He left behind him a debit of some 800,000 francs, so complete a bankruptcy that even the Comédie Française could not set matters right, and therefore lost control of the destiny of her sister theatre. The receivers appointed to deal with the situation, who were anxious to turn what assets there were to good use, sold minor rights to the fairground theatres, among them those of employing singers and musicians, and of using machines and scenery. The fairground theatre-owners were graciously allowed to buy back the privileges stolen from them a few years before.

They were not the persons to stand upon their rights when it was better to forget them. They bought up everything the Receiver General would allow, and began to put on again the musical plays that had created such a furore before the *Comédiens* banned them. Light opera in France was born in the fairground, with Arlequin and the Opéra as doctor and midwife. The new genre was called *Opéra-Comique*, to stress at once its relation to, and difference from, opera of the conventional kind.

At first *opéra-comique* followed the pattern set by Fuzelier in *Les Amours de Tremblotin et de Marinette*. The first of these operas was composed entirely of topical and satirical songs sung by the actors. Arlequin, as before, was the leading player and singer. Since it was difficult to express a whole plot in song, a few phrases of spoken dialogue imperceptibly crept in, linking the solos and explaining the action. Emboldened by success, the companies added to the spoken dialogue until sometimes whole scenes were given without a song sung. The *opéra-comique* written and produced by Lesage in the early years of the eighteenth century shows a balance between speech and song unusual at that time, and bringing his work into line with modern light opera. Paris welcomed these new shows with the same rapturous delight that had been extended a few years before to *Les Amours de Tremblotin et de Marinette*.

Once more, success proved only too disastrous. As in the fairground theatres an increasing company jostled for place, in the Comédie Française there were too many empty seats. In 1718, when, after more than twenty years of unremitting struggle, Arlequin felt secure again, the *Comédiens* stepped in, and robbed him of his success, his dearly bought privileges, and his legitimate hope of an honourable future in the genre he had created. At their instigation, the Supreme Court suppressed all fairground entertainments, with the exception of the marionette shows, and tight-rope walkers. The *Grands Comédiens* presumably saw no dangerous rivalry emanating from those two sources.

The fury and despair of the fairground players can well be imagined. Through the lively but exhausting years of battle, they had managed by hook or by crook to turn aside veto, to avoid the consequences of prohibition upon dialogue, monologue, speech, music, and dancing. With all the big guns loaded on the other side, they had, time and again, snatched victory from their powerful opponents. It was hard to lose the fight at the moment of full success; and this time the veto was absolute. Arlequin was to lose his home, his livelihood, and his future at the fair, without any hope of evading this total prohibition.

Yet Arlequin's career was always as chequered as his coat. While he was engaged upon these last attempts at survival, forces beyond his knowledge or control were working on his behalf, in Italy and in France, at court, and in the Hôtel de Bourgogne, where, twenty years before, other members of his race had been driven into exile.

The battle was not yet lost, or won.

CHAPTER FIVE

Victory and Defeat

THE years that Arlequin spent at the fair had brought radical changes to the social scene in Paris. Louis XIV, whose approbation shone upon Biancolelli, whose decree banished Gherardi, had died, and with him died the scandal of *La Fausse Prude*. By the winter of 1716, the funeral ceremonies and mourning were forgotten. The late King's brother, Philip, Duke of Orleans, was made Regent for the minority of the young Louis XV, and in a position therefore to please himself concerning court amusement. As Monseigneur, he had greatly enjoyed, and been a leading patron of, Italian comedy. In the first year of his Regency he set plans afoot to recall Italian players to court. He was aware that the years of exile, the dubious adventure in the fairground, the constant opposition of all vested theatre interest, had despoiled the quality of the players who remained in France, and had changed their technique, and altered their repertoire. Philip of Orleans would tolerate only the best.

He turned therefore to Italy, birthplace of the improvised comedy, and approached Antonio Farnese, Duke of Parma, whose family from the beginning had been patrons of Italian comedy, and whose company contained the most gifted players of the day. The Duke invited Luigi Riccoboni to form a company of such excellence that it could go to France under court patronage.

Riccoboni, known as Lelio, since he played the Lover, is one of the most interesting personalities in the history of commedia dell'arte. An actor who nearly became a priest, he made his whole career in the theatre a crusade against its decadence, licentiousness, and profligacy. His life was dedicated to the ennobling of drama in Italy and in France, and spent in the service of an art he despised.

At the time he received the Duke of Parma's invitation to form a company of players for France, he had already become a notable figure and had set his mark upon Italian tragedy. He had also sustained a grievous failure with *La Scolastica* of Ariosto, so badly received by the audience that Lelio himself was hissed off the stage, and the curtain came down before the end of the fourth act. The Duke's invitation offered escape from an intolerable situation, and the hope of conquest abroad.

Lelio's company, when it was assembled, contained the best players in the Duke's service, and others drawn from the élite of the leading companies. Both Lelio and his wife Elena Balletti, known as Flaminia, since she played the Lady, belonged by birth, training, and tradition to the ancient and distinguished line of true Italian players. There is a possibility that Flaminia deliberately modelled herself upon her predecessor Isabella Andreini; for, with less talent, she became noted as actress, musician, linguist, a Greek and Latin scholar who was member of several academies, and a frequenter of pedants and courtiers. She had a wide knowledge of European literature; and has recorded in charming verse her unrealised desire to write poetry. She was celebrated from her earliest years in the theatre for her beauty and her wit.

She belonged to a family with a long theatrical ancestry. Her forebears had played at the courts of Germany, Vienna, Poland, Saxony, Bavaria, and Hanover; and while she was still in her 'teens, she had earned the reputation of being the best actress in commedia dell'arte in the whole of Italy. There is a story concerning her that illustrates not only her own prowess but by extension that of all highly qualified players of improvised comedy.

It happened in Venice, where two lawyers, great lovers of comedy, who often put on shows themselves, for their own amusement, saw Flaminia play on several occasions, and were convinced that she was not extemporising but acting after rehearsal with a written script.

They decided, with marked lack of gallantry, to set a trap for her; and having invited her to come to watch one of their own shows, one of them came to her in great distress because the leading lady had been taken ill suddenly. The play could not begin, the audience must go away disappointed. Flaminia, with the ready generosity of the first-rate actress, offered to fill the breach. Her offer was gratefully accepted, she was given a rapid résumé of the plot, and the play began. 'The two lawyers, one of whom played the Dottore and the other Pantalone, believed that they would cause her embarrassment, more especially in a scene where they had to oppose her over the legal rights of a father in making settlements upon his children. Their knowledge of law, and fluency acquired by dint of practice in the courts, served only to stimulate Flaminia's remarkable talents. She upheld the rights of nature and of reason so forcefully, and with so much eloquence that her outwitted opponents cut short the performance in order to make public confession of their defeat.'[1]

Lelio had gained still greater fame than Flaminia. Actor, director, author of several tragedies, of some invaluable studies of the theatre of his time, and of many scenari for improvised comedy, he would seem to combine in his one person the culture of Andreini, the talent of Biancolelli, and the literary value of Gherardi. Antonio Farnese made a wise choice when he placed the future of Italian comedy in France into the dedicated hands of Lelio.

There were ten players in the company brought to France in 1716, among them Thomassin as Arlequin; and a fifteen-year-old girl, Zanetta Benozzi, playing second lead to Flaminia, and destined in due course to become her serious rival and the Silvia for whom Marivaux wrote his subtle comedies.

The choice of Thomassin for the Arlequin of the new company had far-reaching consequences. Arlequin had early gained and kept first place in the affections of French audiences, at court, and, above all, at the Hôtel de Bourgogne: so that to a very large degree the fortunes of any Italian company in France depended upon the excellence of Arlequin. Thomassin, quick, small-boned, supple, a little man, sensitive and subtle, was to follow in the footsteps of Dominique and Gherardi, after an interval twenty years long. He came to Paris at the peak of his career, and at the age of thirty-three. His acrobatic power was unimpaired, his dexterity and muscular control perfected over the years. His years in Italy had enabled him to achieve a classic blending of comedy and pathos in his rôle, and to acquire a number of astonishing *lazzi* never before seen in France.

One of them was to leap from the stage, for fear of pursuit, on to the nearest box, from there to the next above, then on to the balcony rail, running round the vast semi-circle, balanced on the rail many feet

1 *Mercure*. March, 1772.

above the stage. It was not long before his audience begged him to forego this extremely dangerous trick, for they were convinced that it would be only a matter of time before he fell to his death; and he could not be spared.

Paris was so eager to see the Regent's company perform that it was decided to open on May 18th, 1716, at the Palais-Royal, since the Hôtel de Bourgogne was undergoing extensive renovation, and was not yet ready to receive them. So many people were determined to be present on the opening day that although the performance was to be given at five, by noon the boxes, circle, and pit were full. Many who queued for three hours or more were turned away.

The auspices were so far good: but the company knew that on this occasion they would owe success or failure solely to Arlequin, the darling of Paris returned from exile. Comparisons would be drawn between Thomassin and his great predecessors; even more dangerous, between Thomassin and Arlequin of the fairground. One of the gravest preoccupations of Lelio in these circumstances was Thomassin's voice. Since Dominique, all Arlequins had spoken with his parrot-voice; all Arlequins except Thomassin. To the audience accustomed to that voice, Thomassin's clipped straightforward tone would come strangely, and might prove catastrophic while the future of the players hung in the balance on that opening night.

To postpone the evil moment when Thomassin's voice must be heard, the play chosen was *L'Heureuse Surprise*, slightly altered so that it opened with a night scene. Lelio enters and calls for his valet Arlequin, who answers only by sleepy grunts offstage. Lelio, in great anger, goes to him and drags him on to the stage, Arlequin still fast asleep. Lelio, after a considerable struggle, wakens him and begins to speak. Arlequin falls asleep again and slips to the ground. Lelio pulls him up, Arlequin settles his head cosily on his master's shoulder, and snores. Lelio shakes him off and slaps his face to waken him; Arlequin, his arms round his master's knees, settles down again to sleep.

By the time this scene was over, the laughing audience had warmed to the new Arlequin, recognising the foolish witty clown, and were ready to be pleased: so that when at last he spoke, his unfamiliar voice added to their mirth, and the danger point was passed. Lelio was intelligent enough to follow *L'Heureuse Surprise* by *Arlequin Bouffon de Cour*, in which Thomassin was able to employ all the considerable resources of his silent mime. For in this play Arlequin disguises himself as a deaf and dumb jester at court, in order to save his master. He speaks twice only, once at the beginning, and once at the end of the play. Both performances were acclaimed, and it was clear that henceforward there would be no difficulty over Arlequin, with or without voice. By the time the Hôtel de Bourgogne was opened on June 1st, Arlequin in the person of little gentle Thomassin had captured Paris.

The play chosen for the opening was *La Folle Supposée*, based upon an ancient scenario that had been given at the Petit-Bourbon in 1645, and that is to be found in Locatelli's collection. It was a clever choice for this special occasion, linking as it did the traditions of the past with the present performance.

The Hôtel de Bourgogne had been magnificently restored for the new Italian players. Among points of interest was the curtain, showing a phoenix arising newly born from the flames, and, surrounding the fabulous creature, the caption *io rinasco* (I am reborn). Not all the dignity of its massive folds could hide the fact that Arlequin had by this means thumbed his nose at those who had driven him out twenty years before. The New Italian Theatre was opened with pomp and ceremony on June 1st, 1716, and however many attempts were made by Lelio the crusader to introduce serious drama, it became increasingly clear that Paris came to see Arlequin—Arlequin cutting incredible capers with a ladder in *Les Escalades Nocturnes*, somersaulting with a glass of wine in *Le Festin de Pierre*, proving his identity in a group of four Arlequins by walking round the edges of the boxes on all three levels, in peril of his life, in *Les Quatre Arlequins*; or devouring himself in *Arlequin cru prince par magie*, eating his feet with placid enjoyment, working up to knees, thighs, torso, until, with a last convulsive heave, Arlequin had consumed Arlequin, and there was nothing left upon the stage; or, with less cannibalism, eating his own brain in *Arlequin Soldat en Candie*; or catching a flea in *Arlequin feint baron allemand*, twisting his body into amazing knots and contortions until, with his body arched backwards and his head held between his knees and his convoluted arm, he caught the invisible monster and expressed his triumph in a series of double back-springs.

For the next seven years Lelio worked to re-establish the Italian players in Paris; and at the end of that period was rewarded by a royal patent and gratuity of 15,000 francs for the company. Louis XV, following in the steps of his father and his uncle as patron of the Italian players, granted the right to place upon the doors of the Hôtel de Bourgogne, beneath the arms of France, a black marble plaque bearing the inscription:

'Hostel des Comédiens Ordinaires
du Roy, entretenus par sa Majesté
rétablis à Paris en l'année MDCCXVI.'

It would appear then that all was well with the Italian players. They were securely established in their own theatre, fully restored to Paris and to royal favour. Only the players themselves knew the hard struggle they were waging, and the insecurity beneath their apparent success.

Within a year of their triumphant opening of the Hôtel de Bourgogne, their audiences were noticeably smaller and their receipts had fallen so disastrously that they sometimes failed to cover expenses. This decrease in popularity was due in part to the fickleness of the public, who departed once the novelty wore off; and mainly to the language difficulty. The Italian influence had departed from the court of France; the Italian fashion from the social scene. In those years that Arlequin in exile had gone to the fair and flourished there in spite of his many vicissitudes, he had engendered a new branch of his family; a race of Arlequins who spoke French even while they kept closely to the old scenari of commedia dell'arte.

By 1717 Lelio was so much aware of these factors that in *L'Italien Marié à Paris*, a new scenario given only by his company, he interpolated an extra scene, in which the jealous husband took his wife to the theatre. Backstage was placed a small model of the Hôtel de Bourgogne in which sat a French Arlequin. Then the real Arlequin, dressed in his best to go to the play, leapt from the pit to the stage, and was dumbfounded to meet with his double, speaking a foreign tongue, of which he could not understand a word. He called him away from the theatre, discussed with him the qualities that go to make a good Arlequin, each using his mother tongue, and managed not only to offer severe and witty criticism of the French Arlequins at the fair but to prove himself infinitely their superior in all the necessary qualities of a good Arlequin.

In spite of these and similar efforts, it became increasingly clear to

Lelio and his company that Paris preferred a false Arlequin who spoke
French to one in the ancient tradition who spoke Bergamasque. It was
no longer enough to play a few scenes in French, or to use both
languages at once. Arlequin and his fellow Masks were forced to
apply themselves seriously to their studies if they wished to survive.

In this transition period, the members of Lelio's company suffered
more than any others before or afterwards. All highly skilled, accustomed to working closely together, and to delivering fluent
dialogue suitable to each moment of the plot, they discovered that
when they played in French, the intimate relation one with the other
was blunted, dialogue was difficult, and there were too many pauses
covered by a confusion of *lazzi*. Their very excellence as players of
commedia dell'arte impeded their early attempts to play improvised
comedy in French. Their dialogue lost in wit and savour as they
extemporised in a tongue that was not their own. Imperceptibly, the
nature of their work changed. They could only recapture their
former verve by recourse to scripts written by French authors. The
change of language brought with it two others, equally fundamental. Written scripts replaced the traditional scenari; French farce
and wit the former Italian sources. Arlequin no longer spoke Bergamasque; the loss of his mother tongue was the severest he had yet
endured.

Even while the players struggled to acquire in French the technique
they had long since perfected in Italian, they were slowly but surely
undermined by the changes of taste in Paris since their predecessors
had gone into exile twenty years before. Even then, at the end of the
seventeenth century, there were many who found the repertoire of
the Italian players licentious and obscene. The Constantini brothers,
directors of the troupe then installed in the Hôtel de Bourgogne, were
largely responsible for this view. They encouraged the utmost development of the grossest elements in the farces: and imposed little if any
check on those players who went beyond the limits of decency. When
Lelio was first invited to form his company, he had been asked to
choose his players for their moral as well as for their dramatic
excellence. He had moreover signed an agreement that he would
never in any circumstances employ any member of the Constantini
family in his company.

This embargo is certain evidence that those dubious elements in the exiled company had not been forgotten. Lelio, who was himself wholly opposed to that gross indecency which could so easily become part of the comedies, suffered greatly under the stigma handed on by his predecessors. His own company had never merited such criticism: but there were other and subtler ways in which he failed to meet the requirements of the Parisian public in his first few years in France.

The early years of the eighteenth century had been marked by an increasing refinement of taste and spirit in Paris, an elegance of mind springing from the magnificence of the new century opening under the sophisticated influence of the Regent and his court. Women now attended theatres as a matter of course; their presence inevitably brought about changes in the type of drama presented. For the few among the audience who continued to enjoy and appreciate the brilliance of Thomassin, there were many who found Arlequin and Pantalon crude, and the comedies so overloaded with gross farce that they could take no pleasure in them. The Italian tradition of clowning ceased to be amusing in France in the eighteenth century.

These were the disturbances underlying the apparent tranquillity of those years preceding Louis XV's royal gesture. Lelio, sensitive and intelligent, dealt with them ably. He gradually replaced the old Italian scenari with modern French ones, the Italian tongue with French, gross farce with witty satire, coarseness with delicacy, frankness with subtlety. These changes were cumulative, so that Arlequin at first seemed little changed. Marmontel's description of him in the person of Thomassin, in the early years of the century, could be easily applied to Dominique or Gherardi: even to Locatelli and to Martinelli, so sustained was the broad outline of his character and personality through the years—'His character is a mixture of ignorance, naïveness, with stupidity and grace. He is like the merest sketch of a man, a great child visited by flashes of reason and intelligence, in all of whose muddles and awkwardness there is something arresting. The model Arlequin is all suppleness and agility, with the grace of a young cat, yet equipped with a coarseness that makes his performance more amusing. The rôle is that of a valet, patient, faithful, credulous, and gluttonous, always in love, always in difficulties, either on his master's account, or his own, suffering and consoling himself with the readiness of a child, one whose sorrows

are as amusing as his joys. Such a part demands a great deal of natural-
ness and of wit, and a great deal of physical grace and suppleness.']

Marmontel caught Arlequin just before further great changes came
to him. Lelio had laboured mightily to restore commedia dell'arte
to France: but he could not turn a changing tide. By his efforts he
brought success to his company: but only when his players were
engaged upon work fundamentally dissimilar from any they had
undertaken before: when, in fact, they had abandoned commedia
dell'arte.

CHAPTER SIX

The Elegance of Arlequin

UNTIL the early years of the eighteenth century, the potentialities of Arlequin had been developed by those who played him. From Martinelli he received bodily grace; from Locatelli the cunning of Brighella; from Dominique wit and a passable imitation of polite behaviour; from Gherardi intelligence; and pathos from Thomassin. At the fair he acquired a certain polish in language, if not in behaviour. Now a new influence entered his life, different from all others.

In October 1720, Lelio's company gave a one-act comedy by an unknown author, *Arlequin poli par l'Amour*. This was the first of Marivaux's comedies for the Italian players: its first appearance passed almost without comment. Just as Molière, who shared a theatre with the Italians in the previous century, had been aroused and stimulated by them, so Marivaux found in their technique, their scenari, and their Masks, a fertile source of inspiration, which led him first to write plays that breathed the very air and spirit of commedia dell'arte, then to develop a form of comedy that no one since has been able to rival or to imitate.

There was affinity of mind and spirit so tenuous and so powerful between Marivaux and Lelio's company that even when his comedies were wholly shaped by his poetic originality they were still haunted by the atmosphere of the Italian players. Perhaps no other company could have exerted so strong an influence upon him: the personnel of Lelio's troupe were singularly sympathetic. Lelio and Flaminia were friends of culture and intelligence. Their Arlequin, the little gentle Thomassin, in whom tears and laughter fought for mastery, was as sensitive an artist as Marivaux himself. There was, above all, the young Zanetta Benozzi, now nineteen years of age, and perhaps the most enchanting Silvia who ever trod the boards of the Italian

Comedians. Her four years in France were marked by the rapid development of her talents, and by her equally rapid conquest of the Parisian public. She was, from the beginning, the ideal interpreter of his plays. Their long and intimate collaboration was unique; for Silvia became the incarnation of Marivaux's creation, the Galatea to his Pygmalion.

Marivaux gave new life to Lelio's players at a moment when they were most discouraged, and finding it almost impossible to contend with the difficulties besetting them on all sides. He advised and directed them, encouraged and protected them; and began the series of comedies—*Arlequin poli par l'Amour*; *La Surprise de l'Amour*; *La Double Inconstance*; *Le Jeu de l'Amour et du Hasard*—in all, thirty-five comedies all written for Lelio's company, in twelve of which Arlequin appeared, while the rest contained his variant under the names Crispin, Lubin, Frontin, and others. By breaking the confining bands of commedia dell'arte, by extending the gifts of the company and using them differently, Marivaux saved Lelio and his colleagues from disaster.

The way was prepared for radical changes in Arlequin in Marivaux's first comedy, *Arlequin poli par l'Amour*; for in that play the original Arlecchino was shown for the last time, and transformed into a creature of mythology within the brief space of its one act. The beginning of the comedy shows the Bergamask clod of early commedia dell'arte. One of the characters tells how Arlequin is roused from sleep by the dazzlingly beautiful fairy who has kidnapped him for love, a situation reminiscent of Titania's love for Bottom. Arlequin, unmoved by the splendid vision, yawns hugely several times, stretches, turns his back, and goes to sleep again. His dialogue is almost monosyllabic, every word betraying his doltish insensitivity, with several *lazzi* introduced to offer further proof that time had altered nothing in the peasant Arlecchino—his first entry, when he looks like, and behaves like, a sulky gorilla; his indifference as he catches, kills, and eats flies while the fairy is talking; his grotesque attempts to learn to bow under the directions of a skilled dancing master. Throughout the first part, Arlequin is a reversion in type to the original Arlecchino, stupid, childish, with gross manners and speech. The fairy provides music and dancing for him. When she asks him whether the music made him feel anything, he replies, 'Yes—hungry.' Then comes the meeting with Silvia, the little shepherdess, for which the following stage directions are given: 'Arlequin comes in playing with a shuttle-cock. He comes in this manner to the very feet of Silvia; then, still playing, he lets the shuttle-cock fall, and, bending to pick it up, he sees Silvia. He stays bent, and, astonished, little by little and jerkily, he stands upright again. When he is upright, he looks at her. She, a little taken aback, makes to withdraw. In his embarrassment he stops her and says, 'You *are* in a hurry.' Later, kissing her hand, he essays his first compliment, 'I never sucked a sweet as sweet as this!'—in line with Arlequin's natural greed.

There is, in the seventh scene, a curious prescience of Njinski in *L'Après-Midi d'un Faune*. Arlequin had obtained Silvia's handkerchief by accident. He enters rubbing his face gently with it, comes down-stage, puts the handkerchief inside his jacket, stretches out, and rolls in ecstasy on the stage. Njinski, as the faun, shocked his audience with a similar pattern of behaviour. Arlequin, now speaking French as exquisite as the Fairy's own, asks her with great courtesy what are the symptoms of love. For the rest of the play Arlequin shows him-self increasingly intelligent, sensitive, polite, and elegant. He is still himself: but in an idealised version. Marivaux's subsequent comedies continued this process of idealisation until the title of his first—*Arlequin poli par l'Amour*—might well be extended to describe the development of Arlequin in Marivaux's hands.

All those elements that had been added to Arlequin, and developed in him through his sojourn in France, were fused and polished by Marivaux. He reached a degree of subtlety he had never yet attained. His coarseness dropped from him for ever, to be replaced by a delicacy of spirit that was infinitely moving. His wit was as lively, but now never obscene. The element of pathos added and exploited by Thomassin became an integral part of Arlequin's personality. The days of lusty stupidity and gross farce were put by. Marivaux penetrated to the core of poetry that Arlequin had always carried within him, released and shaped it until Arlequin stood forth in all his mystery and all his poetry, much as the dragon-fly emerges from its pupa.

Yet the seeds of his decadence were sown even as he reached this zenith. The refinement of all his gifts, the delicate expression of his enigma, created beauty in him; and destroyed the animal vitality that had sustained him through more than two hundred years of vigorous and exacting life. He wore the traditional costume and mask, carried the well-known bat, practised the old *lazzi*. To all outward appearance he was unchanged. Only, the virtue had gone out of him. Dramatically he had become a complex character subtly presented; the poetic creation of an original genius. He was literate, cultured, with an exquisite taste: and had found a delightful resting place in written comedies that offered every opportunity to him in his newest metamorphosis. Arlecchino had been polished; he became a decadent Mask, an unworthy son of Bergama, with little left in him of the blood and sinews of his ancestors. He was no longer an integral part of commedia dell'arte. He was the elegant French Arlequin, one of those that Thomassin had defeated in *L'Italien Marié à Paris,* but so changed, so much more subtle and so compelling that this time it was Thomassin who suffered defeat: for he himself played the 'false Arlequin'.

De Lisle was another French author of distinction who began to write for Lelio's company at about the same time as Marivaux. He made no radical changes in Arlequin, but continued the process of naturalisation by which Arlequin cast off his Bergamask tongue and origins, and became increasingly French. His first comedy, *Arlequin Sauvage,* given in 1721, was a greater success at first than Marivaux's *Arlequin poli par l'Amour.* In this piece Arlequin was a savage brought to France by Lelio, who had been shipwrecked on a strange shore, and had decided to show one of the natives the delights and advantages of civilisation. This situation gave Arlequin ample scope for a commentary on the social scene as witty as it was satirical, each episode in the play leading him to reach conclusions that reflect little desire to become civilised.

> 'You are mad, for you go to endless trouble to discover a multitude of useless things. You are poverty-stricken, since you limit your wealth to money or devilries of that kind, instead of simply enjoying nature, as we do, we who don't want to own anything, so that we can freely enjoy everything. You are the slaves of your possessions, that you value above your liberty and your fellow-men. Why, you would hang your brother if he dared lay hand upon the smallest part of all these useless belongings. Then you are ignorant, for you declare that wisdom lies in knowledge of laws, and you cannot understand that a knowledge of reason would teach you how to do without laws.'

'You are right, my dear Arlequin,' replies Lelio. 'We are mad, but only because we cannot help ourselves.'

'Your greatest delusion is to imagine that you cannot help being mad.'

In his subsequent comedies, De Lisle allowed Arlequin a similar measure of satiric understanding of the contemporary scene, and used him increasingly to express his own philosophy of life, in which were to be found the germs of rebellion against established institutions, and of romanticism.

The comedies of Marivaux and of De Lisle, and of those who followed in their footsteps—Autreau, Gueulette, D'Allainval, Moni-cault, and others—materially helped the fortunes of the Italian players by creating renewed interest in a dying genre. The burden placed upon Lelio was nevertheless a heavy one. There were the difficulties inherent in choosing a repertoire that would suit both those who were still faithful to the old tradition and those who demanded the new French comedy. There was the hostility of rival theatres to endure, and the fear of attack from the fairground theatre-owners, or from the Comédie Française and the Opéra. In spite of the excellence of the players and the Arlequin of Thomassin, the company found it increasingly hard to make ends meet. On one occasion there was consternation in their midst. They knew that it was the custom to light the theatre with wax candles instead of the ordinary tallow ones, whenever a member of the royal family decided to honour them with a visit. The Regent having announced his intention of being present on a certain evening that came at the end of a very lean period, the company tried the effect of putting wax candles in the three chandeliers nearest the royal box, and keeping the cheaper tallow ones in all the others. There was such a difference in the light given that they dared not do otherwise than provide wax candles for all the chandeliers. Since the funds of the company could not meet the price, the players dipped sadly into their own nearly empty pockets to honour their patron.

The exacting conditions of work, the meagre rewards, and the knowledge that commedia dell'arte had lost its hold in France, fostered quarrels and rivalry among the players, who formerly had enjoyed the closest ties of friendship and relationship. Flaminia saw herself ousted by Silvia: Thomassin resented the presence in the

8

troupe of Pierre François Biancolelli, son of Dominique, who had played Arlequin at the fair and then in 1717 joined Lelio's company as second Arlequin. Lelio's attempts to avoid a clash by allowing Dominique the younger to appear as Trivelin did little to appease the anger of Thomassin, who objected to the similarity in costume and mask. The young Biancolelli, for his part, fresh from the success at the fair, smarted under the treatment he received at the hands of Thomassin. Peace was declared between them only when it became clear that Thomassin had no peer; and that Biancolelli's Trivelin, the sharp gamin born in the fairground, was a lesser creature than Thomassin's complex Arlequin.

Added to these disturbances within and around the company was the perpetual anxiety of wondering how long it would be possible to continue with increased costs, a diminishing audience, and the impossibility of offering a repertoire suited to all the demands of the transition period.

In 1731, Lelio retired at the age of fifty-five, a weary and disappointed man.

CHAPTER SEVEN

Liberty, Equality, Fraternity

WHILE Lelio was waging his heartbreaking struggle, and Thomassin, under the influence of Marivaux and De Lisle, was becoming the first French Arlequin of the New Italian Theatre, the fairground theatre-owners were recovering, in a somewhat curious manner, from the veto on all fairground amusements. They were saved, as they had earlier been saved, by the debts with which the Opéra was once more heavily loaded. For some time before the suppression of fairground entertainment the administration of the Opéra had been casting covetous eyes upon the highly successful *opéra-comique* evolved by the showmen at the fairs.

In 1720, the year of *Arlequin poli par l'Amour*, it was decided, by a tacit agreement between the Supreme Court, the Opéra, and certain of the fairground showmen, that the possibilities of *opéra-comique* should be exploited to the profit of both theatrical parties involved. Four years later, the first theatre ever to be called the Opéra-Comique was established at the St. Laurent Fair under the direction of Maurice Honoré, one of the two leading showmen tacitly permitted to ignore the veto imposed in 1718 by the Supreme Court. With official backing, however silent, with willing cooperation from the Opéra, the spectacles at the New Opéra-Comique became increasingly lavish. The themes of these shows were drawn from classical mythology, allegory, folklore, legend, Oriental and mediæval romances, from any source which would yield a basis upon which to build a show reminiscent of a modern musical, with amazing décor, fabulous machines, fearsome or magical effects of all kinds, wonderful costumes, the whole enlivened with music and dancing and elaborate *divertissements* rather like an early Augustus Harris pageant. While Arlequin in town was acquiring refinement and delicacy, his brother at the fair was singing lustily, and playing his musical rôle with all the old vitality, and a large part of the early crudity of Arlecchino, whence they both sprang.

No expense was spared in mounting a spectacle at the Opéra-Comique: and the machinists vied with each other in producing original and magical effects. In *Arlequin Mahomet*, our hero sailed through the air in a magic flying trunk which took him wherever he wished to go; in *Le Tombeau de Nostradamus* demons flew off into the night: in *Le Monde Renversé* Arlequin and Pierrot crossed the stage several times high in the air upon the back of a winged gryphon. When they wished for food, a laden table shot out of the earth, bearing every imaginable delicacy; and while they consumed this with all their natural greed, food rained down upon them from the heavens. The stage of the Opéra-Comique was crowded with monsters belching forth flame and smoke; with yawning caverns filled with lurid light, from the opening of which came forth flying demons; with cascades tumbling down sinister hillsides, with fountains shooting water twenty feet high. Arlequin took enough journeys to the moon or to the caves of Vulcan on the back of eagles, dragons, swans, dolphins, whales, or serpents to have shaken mortal man. Nor was he unfamiliar with travels upon clouds, in flying baskets, on magic carpets, or upon the broad shoulders of Jove himself. *La Princesse de Carizme* was noteworthy for its macabre décor. The curtain rose upon a construction resembling the gateway to an ancient town. On each side of the gate were three small towers; and at the window of each a madman, violently gesticulating and showing every symptom of his mania. These were the men who had lost their wits simply through having caught sight of the beautiful Princess of Carizme.

While the Opéra-Comique flourished, the New Italian players lost ground. By the middle of the eighteenth century, the company recalled by the Regent was very much changed. Lelio and Flaminia had long since retired to Parma, several others had given up the struggle in France, and had returned to Italy, some were dead, and the direction of the company had several times changed hands. Their repertoire showed how anxiously they had tried to suit all tastes. They were giving shows entirely in Italian, and in the old tradition of gross farce; in Italian with French scenes interpolated; wholly in French;

CARLO ANTONIO BERTINAZZI, KNOWN AS CARLIN,

1710–1783

they were offering parody, farce, satire, French comedy of a philoso-
phical or psychological kind derived from the schools of De Lisle and
Marivaux. They introduced singing, dancing, and even firework
displays into their shows, in a vain attempt to stem the tide against
them. Yet even while they declined in powers of attraction, they were,
as always, subject to the persecution of the rival theatres, who never
ceased to complain that the Italians were stealing their thunder.

Singing was encroaching more upon dialogue; and while the taste
for Italian plays was fast declining, the new French comedy was
attracting new audiences that had never before shown interest in the
Italian players. Their Arlequin now was Carlo Antonio Bertinazzi,
known as Carlin. He was born in Turin in 1710, the son of an officer
in the army of the King of Sardinia. The father died when the boy was
only three years old. His mother devoted herself to her only child, and
secured for him an excellent education that included fencing and
dancing. At fourteen, following in his dead father's footsteps, the
young Carlo became an ensign. It would seem that his entry into an
army career was undertaken solely to please his mother, for upon her
death he immediately resigned his commission to become an actor.
After a careful study of technique, he successfully played Arlecchino
in the theatres of Bologna and Venice.

When Thomassin died in 1739, Carlin was celebrated enough for
the Italian players in Paris to invite him to replace their lost Arlequin.
His commitments in Italy were such that he was not able to accept the
invitation for two years. He made his first appearance in Paris in
Lelio's play *Arlecchino muto per forza*, one of Thomassin's early
successes. He was an excellent mime and a charming dancer, with
great wit and a fertile imagination. He showed the jaded public of
Paris what improvised dialogue could be and had been in the days of
its triumph. David Garrick, who saw him perform, was enchanted
with his technique, and very much impressed with his mime. 'Carlin's
back,' he is reported to have said, 'is more expressive than any other
actor's whole body.' Like all the great Arlequins, Carlin was a
cultured and gifted man. He played several instruments, was a painter
and engraver of considerable ability.

Only Carlin's mime kept the old tradition alive at all: for by the
time he joined the company the New Italian Theatre was, in all but
name, giving light operas based upon libretti by Fuzelier, De Lisle,

Favart, and Marivaux in a desperate attempt to attract the public of the Opéra-Comique.

In 1745, when the Fair of St. Germain ended, the Opéra-Comique closed, probably due to the joint exigencies of the Comédie Française and the Italian players, both of whom were suffering from the competition, and it was only with extreme difficulty that Favart obtained reluctant permission from the Opéra to give a few pantomimes at the Fair of St. Laurent when it opened in the summer. These were immediately so successful that the Royal Academy of Music, always ready to profit from someone else's inspiration, turned the Opéra-Comique into the Théâtre du Nouveau Spectacle Pantomime, and for three years produced ballets and pantomimes in the former fairground theatre.

Seven years after the abolition of *opéra-comique* at the fairs, in 1752, the civic authorities of Paris took over the Opéra and its shaky fortunes, and, with the simple common sense of the outsider, cut through rivalries, hostilities, and veto, restored the name Opéra-Comique to the theatre at St. Laurent; and allowed shows at both fairs.

Lively quarrels still took place between the Opéra, the Comédie Française, the Opéra-Comique, and the Italian players. The battle raged across the fairgrounds and along the boulevards, where theatres were beginning to spring up again, in spite of rivalry, veto, and persecution.

Through all this turmoil, public taste continued to change, and to grow away from the Italians. In despair, the company invited Carlo Goldoni, a leading Italian dramatist, to come to Paris to write plays for them: perhaps the fact that he was known as 'the Italian Molière' inspired their choice.

When Goldoni came to Paris in 1760, he was fifty-three years of age, and enjoyed a considerable reputation in his native land. His memoirs show how horrified he was to discover into what dire straits the Italian players had fallen, artistically and financially: 'I saw, on the days when light opera was given, an astonishing concourse of people; and on the days when the Italians played, an empty auditorium.' He noted, however, that Carlin wove a magic web of intimacy between himself and his audiences, and wrote of him with respect and affection: 'He was a man of great moral rectitude, famous for his playing of Arlequin, and equal in reputation to Dominique and Thomassin in France, and to Sacchi in Italy. Nature had endowed him with inimitable grace. His face, his gestures, his physical grace gave him great stage presence. His technique and his talent made him as much admired on the stage as he was loved in Society.' But Carlin was not enough. Goldoni discovered that the players had fallen back upon ancient scenari worn threadbare with use, that were completely out of touch with the times. A revolutionary at heart, Goldoni suggested a total change of technique and repertoire, and that only written plays should be given. As might be expected, the Masks opposed him, the romantic leads supported him. Gradually, and working with infinite tact and patience, the genial Goldoni achieved his ends.

He wrote for the Italian players scenari as brief as those of ancient tradition; then scenari with a certain amount of dialogue; and finally full play scripts. He felt that since their technique of acting was changing to come more nearly into line with contemporary taste, the wearing of masks was outmoded. Gradually he abolished their use, even while, in his plays, he retained all the other characteristics of each type. By the time his written plays were being presented, the clowns had lost their strangeness with their masks, and were no longer types, but full persons. His reforms, which in effect brought about the final destruction of commedia dell'arte in France, aroused the enmity of the lovers of the old tradition: and among these he found his bitterest opponent in Carlo Gozzi, who from Italy launched himself into active opposition, writing and producing plays in which he kept closely to the pattern of traditional commedia dell'arte.

The efforts of both were doomed to failure in so far as improvised comedy was concerned. Gozzi could not stem nor even impede the death of national comedy at home or abroad by striving to revitalise the ashes of the dead past. Nor could Goldoni bolster up a declining drama by transforming it into written comedy of manners played without masks. The long day of commedia dell'arte was done. A few Masks would survive, and be discovered in strange places. Molière, Lesage, Marivaux, and De Lisle had immortalised certain aspects, the history of the theatre would give it an honoured place. But the form itself died in the eighteenth century. Fundamental changes in the social spirit and temper, the first burgeoning of romanticism, the muffled drums of approaching revolution, the movement of history, conspired to defeat Gozzi, and to render Goldoni's efforts useless.

There was moreover a natural unification afoot. By now the Italian players under the King's patent, and the Opéra-Comique arisen from Arlequin's sojourn at the fair were rapidly converging, with a third stream drawing near the point of unity.

When Arlequin went into exile, he found shelter not only in the fairs but also in the boulevard theatres that were to be found on the fringe of the sites of St. Germain and St. Laurent, and to which the hucksters brought their shows when the fairs were closed.

By 1759, new and interesting theatres had been opened, among them one owned by Jean Baptiste Nicolet. The latter, who had himself played Arlequin in a minor company, was the son of a marionette showman, and through his lifelong association with fairground folk was able to establish himself in their show business, and later on the Boulevard du Temple, where he presented comedies in the Italian manner, some straight plays, and various acts—jugglers, tight-rope walker, ventriloquists, and sword-swallowers. The suppression of *opéra-comique* in 1745 had brought him an increased public, and by the time Goldoni reached France, Nicolet's theatre was the leading one of its kind along the boulevards. Louis XV had deigned to show approval, so that the tight-rope walkers were able to claim that they were 'appointed to His Majesty the King'.

Goldoni tells an amusing story of this theatre. Attracted there one day by playbills advertising *Coriolan, a tragedy in one act* as the third play, he entered the place early, and found himself with a few other scattered patrons in the circle. Later, as the audience streamed in, he was approached by a well-set up young man in very shabby clothes, Goldoni, believing him to be a fellow spectator, made room for him on the bench. The young man, however, turned out to be a member of Nicolet's company, and the one destined to play Coriolanus. Not having been able to discover among the company's properties a sword suitable for the part, he had come to beg loan of the handsome Italian dress sword Goldoni was wearing at the time. The latter, prudently, made quite sure that the young man spoke the truth and then loaned his sword. Goldoni watched the tight-rope walkers with shuddering fascination, dozed through the dreary playlets that followed, and awoke only for Coriolanus, which was, in his

DAVID GARRICK DRESSED AS HARLEQUIN

Photo Rigal, Paris *Courtesy Bibliothèque de l'Opéra, Paris*

GRIMALDI THE CLOWN WITH BOLOGNA JUNIOR
AS HARLEQUIN

opinion 'very badly dressed and acted, yet not without a certain merit'.

Nicolet's theatre, ultimately called Théâtre de la Gaieté, was the forerunner of others. One of the most interesting was the Ambigu-Comique in which Nicholas Médard Audinot gave marionette shows where every puppet represented an Italian Mask. Later, he engaged a fourteen-year-old dwarf, Adrien Moreau, a beautifully made child of exceptional agility, who played Arlequin among his wooden fellow-players. Moreau was certainly the youngest Arlequin ever known, and playing in the oddest form of Italian comedy on record. Later still, the marionettes were superseded by children, with the young dwarf still playing Arlequin at the head of a miniature company that brought good fortune to Audinot and the Ambigu-Comique.

Two similar theatres, the Variétés-Amusantes and the Théâtre des Petits Comédiens, which, like the Ambigu-Comique, employed children, were transferred to the Palais Royal, the first because of the excellence of its shows, the second because of the novelty of children playing in *opéra-comique*. The singing for these shows was done by adults backstage and in the wings; and the children timed their gestures so perfectly that for a long time many people believed that they were singing, so that bets were taken on it at most performances.

The first result of this slow convergence of the three streams from the court, the fairs, and the boulevards was shown when in 1762 the Italian Comedy at the Hôtel de Bourgogne obtained that the *opéra-comique* should be incorporated in them: two of the three affluents were now one.

Yet in spite of this promising amalgamation, receipts steadily declined through the next five years. Tastes changed so rapidly, the ferment of the coming revolution was already at work, the theatre had so many rivals that the players, switching from Italian to French comedy and back again, then to operettes and vaudevilles mounted with costly décor and machines, could only catch the attention of a fickle public for a moment. Part of the decline was due to the company itself, which had lost heart and abandoned the struggle.

The public had shown clearly that it was heartily sick of the shabby fare offered, and clamoured for a revival of French plays. This was the ringing of the death-knell of Italian comedy in France. The Italian repetoire was never given again. Those actors who could only play in Italian were pensioned off. In December 1779, the State Council ordered that the Company of Italian players, now sixty-three years old, should be abolished, the mandate to take effect from Easter of the following year. Provision was made for the formation of a new company, playing only French comedy and opera and retaining the status of the company that was to be liquidated. Among those actors retained in the new company (according to Goldoni, the only one retained) was the seventy-year-old Carlin. It is not certain whether he was retained to play Arlequin himself, or to train younger players in the complex requirements for the rôle in French comedy.

A few years later, when for the first time in its history the theatre of the defunct company was called the Théâtre des Italiens, there was no longer a single Italian member in the company, Carlin having died of apoplexy in 1783.

In 1781, exactly a year after the disbanding of the Italian company, the major French theatrical troupes moved into new theatres. The Comédie Française left the Tuileries for the Faubourg St. Germain, while the newly formed company at the Hôtel de Bourgogne took over and adapted the estate and house of the Duc de Choiseul, where the Salle Favart, home of *opéra-comique*, stands at the present day.

While the two affluents that had merged were abolished, the third throve and prospered on the boulevards. Many more theatres had been established since the days of the Gaieté, the Petits Comédiens, and the Ambigu. Many of the actors dismissed when the Italian company broke up opened boulevard theatres. Some presented shows that were disgracefully bad; others were so good that they brought down upon themselves the wrath of the Comédie Française, who still held their power of veto. Arlequin on the boulevards began to suffer the fate meted out to Arlequin at the fair. Interdiction followed veto, veto followed prohibition. The actors were forbidden to speak, to move about on the stage, to be more than two on the stage at a time, to dance, to sing, to perform acrobatic tricks. When all other embargoes had been applied, and the boulevard theatres nevertheless continued to open and attract a large public, the Comédie Française ordered that the actors be separated from the audience by a gauze curtain.

On July 14th, 1789, a certain Plancher-Valcour, director of the Délassements Comiques sur le Boulevard and chief sufferer from the persecution of the Comédie Française, was playing Arlequin in his own theatre. Backstage a moment, he received the awe-inspiring news of the taking of the Bastille. Straightway he went on stage, scattering the players right and left, put his fist through the gauze curtain, and tore it open along its whole length, shouting at the top of his voice. 'The Bastille is taken! Long live Liberty!'

A riot ensued. The audience mounted onto the stage, embraced the players, shredded the gauze curtain and trampled it underfoot. The actors, still in motley, linked arms with the public and joined the mob exulting in the streets.

Within less than two years, on January 13th, 1791, the National Assembly broke for all time the powers and patents that had trammelled Arlequin and his fellows through all their struggling years. Liberty, equality, and fraternity reached the theatres in these terms: 'Any citizen has the right to build a public theatre and there present and perform plays of all kinds provided that, before establishing his theatre, he declares and registers his intention at the local town hall.'

PART THREE

———————◄◄✴►►———————

Harlequin in England

CHAPTER ONE

Arlecchino in England

ARLECCHINO and his company reached England in the sixteenth century, in the ordinary course of their travels abroad. If he had hoped to arouse immediately the enthusiasm, and enjoy the popularity he had already gained in France, he was swiftly disillusioned. The way had been prepared for him in France by the royal alliance with the House of Medici, and the subsequent adoption of Italian fashion at court. There was no such preparation in Elizabethan England, where both Italy and France were considered 'foreign' by all but a few well-travelled gentlemen.

The English, moreover, by the sixteenth century already possessed a well-established tradition of clowns and clownship derived from the comic element in the old miracle and mystery plays, and the Church pageants. In these, the Devil himself and the Vices and Follies of mankind were very often the source of ribald mirth. The English clown had much of the Devil in him, and delighted his audiences with a native form of broad, coarse humour that endures to this day in the few remaining music halls, and in the radio variety shows.

The company who arrived in 1582, at the time Francesco and Isabella Andreini were delighting French audiences, found themselves playing to a frigid public who showed clearly that they found their own tradition infinitely superior to that of the Italians.

The company, of no great distinction, since the best companies and players went straight to the French court, suffered from the antagonism of their audiences, and missed the exhilaration of playing before the demonstrative French. Their performances suffered from this lack of sympathy, and a considerable time elapsed before the players felt sufficiently at home to show what improvised comedy was really like.

Yet Arlecchino, if he failed to take the placid English by storm, nevertheless managed subtly to influence trends in the theatre, as he had done in every other European country into which he had set foot. His influence was due not only to the coming of the Italian players to England, but also to the intercourse between actors of both nations, the travels of wealthy young men, and members of the diplomatic mission in Italy and France. In February 1571 the *Gelosi* were in Paris, and early in March Lord Buckhurst, invited to the wedding of Charles IX, was entertained by the Duke of Nevers 'with a comedie of Italians that for the mirth and handling thereof deserved singular commendacion'.[1] In the year following, the Earl of Lincoln, sent with full ambassadorial dignity to Paris to ratify the League with France, was royally entertained during his stay, and was present on at least one occasion at an Italian play which he found 'vearie excelent'.[1] It is clear from contemporary evidence of this kind that English noblemen were present at the French court on every political or social occasion of importance, and were entertained by performances of the great companies under royal patronage.

Private travellers have also left some evidence of their interest in seeing the players in the urban centres of Italy, and in Paris: while it is certain that notable English actors toured abroad. Will Kempe, the celebrated clown of the Burbage company, whose free interpretation of his lines and frequent ad libbing was often deplored by Shakespeare, chief playwright to the company, toured widely on the continent. He is reported to have seen Tristano Martinelli playing Arlecchino in Rome in 1600; and to have returned again and again to the theatre to watch a technique and a dexterity that filled him with admiration. It is certain that the Italian players, and notably Martinelli, made a lasting impression upon him; for in 1607, six years after his experiences in Rome, Kempe took part in an historical play entitled *The Travels of English Brothers, Sir Thomas, Sir Anthony, and Mr. Robert Shirley*. During a conversation between Kempe and Sir Anthony Shirley on trends in the contemporary London theatre, an Italian Harlequin is announced, who offers to provide a *commedia al improviso*. Kempe is persuaded by Sir Anthony to take part in the proposed entertainment, and replies, 'I am somewhat hard of study; but if they will

1 Quoted by K. M. Lea. *Italian Popular Comedy*, Vol. II.

invent any extemporal merriment, I'll put out the small sack of wit I ha' left in venture with them.'

Dutton Cook, who gives this story in *A Book of the Play*, continues: 'It is likely that the Italian Harlequin who appears in Day's play was introduced expressly at the suggestion of the travelled actor Kempe. Did Shakespear take his seat among the spectators at the Curtain Theatre in 1607 to note the character his Dogberry had brought from Venice? Surely that, too, is likely.'

Italian comedy became a familiar part of the Elizabethan theatre scene, and exerted its influence over the plots and structure of contemporary drama in England. Playwrights were clearly aware of the foreign invasion. Shakespeare begins to call his clowns zanies, the name given to Arlecchino, Brighella, and their variants. His 'dagger of lath' is Arlecchino's own; and in his dissertation on the seven ages of man in *As You Like It* we find the sixth age 'like to the lean and slippered Pantaloon with spectacles on nose, and pouch on side'.

Among similar examples with which Elizabethan drama is studded, there is the interesting allusion in Thomas Middleton's *Spanish Gipsy* (*Act IV*, *Scene* 2), which was written in collaboration with William Rowley. The scene is set in Spain, and Fernando is arranging for a performance by a company of strolling players. Alvarez is the director of this company, and Roderigo its poet-dramatist:

> *Fernando* . . . there is a way
>   Which the Italians and the Frenchmen use
>   That is, on a word given, or some slight plot
>   The actors will extempore fashion out
>   Scenes neat and witty.
> *Alvarez* We can do that, my lord;
>   Please you bestow the subject.
> *Fernando* Can you?—Come hither,
>   You Master poet: to save you a labour
>   Look you, against your coming I projected
>   This comic passage (*producing a paper*)
>   Your drama; that's the scene—
> *Roderigo* Ay, ay, my lord.
> *Fernando* I lay in our own country, Spain.
> *Roderigo* T'is best so.

JOHN RICH (1692–1761) AS HARLEQUIN
Water-colour by an unknown artist, 1753

LUPINO LANE AS HARLEQUIN

Showing Five Attitudes.   From a photograph in the Mander and Mitchenson Theatre Collection

> *Fernando*   Here's a brave part for this old gypsy; look you,
>   The father: read the plot; this young she-gypsy,
>   This lady: now the son, play him yourself.
> *Roderigo*   My lord, I am no Player.
> *Fernando*   Pray, at this time
>   The plot being full, to please my noble friends,
>   Because your brains must into theirs put language,
>   Act you the Son's part; I'll reward your pains.
> *Roderigo*   I'll venture.
> *Fernando*   I thank you: let this father be a Don
>   Of a brave spirit.—Old gypsy, observe me.
> *Alvarez*   Yes, my lord.
> *Fernando*   Play him up high: not like a pantaloon
>   But, hotly, nobly, checking this his Son . . .

This extract serves to show that Middleton knew not only the characters of Italian comedy but also its technique. Fernando would clearly have made an excellent director of a company.

Long before Arlequin took to the fairs in Paris, after his exile from the Hôtel de Bourgogne in 1697, acrobatic Harlequins—tumblers, dancers, and tight-rope walkers—were becoming a common feature of the great English fairs in London and the provinces, in the early years of the seventeenth century. There he achieved the immediate popularity he had hoped for, but not found, in the theatre. By the end of the century the fairground showmen in London began to engage French Arlequins from the Paris fairs, so great was the demand for him: they thus provided a healthy competitive spirit that gave rise to English companies determined to meet the increased demand from native, not foreign, sources. The fairground Harlequin was remote from the Bergamask valet of commedia dell'arte. He was any performer at the fair who chose, for financial reasons, to wear Arlecchino's motley and mask. The enthusiasm aroused by this primitive and English tumbling Harlequin gradually extended to the Italian Arlecchino in the theatre. He seemed less foreign, less alien, once his brother was established in the familiar setting of fairground booths and trestles, and the known company of hucksters. So great was Harlequin's success at the fair that when in 1701–1702 the Sieurs Alard, the brothers who had fought the Comédie Française and established their theatre at the Foire St. Laurent, came to London and

9

presented *An Italian Night Scene* at Drury Lane, they played to packed houses and highly appreciative audiences.

Harlequin's progress in the theatre was slower. By the end of the sixteenth century he had done no more than achieve a precarious footing in England, and become a fairly familiar but not greatly loved figure of contemporary theatre. In the next century, his infiltration into English tradition received new impetus, and he quickly threw off his Bergamask characteristics to become English.

The beginning of the seventeenth century was marked by the development of court entertainments under the influence of Inigo Jones, who was responsible for mounting them from 1605–1640, a period long enough to enable him to achieve magnificent results. Before his court appointment he had on several occasions visited Italy, where he found, in Italian theatre, the inspiration for his own work. Under his direction, a glittering series of masques, pageants, plays, and operas was given at court; and among them one of particular interest to the biographer of Harlequin.

In 1637, on the Sunday after Twelfth Night, *Britannia Triumphans*, a masque by Inigo Jones and Sir William D'Avenant, was presented at Whitehall before Charles I and his court. There is to be found in the description of the comic characters the following passage:

> In the bottom row on the left is a Mountebank's
> man or zany . . . Cap, with two feathers and long
> peak, drawn over his brow; loose blouse with hanging
> sleeves, and baggy trousers. Next to him is a
> Harlekin . . . he has beard and moustaches. Flat
> cap; long loose jacket with sleeves covering hands;
> and trousers. Inscribed Harlekin. On the right is a clown
> with moustaches and peaked beard. Close round cap
> or hood, loose jacket with large round buttons
> and belt, and trousers. Inscribed John Farino.[1]

The haunting presence of the Italian players continued. In 1660, *Salmacida Spolia* was presented. Among its characters were a Pedant of Francolin, easily recognised as our old friend *Il Dottore*; and a certain Doctor Tartaglia. In the original commedia dell'arte, Tartaglia was a talkative valet with a stammer. Later he played, still with his stammer, any functionary—lawyer, apothecary, officer of the watch—necessary

[1] *Walpole Society*, XII, p. 105. Quoted by Sir James Laver in his *Drama: Its Costume and Décor*. Gian Farino was a Pagliaccio variant.

to the plot. Here he is then, borrowed by an English dramatist, and given academic status.

Seven years later, Joseph Haynes made history as the first English Harlequin to appear in a theatre. The occasion was the presentation at Drury Lane of Ravenscroft's *Scaramouch, a Philosopher; Harlequin as Schoolboy, Bravo, Merchant, and Magician, after the Italian Manner*, a florid title for a playbill. Legend has it that Edward Ravenscroft, a minor dramatist of Charles II's time, being hard put to it to think of a new attraction for Drury Lane, then under his management, suddenly recalled the resounding success of Tiberio Fiorelli when in 1663 he had come and conquered London with his playing of Scaramouch. With Fiorelli in mind, Ravenscroft compiled his five-act comedy, announced that it was 'based upon Molière's *Fourberies de Scapin*' and neglected to add that *Le Bourgeois Gentilhomme* and *Le Mariage Forcé* of the same dramatist had also been heavily plundered. The scenes in which Harlequin appeared were of Italian origin, drawn from Ravenscroft's memory of Fiorelli's company and technique. Much to his chagrin, Dorset Gardens Theatre, a rival house, opened with Otway's version of *Les Fourberies de Scapin* a few days before the curtain rose on *Scaramouch a Philosopher*, etc., at Drury Lane. Ravenscroft, bent on showing that his was an original undertaking, added the following lines to his prologue:

> The poet does a dangerous trial make
> And all the common roads of plays forsake;
> Upon the actors it depends too much;
> For who can ever hope to see two such
> As the famed Harlequin and Scaramouch.

A strange little wheel has come full circle here. Originally, Scapin was a variant of Brighella, Arlecchino's own half-brother, whose identity merged with his when Locatelli created Trivelino. Locatelli was the Arlequin of the company installed in the theatre of the Palais Royal, which they shared with Molière's company. Molière's Scapin was inspired by Arlequin; and in due course inspired, however remotely, the first English Harlequin.

In 1687 came another piece taken from the French—a three-act farce by Mrs. Aphra Behn, *The Emperor of the Moon*, and presented at the Dorset Gardens Theatre. The play, taken from de Fatonville's *Arlequin Empereur dans la Lune*, which in turn had been based upon an old scenario of the Italian players, contained a Harlequin and a Scaramouch, the former played by Tom Jevons. The French version had been presented in Paris for the first time in 1684, with Dominique Biancolelli playing Arlequin. Aphra Behn, in her English version, drew upon Biancolelli's characteristic *lazzi*, which Tom Jevons adapted to his own style. One which was greatly enjoyed by his audiences was the *lazzi* of the suicide. Harlequin, despondent over the failure of his schemes, attempts to commit suicide first by holding his mouth closed with one hand, and his nose by the other, so that he can no longer draw breath: then, when that fails in a vast explosion and inhalation of air, by tickling himself to death. The sight of Harlequin rolling round the stage, tickling himself vigorously and roaring with helpless laughter, was enough to set his public laughing until it cried. It was this play also which showed a schoolroom scene in which Harlequin and Scaramouch played the fool, and were suitably chastised. The classroom scene is now a classic in the modern pantomimes *Red Riding Hood* and *Babes in the Wood*.

A curious play given in 1697 at Lincoln's Inn Fields had among its characters the four destined to become the celebrated quartette of early pantomime. The play was Motteaux's *Novelty: or Every Act a Play*, in which appeared Harlequin, Pantalone an old miser, Colombina his maid, Nicholas a clown, Pasquarel, and Mezzetin. This play, given in London in the year in which the Italian players were exiled from the Hôtel de Bourgogne in Paris, was a forerunner of those written by Lesage and others at a later stage for the fairground Arlequins of Paris, when they were engaged in bitter struggle with Parlement and the Comédie Française. Each act of *Novelty* was, as its subtitle proclaimed, a full play. The five acts offered a Pastoral Drama, a Comedy, a Masque, a Tragedy, and a Farce in the Italian manner, loosely linked together by the characters, who played throughout. It would be difficult to discover whether *Novelty* was known to the French fairground folk; or whether they employed similar play construction accidentally, and only because they were forbidden to present plays.

The English Harlequin was slowly coming to birth, not freed yet from his Italian and French forebears, but with each new play moving a little farther away from them. It is noticeable that he is infinitely less than his counterpart in France. Locatelli, Biancolelli, and Gherardi had each given of their own artistry and originality to Arlequin, so that ever afterwards he bore their mark upon him. Harlequin in England at this stage was only the shadow of the scintillating Arlequin of France. Joe Haynes, Tom Jevons, William Pinkethman, those first English Harlequins, were nimble acrobats and supple dancers. They were imitative, not creative, applying English training and technique to foreign comedy. They neither understood nor assimilated the long tradition that had evolved Arlecchino and through him Arlequin: it reached them only through France, not from its Italian source. They borrowed from the ancient commedia dell'arte, about which they knew little, if anything, as much of the technique, *lazzi*, tricks, plots, and presentation as reached them through France. There resulted an amorphous Harlequin much closer to the Arlequin of the fair, the tumbler, the dancer, than to the witty Arlequin of the Hôtel de Bourgogne. Harlequin was maintained, but not developed by them. It was as if, at the end of a long and honourable career, he was held for a moment in check, before his inevitable decline into old age.

Yet, paradoxically, had his survival depended upon France, he would have died early in the nineteenth century. Fate, however, held in store his English metamorphosis. In France, in the seventeenth century, he reached a peak to which he could not climb again in England. There he had another destiny to play out. John Rich set his feet upon the path that was to lead him into the creation of an original form of theatre, fated to become traditionally English, and to endure to our own time.

CHAPTER TWO

Immortal Lun

AFTER a century of sluggish progress in the affections of the English public, Harlequin's pace began to quicken.

In 1702, John Weaver, a dancing master of Shrewsbury, and friend of Addison and Steele, produced *The Tavern Bilkers* at Drury Lane, and fourteen years afterwards presented *The Loves of Mars and Venus* at the same theatre, the length of time elapsing between the two being in part due to discouragement over the lukewarm reception accorded *The Tavern Bilkers*. In his later *History of Mimes and Pantomimes*, published in 1728, Weaver describes his plays in the following terms:

> The first Entertainment that appeared on the English stage where the Representation and the Story were carried on by Dancing, Action, and Motion only was performed with Grotesque Characters after the Modern Italians such as Harlequin, Scaramouch, etc.; and was called *The Tavern Bilkers*, composed by Weaver and first performed at Drury Lane Theatre, 1702. The next was many years after, and was an attempt in imitation of the ancient pantomimes and the first of the kind that has appeared since the time of the Roman Emperors.

He asserts that *The Tavern Bilkers* was the first English pantomime; and that he was the originator of the new genre. Yet neither a play based upon partial understanding of Italian comedy nor another in imitation of ancient Roman mime can truly be said to have created a new form. They should rather be regarded as entertainments of exceptional interest belonging to the preparatory period which lasted for the whole of the seventeenth century and into the early years of the eighteenth century.

Moreover, Weaver's claim to originality is invalidated when we discover that his memory played him false concerning the date of presentation of *The Tavern Bilkers*. In 1702, the year he gives, he was at Lincoln's Inn Fields Theatre, and not at Drury Lane. There is no proof therefore that he was early or first in the field even with *The Tavern Bilkers*. As late as 1715, the only known forms of Harlequinade were dancing entertainments in which characters dressed in the traditional costumes of the Masks took part. These were given after the main play, or as an intermission between two plays. A contemporary playbill announces, in addition to its more serious items, a *Dance of Two Scaramouchs*; another *An Entertainment between a Harlequin and Two Punches*. These dancing interludes were gradually developed and lengthened, but were only a bastard form, half-way between the earliest scenari of commedia dell'arte and the later dancing and tumbling entertainments at the fairs. Examination of *The Tavern Bilkers* shows it to be no more than an uncertain transposition of a few Masks into an 'entertainment of Dancing' somewhat longer than usual.

Apart from *The Tavern Bilkers* in the Italian manner, Weaver, throughout his career in the theatre, sought his themes in Roman mythology, and tried to reproduce the old Roman mimes. His attempts were various, and of peculiar interest to the theatre historian; but their very nature prevented him from establishing new dramatic forms.

It was left to John Rich to take over the dancing Harlequinades of his time and transform them into a national theatre that was as native as the air he breathed, in spite of its foreign origins. In its earliest form, English pantomime is a recapitulation of Italian comedy from its crude beginnings to its subtle apotheosis, so that even when John Rich had set his English mark upon it, pantomime was haunted by that long-dead commedia dell'arte, and bears its imprint to this day.

The fiery dragons, great sea monsters, eagles, and swans of early pantomime, the later comic horse, donkey, cow, and cat were all derived from early scenari. It would be difficult, if not impossible, to trace the exact means by which pantomime took over certain effects and situations from commedia dell'arte. Traveller's tales, touring companies at home and abroad, the Harlequins at the fair no doubt played some part in the secret processes by which theatre tradition travels through the years, and from one country to another. Jack's cow, for example, in *Jack and the Beanstalk* is an odd descendant by mythological procreation of Arlequin's ass, which in *Arlequin Mercure Galant*[1] (1682) broke in two when Pan endeavoured to clamber upon it. The pillars of cloud, the eagles upon whose back Arlequin, and Arlecchino before him, were accustomed to fly, the chariots led by swans are today replaced by streamlined aeroplanes, unexcitingly static upon the stages they nearly fill, or by rocket ships worked by jet propulsion. Arlecchino's modern descendant has exchanged magic for science.

The scenari of early Italian commedia dell'arte, and the scripts of the early English pantomimes show similar themes. The Italians drew upon the recrudescence of humanism, the renaissance of interest in classical culture, the exoticism of the East, made known to them by the exiles from Byzantium, mythology, legend, and folklore. These themes were handed down, taken abroad, adapted for use in the fairgrounds, and disseminated through Europe wherever the Italian players had set up their trestles. The early pantomime scripts draw upon the same sources, with here and there a touch of local colour: for to the range of adventure open to him in mythology and the Orient, Harlequin pursues others under the guise of Robin Hood, Jack Sheppard, or Dick Turpin.

Both Arlecchino and Arlequin were great travellers. Similarly, Harlequin shares the exploits of Don Quixote, Baron Munchausen, and Haroun al Raschid; while the innocent lovers so strangely evolved from the Bergamask clown and the wanton Colombina were pursued, in English pantomime, to most countries of the earth, to Mount Olympus, or to Hell, from the moon to the depths of the oceans, with a total disregard for the limitations of time and space.

The traditional 'business' of pantomime is derived from specific scenari to be found among those that were collected and published by Gherardi in the seventeenth century. There is no pantomime worthy of the name that, even today, would be without a humorous interlude in a shop, a schoolroom, or a kitchen. The forerunner of the shop scenes is to be found in *Arlequin Lingère du Palais* (1682), in which scenario Arlequin appeared in hermaphroditic form, confusing his customers with his half-male, half-female presentation, since each half ran a different shop. Similarly, the cloth-rolling episode of *Le*

---

[1] For text seem Appendix B, p. 194.

A TOY THEATRE PRINT, DATED 1854

Showing the 'Heads' worn by pantomime characters before their transformation into the Harlequinade quartet

Marchand Duppé (1688) is with us still, every time *Dick Whittington* is shown.

Both *Le Tombeau de Maître André* (1695) and *L'Opéra de Campagne* (1692) contain that element of tomfoolery in the kitchen that has gone down the years with *Cinderella* and *Jack and the Beanstalk*; while from Mrs. Aphra Behn's English version of *Arlequin Empereur dans la Lune* (1684) comes the schoolroom scene, a transposition of the scene in the French version in which Arlequin instructs the credulous Doctor about the habits and customs of the inhabitants of the moon.

Pantomime might never have been evolved were it not for the fact that John Rich and his brother became, upon the death of their father, joint patentees of Lincoln's Inn Fields Theatre at a time when the company established there was very much inferior to that of the rival theatre, Drury Lane. Audiences had dropped off so badly that the brothers in effect inherited a dying concern. Rich's robust energy was wholly given to pouring new life into the company. He made full use of the fashionable dancing interludes with Harlequin and Punch and Scaramouch in his endeavours to attract audiences to the all-but deserted theatre. Within a very short space of time he discovered in them a source of stimulation to his dramatic imagination; and a framework in which his own talents showed to best advantage.

The word 'pantomime' appeared in connection with the new form of entertainment in 1717 on the bills advertising Rich's first essay in the genre—*Harlequin Sorcerer*, a piece consisting of two parts, one grave, one gay. It was well mounted, with lively décor, beautiful costumes, a great deal of music and dancing; and scenic effects of considerable ingenuity. Between the acts of the serious part, Rich wove scenes of a comical story chiefly concerned with the courtship of Harlequin and Columbine. One of the novelties of the piece arose from the magical powers of Harlequin's bat. Whenever he and Columbine found themselves in difficulties, Harlequin's magic bat came into play, transforming palaces into cottages, men into statues, into wheelbarrows and baskets. Trees were changed into houses, beds of flowers into lakes, and the contents of a grocer's shop into snakes and ostriches.

The word 'pantomime', applied to this form of entertainment, was adopted forthwith, in spite of its verbal solecism, first perpetrated, so it was said, by the pretty young Duchesse de Maine, a lady with pretensions to learning. A pantomime, in the original meaning of the term, was an actor who could play any part, or all the parts, in any tragedy, comedy, farce, or burlesque. The enchanting Duchesse, presenting part of Corneille's *Horace* as a ballet, decided to call her entertainment a ballet-pantomime on the grounds that dumbshow was an art much practised in the theatres of ancient Rome. From this cultural gaffe, so legend has it, grew the popular idea that a pantomime was an entertainment without speech. John Weaver accepted that meaning of the term, referring often in his writings to 'pantomime' acted in dumbshow. The term was generally applied, so that from the time of Rich and Weaver until the beginning of the nineteenth century, a pantomime in England was a dumbshow entertainment in which Harlequin mimed a leading rôle. The only exception to this was the talking Harlequin Woodward, employed by Garrick at Drury Lane.

John Rich, like the original Arlecchino from Bergama, had wit only in his body. He was born in 1692, the son of Christopher Rich, an attorney, who in 1668 had bought a share in the patent of Drury Lane Theatre for eighty pounds. This turned out to be so profitable a transaction that he shortly afterwards acquired the patent of Lincoln's Inn Fields, and continued to make more from the theatre than from law. His son John turned early to the stage in search of a career, and after one or two failures in tragic or dramatic rôles, appeared as a comic actor. His uncouth appearance and illiterate speech closed all other avenues to him.

He became in the course of time one of the theatre's great eccentrics. There seems little doubt that his early humiliating experiences on the stage fostered the growth of a feeling of inferiority which nothing in his later successful career served to counteract. If he could not be like other people, he would be as different as possible; and throughout his life he nursed a bitter loathing of straight actors, reaching to the point of hatred where the great ones among them were concerned. He also disliked full length plays of a serious kind; and insisted on absolute autocracy in the theatre when he was in control.

Soon after he became actor-manager at Lincoln's Inn Fields he had found his niche as the mute Harlequin. His roughness of speech was irrelevant, his unprepossessing looks were covered by the black mask. Released from the burden of his physical deficiencies in speech and beauty, he rapidly developed into a dancing Harlequin in the old tradition of the fairs. The wit of his well-formed body expressed itself in his acrobatic dancing, his leaping and tumbling, and in the detail of his mime. His Harlequin was as expressive and as graceful as his straight rôles had been gauche, self-conscious, and inhibited. Under the stage name of Lun, he soon gained such a place for himself that even Garrick, who intensely disliked pantomime, wrote of him after his death:

> *When Lun appeared with faultless art and whim*
> *He gave the power of speech to every limb.*
> *Though masked and mute, conveyed his quick intent*
> *And told in frolic gestures all he meant;*
> *But now the motley coat and sword of wood*
> *Require a tongue to make them understood.*

Harlequin Sorcerer took the town by storm, and created overnight the audiences Rich had despaired of attracting, as well as a thirst for pantomime which nothing seemed able to quench. This overwhelming success after so much failure, and the release the playing of Harlequin had brought to him, combined to liberate Rich's potential genius in the theatre. Not only did he become the first creative English Harlequin but he developed the resources of pantomime until in his own lifetime it became a form of national popular drama of a kind hitherto unknown.

The costume in which he played Harlequin marked the transition period between the loose jackets and trousers and the full mask of seventeenth-century Italian Comedy and the vivid lozenge-patterned tights and black eye-mask of the later Regency Harlequins. He wore a short jacket and fairly tight trousers with a criss-cross design, based upon those of preceding Harlequins, but fitting him more closely; a cap that concealed his hair; and a black vizard, not the traditional mask.

Here at last was the originator without whom Harlequin must have dwindled and died much earlier than he did. As it was, he was saved by Rich's lack of culture, and by his sense of inferiority. Since there was no future for Rich in straight theatre, he was led quite naturally into developing the Harlequinade of his time into something that would give his special gifts the fullest scope. All his innovations were subjective. Harlequin was mute because Rich spoke badly; he danced because Rich danced superbly. Among the wonderful *lazzi* he invented, thus proving himself in the great line of Harlequins, was one that most captured the imagination of those who watched it. Harlequin was explaining to a young Harlequin how the first man came to be hatched from an egg by the heat of the sun:

> From the first chipping of the egg, his receiving
> motion, his feeling the ground, his standing
> upright, to his quick Harlequin trip round the
> empty shell, through the whole progression, every
> limb had its tongue, and every motion a voice,
> which spoke with most miraculous organ to
> the understanding and sensations of the observers.[1]

Rich greatly encouraged the artistic and mechanical sides of production. Any inventor of a new device for his pantomimes was as sure of a warm welcome as a straight actor could be sure of a frigid one. In 1739 his chief machinist, Samuel Hoole, produced a mechanical serpent for *Orpheus and Eurydice*, in which piece Rich played Harlequin to the Pantaloon of Grimaldi, father of the famous clown. The serpent, thrashing with its scaly tail, opening wide its cavernous jaws, darting flames of sulphurous fire from its eyes, sent the audience into pleasant paroxysms of terror, and delighted Lun so much that Hoole received a handsome bonus.

It was Lun who abolished the custom, up to that time unchecked, of allowing mashers and the flower of the nobility to walk across the stage, or sit chatting to friends and actors, during a performance, whenever they felt so disposed. In Rich's theatre, they no longer felt disposed.

Offstage, he was legendary, even in his own time. His dislike of anything approaching culture drove him to strange lengths. Any author bold enough to call upon him for his verdict on a play sent in would be fixed with a baleful glare, coldly invited to find his own manuscript in a vast pile obviously untouched, and told to take it away with him, or to take someone else's if he preferred to.

When in 1746 Garrick joined him for a season, bringing with him a company that included Quin, Mrs. Cibber, Mrs. Pritchard, and Henry Woodward, Rich was so enraged by the triumph of these straight actors, who actually netted for him £8,500, a stupendous profit in terms of the currency of the time, that every evening he stood upon the stage, between the closed curtains, looking through

[1] Jackson, contemporary historian of the Scottish stage.

with a jaundiced eye upon the crowded house, and muttering impreca-
tions. In spite of the financial success of the season, he could not
bring himself to re-engage Garrick, so allowing him to set up in
rivalry at Drury Lane.

Though many of his contemporaries bear witness to the fact of
his illiteracy, and quote the syntactical innovations he unconsciously
made, it is possible that he was the Sam Goldwyn of his day, and that
some of his mistakes were deliberate.

He was, like Carlin, a great lover of cats, a most suitable interest
for the feline Harlequin. There is the delightful story of his meeting
with Peg Woffington—lovely, graceless Peg, who, at the age of
twenty-six, came to try her fortune in the London theatre. She went
straight to John Rich, by now manager of Covent Garden Theatre,
and so self-important that he refused to see anyone under the rank of
baronet.

Nothing daunted, Peg forced her way into his room and found the
great man in a startling state of undress, holding the manuscript of a
play in one hand and a bowl of tea in the other. Around him, beneath
him, beside him, and on top of him, about thirty cats, of all sizes,
colours, and kinds, disported themselves. One chewed the manuscript,
another daintily lapped the tea. Two were on his knees, one asleep
on his shoulder, and a fourth was neatly curled like a fur toque upon
his head. Even Peg realised that it would be wiser to withdraw.

Rich's pantomimes soon took on a definite shape. The first and
shorter part held the serious theme, taken from Greek and Roman
mythology, or legend nearer his own time. The second and longer
part consisted of the serio-comic love affair of Harlequin and Columbine, in the course of which the lovers were pursued, by Columbine's
father, or guardian, or suitor Pantaloon, into extraordinary and
unlikely places. Harlequin invariably effected transformations and
enchantments with his magic bat, and it was certain that in the
end the lovers would be united, and their enemies routed.

These early pantomimes echoed the rustic origins of commedia
dell'arte. Rich's shows were filled with scenes taken from country
and farmyard, were peopled with louts and peasants and yokels; and
offered the same uninhibited humour, based upon rural life, that we
find in the early scenari.

The dark opening common to many of the seventeenth-century

scenari persisted in Rich's pantomimes, where the curtain rose upon murky caverns, deserted moorland, derelict ruins open to the night, Vulcan's smoke-filled cave in the bowels of the earth, or Pluto's kingdom of impenetrable night. Across the darkened stage flashed lightning or lurid flame, over which hovered birds of ill-omen, bats, and demons of ill-repute.

His stage effects were always worthy of note. In 1726, when he presented *The Sultan*, the first pantomime with an Arabian theme ever to be seen in London, he employed every possible form of flying machine—and his machinists saw to it that they were many. Paris descended on chariots of rosy cloud: the sun came out of the sky, bearing golden-skinned dancing girls. Harlequin entered from above on a magic carpet. Exotic birds brought other beautiful maidens, while Pantaloon made his exit hanging perilously from the sides of a flying coffer. Rich filled the stage with magic, and an Oriental splendour that would have made a real Sultan envious, or surprised. A year later he mounted *The Rape of Proserpine*, and excited his audience with cataclysmic effects. Hell itself rose from the infernal regions, heaven descended to dance upon the earth, and a cornfield was set on fire and reduced to ashes before the amazed eyes of the spectators.

Rich not only founded English pantomime. He created, in England, a Harlequin of fantasy who in the end was kin to, though different from, Marivaux's Arlequin. Marivaux's literary Arlequin was poetic in mind and spirit as well as in body. Rich had too crude a personality to be able to create a Harlequin that was poetic in conception: but he was able to seize the thread of poetry that is always present in Harlequin, and weave it into fantasy. His Harlequin was a creature of magical power and whimsical humour. The material world assumed strange shapes, underwent transformation, ceased to exist, and then returned in different form at the clap of his magic bat. He could take and give life, turn men into things, and things into men. No power on earth, in heaven, or in hell, through all the wide spaces of eternity and all the slow years of infinity, could alter or damage Rich's Harlequin, who was closer to Mercury, his patron god, than at any other time, and more magical than any other.

To compensate himself for his inferiority, Rich created a superman with absolute power over all the elements: and, by so doing, set a pattern that the English Harlequin was to follow to the end.

CHAPTER THREE

The Two Harlequins

IT must not be supposed that Rich had it all his own way in the theatre of his time. Harlequin was, like his ancestors, doomed to a troubled life, and bound to be the subject of controversy and rivalry.

In England the struggle waged was the same as the one in France: and one of the leaders of the battle against him was David Garrick, one of the greatest actors of the English stage.

Garrick himself had once appeared as Harlequin, but very few people knew of it. In his early days, when family commitments kept him in the wine business with his brother, and his increasing passion to be an actor caused him to haunt the theatre at Goodman's Fields, he became well known to the owner of the theatre, who, from good nature, or a natural desire to take advantage of cheap labour, sometimes made use of him in crowd scenes, or in a backstage emergency. One evening Yates, the Harlequin playing at the theatre, fell suddenly sick just before the curtain was due to rise. The young Garrick, as usual lingering in the wings, was pressed into service; and for a single performance, his incognito preserved behind the mask, played Harlequin so well that no one apparently suspected that he was not Yates. This experience did not prevent him from referring to Rich's pantomimes as 'mummery and toys', nor from deploring the public taste that not only attended, but clamoured for, such empty trivialities. His aversion was not in any way lessened by the fact that, in view of popular demand, he was himself compelled to stage pantomime at Drury Lane in order to keep his audiences. Garrick's Harlequin was Henry Woodward, who had appeared in 1729, when he was fifteen years old, in *The Beggar's Opera*, staged by Rich at Lincoln's Inn Fields with a cast of children. The boy Woodward had played the Beggar, and little Peg Woffington, then aged about thirteen, had played Polly.

When in 1732 Rich opened Covent Garden Theatre, which he had built on a plot of land leased from the Duke of Bedford at a ground rent of £100 per annum, he engaged the young Woodward as junior Harlequin, so that he received his training from Lun himself. It was probably Woodward who was playing the young Harlequin to whom Lun explained the hatching from the egg.

Soon after Garrick took over the management of Drury Lane, Woodward joined him, and became second only to Lun in playing Harlequin. Since Lun was so wonderful a mime, Garrick in his wisdom made Woodward a talking Harlequin, to distract the mind of his audience from comparisons in which Woodward was certain to lose face.

Henry Woodward was an innovator rather than a creator. He played the traditional Harlequin known to the English public, but, knowing himself incapable of outrivalling Lun in mime or in artistry, he made use of various tricks that added something hereafter to the English Harlequin that was emerging. Like Thomassin before him, he used special postures to denote different emotions—'poses he struck in rhythm to music, each portraying anger, jealousy, fear, or grief'. These came to be known as 'attitudes'; and though later James Byrne was called 'the attitude Harlequin', Thomassin and Woodward before him had made use of the special poses.

Another of Woodward's specialities was also derived from a scenario of the Italian players. When pursued, he would leap through walls, or similarly impenetrable objects. To create this illusion, he did not use a pivot or a trap, as did Arlecchino, but employed a second Harlequin. On one occasion, through a slight mistiming, both were on the stage together: and the audience greatly enjoyed the breakdown of the illusion.

Woodward had a fine stage presence, due in part to his well-proportioned figure, in part to his personal charm. He enjoyed that curious duality some actors possess, in that his stage and private personalities were different. In the early years of his career, before he assumed Harlequin's motley, he had played elegant young gentlemen to perfection, both looking and seeming the part, and giving every appearance of good birth and breeding. He was in truth cultured and

The Intimate Theatre Group in a scene from *Pinocchio,* showing the puppets who danced
the Harlequinade with which the show ended, 1950

A scene from Val Parnell's pantomime *Dick Whittington*, presented at the Palladium in 1952.
Harlequin (William Barrett) and Columbine (Lynne Golding) are in the foreground as the
curtain falls on the finale of the first-half curtain

intelligent, a pleasant companion to those who shared his intellectual interests. But once away from the stage, his fine manners and noble appearance dropped from him. To all save a few rare spirits, he was violently disagreeable: and, even in those coarser days, he was noted for vile and obscene language.

He contributed to the success of Drury Lane during the years he remained with Garrick, not only by his playing of Harlequin but also with the Harlequinades he devised for the theatre, in which he made use of themes drawn from fairy tales, in an effort to offer something different from Rich's classical and legendary subjects.

One of his most admired *lazzi*, well known to the Italians, was the eating of fruit—'Soft music was played: he came on, sat at a table (on which nothing was placed) and made a pretence of taking up a bunch of grapes by its stem. Then, holding his hand, with the points of finger and thumb compressed, he seemed to shake the stem, and strip off the grapes into his mouth. In like manner, he would hold up a cherry by the stalk, and, after eating, spurt the stone from his lips. Eating a gooseberry, paring an apple, sucking an orange, or a peach— all were simulated in the same marvellous fashion. In short, the audience seemed to know what fruit he was eating by the highly ingenious deception of his acting.'[1]

Woodward's first appearance as Harlequin at Drury Lane was in 1750 in *Queen Mab*, described on the playbills as 'A Gorgeous Pantomime in Italian Grotesque Characters'. By that time Lun was well established at Covent Garden. So spectacular had been his success at Lincoln's Inn Fields that he had been forced to find another site and build a larger theatre. Lincoln's Inn Fields had rapidly become too small to contain his shows or his audiences.

The rivalry that henceforward persisted between the two theatres, Drury Lane and Covent Garden, gave considerable impetus to the growth of pantomime, and to the elaborate staging of entertainment, a trend that influenced all forms of drama. Once Lun had introduced magic into the Harlequin story, and Garrick with Woodward was forced to follow suit, ample excuse was afforded for ingenious transformations, trapdoor work, and machines of all kinds. The rivalry between Harlequin Lun at Covent Garden and Harlequin Woodward at Drury Lane meant in effect that pantomime came to birth with

1 *The Hunters and the Hunted*, Sacheverell Sitwell, Macmillan, 1947.

far more elaborate scenery, costumes, and effects than had ever been provided for straight plays.

We who are accustomed to modern panto, with its elaborate stagecraft, would think little of the crude plays, only half an hour long, embellished with unwieldy machines, that were given in those two theatres under Rich and Garrick: but in their own day they heralded a revolution in spectacle and stagecraft, and were the attraction compelling large audiences.

Lun continued to range far and wide for the themes of his pantomimes, while Woodward drew his inspiration wholly from fairy tales, thus preparing the ground from which Blanchard later drew such a rich harvest. One interesting Drury Lane show may perhaps be mentioned here, since Garrick himself devised it while Woodward was absent in Dublin. It carries haunting memories of one produced at Goodman's Fields: it may even have been the very one in which Garrick made his unique appearance as Harlequin.

In 1741 an early pantomime, *Harlequin Student: or the Fall of Pantomime with the Restoration of the Drama*,[1] was put on at Goodman's Fields to celebrate the recent erection of a monument to Shakespeare in Westminster Abbey. Eighteen years later, Garrick staged *Harlequin's Invasion* at Drury Lane. The theme was of a battle between Harlequin and Shakespeare, ending in Shakespeare's victory. It served to show that, in spite of the many successful pantomimes staged in his theatre, Garrick still deplored its form and popularity. All that remains of this pantomime today is the proud song *Hearts of Oak*, for which Garrick wrote the words.

While Woodward was away in Dublin, Sheridan wrote pantomimes for Garrick; and his treatment of the *Robinson Crusoe* story marked a further development of this new theatre form. Until Sheridan took a hand in the game, the business of the Harlequinade —the pursuit and triumph of Harlequin and Columbine—had no connection with the theme from which the shows drew their titles, and was introduced at random, often interrupting the progress of the action.

Sheridan's *Robinson Crusoe* was a four-act play, produced in 1789, the first stage adaption of the story, and the first pantomime in which Harlequin, Columbine, Pantaloon, and Clown took parts, however

---

[1] See Appendix, B, p. 200.

minor, in the actual story. The Harlequinade was therefore linked to the theme, and not developed, as hitherto, in alternate acts. The first two acts were wholly occupied with the adventures of Robinson Crusoe, the last two took place in Spain, and were mainly concerned with Harlequin in his own person. The innovation was accepted by the public generally: while Horace Walpole expressed his distaste in a vivid letter which shows clearly how the linking of theme and Harlequinade was achieved:

'How unlike the pantomimes of Rich, which were full of wit, and carried on the story! What I now saw was *Robinson Crusoe*. How Aristotle and Bossuet, had they written on pantomimes, would swear! It was a heap of contradictions and violations of the custom. Friday is turned into Harlequin, and falls down at an old man's feet that I took for Pantaloon, but they told me that it was Friday's father. I said, "Then it must be Thursday, yet still it seemed to be Pantaloon. I see I understand nothing, from astronomy to a Harlequin-farce."'[1]

Although Rich had died in 1761, Garrick had continued to stage pantomimes because of their popular success. In 1762, he revived *Queen Mab*, the first to be given at Drury Lane, and one of his triumphs: and in the same year staged three new pieces—*The Witches; or Harlequin Cherokee*: *The Magician of the Mountain*: and *The Rites of Hecate; or Harlequin from the Moon*, this last echoing the old Italian comedy known in France as *Arlequin, Empereur dans la Lune* (and Mrs. Aphra Behn's adaptation of it, which had been shown in the previous century).

Woodward, returning from Dublin, gave a twist to the rivalry existing between Drury Lane and Covent Garden by accepting an engagement at the latter theatre. There had clearly been a serious quarrel between Woodward and Garrick, possibly at the time Woodward left for Dublin. For now, when Garrick staged a spectacular *Jubilee Pageant* at Drury Lane, Woodward brought ridicule upon it by devising a pantomime at Covent Garden, *Harlequin's Jubilee*, in which all the magic properties from well-known pantomimes came to pay homage to a statue of Lun, which finally descended from its plinth and walked among them.

Charles Lamb, as a child, saw a revival of *Harlequin's Jubilee* and recorded the experience in vivid terms: 'To my apprehension (too

[1] Quoted by A. E. Wilson in *Christmas Pantomime*, George Allen and Unwin, 1934.

sincere for satire) Lun was as remote a piece of antiquity as Lud—the father of a line of Harlequins—transmitting his dagger of lath (the wooden sceptre) through countless ages. I saw the Primæval Motley come from his silent tomb in a ghostly vest of white patchwork, like the apparition of a dead rainbow. So Harlequins look, thought I, when they are dead.'

Lun had died indeed. Seventeen years after his death, Covent Garden presented a mixture of his pantomimes under the title *The Medley*, which reminds us irresistibly of Colley Cibber's apology for having allowed pantomime at Drury Lane, in which he refers to 'These monstrous medlies that have so long infected the stage.' Twelve years after *The Medley*, in 1800, *Harlequin's Chaplet*, consisting of scenes taken from a dozen different pantomimes, was staged in Lun's theatre. But 'the primæval Motley in his ghostly vest of white patchwork' was not there to animate these piteous ghosts of dead pantomime. For in the years since Rich's passing, the genre he created had developed so rapidly, and upon such different lines that *The Medley* and *Harlequin's Chaplet* had the same effect upon the audience as reissues of silent films have today upon the public used to talkies.

Lun's immortality was of a different kind. He had, as Lamb much later wrote, handed on his wooden sceptre, his dagger of lath: and with it the potentialities of pantomime. By the end of the eighteenth century, it had become a novel but accepted part of English theatre, and the public had forgotten that Harlequin was a foreigner who once bore the outlandish name of Arlecchino. Pantomime was the most popular form of entertainment all through the year, the length and breadth of the land. Touring companies took it in inferior form to remote corners, every travelling show incorporated a pantomime with its songs, dances, juggling, and melodrama, every huckster had his Harlequin.

Several of Rich's successors were mute Harlequins, partly because of Lun, partly because speech unaccompanied by music was a monopoly owned in those days by patent theatres like Drury Lane and Covent Garden; while Woodward influenced a number of talking Harlequins. As pantomime developed the change in form heralded by Sheridan's *Robinson Crusoe*, Harlequin became mute.

Other London theatres were now presenting pantomimes. The

Norman Rose as Arlecchino in *The Disguises of Arlecchino*, presented by the Mime Theatre Company in 1952

Harlequin (Michael Charnley) with Clown (John Rutland) and
Columbine (Sonya Hana) in the pantomime *Babes in the Wood*,
given at the Players' Theatre, 1952

Haymarket Theatre became renowned for its spectacular shows, and was closely rivalled by the Sadler's Wells Theatre, which in 1773 broke all records with *The Whim Wham*, a piece in which Harlequin and Columbine figured as Christian slaves sold to a Turk.

The end of the century saw pantomime firmly established; and about to start a new phase of existence.

CHAPTER FOUR

The Satirical Harlequin

WHILE Harlequin was engaged in establishing himself in England, certain *beaux esprits* of the eighteenth century saw how they could use him for their own ends. Both in Italy and in France he had, upon occasion, satirised certain aspects of contemporary society: but only in passing, and because he was played by men of wit and intelligence who fell naturally into the satirical expression of social criticism. The wits of eighteenth-century England realised that the enigmatic Harlequin could be made to serve as a symbol of anything they chose, and, if the choice were well made, could easily be used to express opinion that could not otherwise safely be put forward.

The method employed is clearly shown in a mock-farce intended for the study, not the stage, which in 1724 was put into circulation at sixpence the copy by Warner of Paternoster Row. In 1723, when Drury Lane presented Thurmond's *Harlequin Doctor Faustus*, John Rich, then at Lincoln's Inn Fields, had immediately staged *Harlequin Necromancer and Doctor Faustus*, based on the same well-known story. Both pantomimes took the town by storm, much to the dismay of all who disliked this new and garish form of theatre as much as they favoured straight drama. The published farce announced itself on the title page as:

THE BRITISH STAGE
or
THE EXPLOITS OF HARLEQUIN
A Farce

As it is performed by a company of Wonderful Comedians at both Theatres with Universal Applause: with all its original Songs, Scenes, and Machines.

Designed as an After-Entertainment for the Audiences of

HARLEQUINADE DOCTOR FAUSTUS AND THE NECROMANCER

> Here you've a Dragon, a Windmill and a Devil,
> A Doctor, A Conjuror, all wondrous civil,
> A Harlequin and Puppets, Ghosts and Fiends
> And Raree-show to gain some Actors Ends:
> So perfectly polite is grown this town,
> No play, without a Windmill, will go down.

The author of the farce, with heavy humour, then makes it abundantly clear in a preface that he is no lover of pantomimes. If it be true to state that the history of the theatre in the eighteenth century is the struggle of Harlequin and Shakespeare for supremacy, then our author is definitely in the second camp, and serves, in a manner however pompous, to demonstrate the feeling of his time and kind against the new form.

'The Entertainments of Harlequin and Doctor Faustus having been lately introduced to both our Theatres, with the most universal Approbation, it heightened my curiosity to see what had occasioned so much mirth and diversion to others; but notwithstanding there was a crowded audience each night when I was present, and the whole company distributed applauses, they were so far from giving me any real pleasure that I frequently bit my lips whilst others were laughing, and often laughed when others were silent.

'I could not sometimes forebear grinning and extorting my muscles at a sight which indeed excited my surprise; a representation of Puppets I did not expect, nor a Windmill nor a Dragon, on our polite stages: but such I found there, and to the Immortal Honour of this Age be it recorded that they were represented a month together, and met with far greater applause than the politest and most elegant play that ever appeared upon the British Theatre.

'The following whimsical humorous scenes, I confess, are taken from those witty entertainments; and I hope the Town will vouchsafe to countenance a Dramatic Piece which has everywhere kept true to the wit and humour of what they have been so much pleased with, the famous Doctor Faustus, the Dragon, and the Windmill.

'And the reader is desired to be informed that the latter of these actors, with others their Companions are made by the Author to speak in this performance, to Atone for those Characters which are Dumb in the Original Entertainments.'

There follows a list of characters, in which the Town figures as an Ass, and the Theatre an Owl, and the names of the actors playing them are drawn from the two companies concerned, and thinly disguised by hyphens, Rich appearing for example as Mr. R- -h.

The dialogue is loaded with a very heavy satire, as the following extract will show:

> *Ass*   Well, but how have you employed yourselves of late, Mr. Dragon and Mr. Windmill?
>
> *Windmill*   Wondrously advantageously, Sir. Mr. Dragon has been singing for a whole Month together, and I have been dancing like a Jack in the Lanthorn all the time: every night of our celebrated representation we were honoured with an audience of fifteen hundred persons, and we put above one hundred pieces into our pockets of ready Rhino, for our wonderful performances.
>
> *Ass*   The judgment of this town is so very excellent that I cannot too much applaud it—we now see how wit flourishes.
>
> *Dragon*   Beside my singing, I've constantly spit fire, flew about the air, mounted a giant on my back and squirted a Dancing Master at every Fizzle.
>
> *Ass*   Wondrous witty. I'm amazed at the invention.
>
> *Windmill*   Then the Harlequin conjuror jumped over the moon without breaking his shins. We had Shades that could sing, and Ghosts which could dance; Puppets that were men, and men who were puppets. And as to my part it was so exceeding dextrous that all people were amazed, and ushered me in with the loudest applauses.
>
> *Ass*   Adzooks! I would not give a farthing for a play without a Windmill in't. Methinks there's so much wit in it that the Author of it deserves a Statue of Brass.

The two pantomimes given at Drury Lane and Lincoln's Inn Fields are parodied throughout with a pedestrian humour that nowhere approaches wit: but the farce clearly presents the opposition to pantomime so strongly felt by many literary celebrities of the time and by Garrick, even while he was forced to stage them in order to keep his theatre open. Harlequin is satirised in his own person—first, in a parody of the usual dark opening, when Pluto and his attendant demons are discovered, together with the shades of several beautiful women. Harlequin comes in, and the following dialogue takes place:

Le Capitan (Julien Giuomar), Polichinelle (André Weber), Brighella (Jacques Fabbri), Pedrolino (Raymond Devos), Arlequin (André Gille), and Colombine (Rose Varte) in
La Famille Arlequin

Photo Bernand, Paris

The Three Arlequins (André Gille, Raymond Devos, André Weber) in the 'lazzi des trois Arlequins'

Pluto Here, sign this contract, Faustus, and all the Whores of the Universe are yours.

Harlequin His terms are good. Agreed, my friend. (*He signs.*)

Pluto Here, take this wand (*giving him a small stick*) and you're then installed with a Daemon's power. Now, Sir—I have you in my net. (*Aside.*) Beauties, fly to the Plutonian shades! (*Shades vanish.*)

Harlequin Ah! Am I so soon deceived?

Dragon You are, my son! Ha! Ha! I'll sing you a song, and leave you.

The above passage is perhaps the happiest in the whole farce; and the following the most revealing of the tricks Harlequin practised in his early days in England, as well as being an amusing parody of his transformation.

Harlequin Now I'll commence my show. Ass, be you instantly transformed into a modish citizen with Horns exalted on your forehead. (*Striking him with his wand.*)

Ass I'm changed, transformed. This is wonderful!

Harlequin Owl, be you no longer a bird of Prey, but assume the fine gentleman. (*Transformed.*)

Ass This is astonishing. The Wonder of Wonders!

Harlequin Observe my Power, Gentlemen! This leg I can sever from my body, and without any inconvenience put it on again. (*Cuts off a false wooden leg and his right leg appears in its place.*)

Ass Stupendous is the sight I now view. None but Faustus or a Harlequin could effect it.

Harlequin You, Mr. Book on yonder shelf, repair to your master at the word of command. (*Book tossed to him by hand behind shelf.*)

The greater Harlequin's popularity grew, the more tempting it became to use him for purposes of satire; and when Fielding took a hand the results were at once delightful, from a literary point of view, and troublesome from the point of view of those he satirised. His first venture was *The Author's Farce*, given at the Haymarket in 1729: and in a puppet show contained within it called *The Pleasures of the Town* he was able not only to satirise certain quirks and foibles of his age—gambling, drinking, and easy morals—but also to add a political tang by presenting Walpole as Punch, in the usual entertainment of singing and dancing and juggling. Sir Robert Walpole suffered much at the hands of these panto-satirists. Four years after *The Author's Farce* had appeared, he was present at a pantomime *Love Ruins all*

Dangers. During the course of the show, Harlequin hinted at Walpole's intended Excise Act. The latter in a great rage went backstage, and when he discovered the line to be an impromptu, he beat up Harlequin until he yelled for mercy.

Meanwhile Fielding had discovered that the stage is an excellent place for disseminating propaganda, and that Harlequin the unknown quantity could equal almost anything. In 1736, he installed in his theatre in the Haymarket a company to which he gave the grandiloquent title of *The Great Mogul's Company of Comedians*. With this company, he staged shows which satirised both politics and pantomime with a fine catholicism. One of the most successful of the latter kind was *Tumble down Dick: or Phaeton in the Suds*, the very title a satire of those in vogue. Here were interpolated interludes called *Harlequin a Pick Pocket*, in which Fielding excelled himself. Clearly, the scenes poked fun at Lun, with scintillating satire on his love of spectacle, tricks, machines, and magic. To the well-informed observer, they also presented an hilarious and biting comment on the political chicanery of the age.

The result of these satirical pantomimes carries haunting echoes of the troubles of that other Arlequin in France. Walpole, who had been the greatest victim, was the most anxious to check this new development. He bribed Giffard, of Goodman's Fields, who was as usual in great financial stress, to pass over to him the manuscript of a play called *The Golden Rump*. It was a masterpiece of its kind, noteworthy even in those times for its salacity, its all too frequent blasphemy and its unblushing sedition. Walpole, by reading well-chosen extracts, was able to induce Parliament to pass a Licensing Bill, by which the entertainments of the Royal Companies were prohibited, unless a true copy of the intended show were sent to the Lord Chamberlain, and restricted to Westminster, or wherever else the King might reside. The fact that Walpole was anxious to secure the establishment of so stringent an act is proof of the success of the satirical Harlequin.

Two other curious documents may be cited here, since they give evidence of the manner in which Harlequin penetrated into controversy outside the theatre as well as on the stage. The first was a pamphlet, *Harlequin Methodist*, sold at the Print and Pamphlet Shop for sixpence in 1750. An engraving covering the whole width of the sheet shows Harlequin, mounted on a small stool and wearing a preacher's cravat, preaching to an assorted crowd—artisans, gentry, men, women, and children. Beneath are printed in three columns the following satirical verses, which speak for themselves:

> *Thro' all the whole circle of Vice,*
> *Dear Brethren, I often have run*
> *Whores, Horses, and Drinking and Dice*
> *And thought all Religion but Fun:*
> *But now, so my stars have decreed,*
> *My Follies I see, tho' full late,*
> *I'm made a new Man, ah! indeed,*
> *And faithfully regenerate.*

> *Then come, all Good Folks, to my school;*
> *Near Bedlam my tripod I'll place,*
> *And hear me hold forth from my stool*
> *Of Truth and of Daylight and Grace.*
> *Go no more to the old House, I pray,*
> *Where Satan has Ta'en his abode*
> *But come if you please every day*
> *To mine, it will soon be the Mode.*

> *How sweet it will be in the news*
> *Instead of Box, Gall'ry and Pit*
> *To read what's the Price of my Pews*
> *For Lords that are converts to fit.*
> *The Ladies who flaunted before*
> *In Hoops, Sacks, and proud Solitaires,*
> *Will crowd about every door*
> *To see who can first come to prayers.*

> *To G—rr—k my Rachel I'll spouse*
> *And hope she will bring him much Grace;*
> *He shall have my right in the House*
> *Provided our Faith he'll embrace.*
> *Then when of one stage he is tired*
> *The Methodist stage he may tread,*
> *Oh, how he will then be admired*
> *For playing in great Wh—tf—d's stead.*

The other, bearing no date, but set roughly in its period by the references to politicians of the time, and to the French Revolution, is a fake bill sheet anouncing a pantomime:

Pro Bono Publico
Speedily will be Performed on the Vast
Theatre of the World
A Grand Ballet Pantomime Called
HARLEQUIN IMPEACHER
or
JOHN BULL WILL HAVE HIS OWN

Part I.

Scene I. France. A Gallic Explosion comprising the Downfall of the Bastille and the Erection of the Temple of Freedom on its Ruins.

Scene II. England. A Council of Evil Genii in the Palace of Pandemonium; after violent debates they concert a plan for beheading Louis and setting Europe in a Blaze.

(This political lampoon is continued in descriptive scenes set in Pilnitz—Europe—Flanders.)

Part II.

Scene I. The Low Countries. Alarms, Retreats. English, Dutch, and Austrian Soldiers cross stage in confusion. Harlequin Vuidhans leaps the dykes with astonishing agility, etc.

Scene II. Concert of Vocal Music called The Fall of Babylon.

Humbug, Mr. Pitto
Backall, Master Channing
Nonblush, Mr. Dundaffio
Flamer, Mr. Windy
Honesty, Mr. Fox
Detector, Mr. Gray
and True Tongue, Mr. Sherry

Scene III. Great Britain—Universal Fermentation, etc.

The whole to conclude with a Sublime and Animating Spectacle, the Storming of the Cabinet.

The rest of the bill is set out to resemble a normal theatre bill of the time, giving details of the spectacle to be witnessed as the grand finale, and continuing the political satire throughout.

The eighteenth century was peppered with similar pamphlets, news-sheets and broadsheets, rapidly produced, filled with topical allusions of a theatrical, political or scandalous kind, and sure of lively sales, since all of them featured Harlequin, the most popular figure in eighteenth-century England.

Patricia Miller and David Blair in *Harlequin in April*, a ballet
devised by Johnny Cranko for the Festival of Britain in 1951, and
presented by the junior company of Sadler's Wells

Photo by Baron

Robert Helpmann as Harlequin in Fokine's *Carnaval*, presented by
the Sadler's Wells Ballet Company

CHAPTER FIVE

Harlequin in Decline

HARLEQUIN, then over three hundred years old, was still active, alert, and adaptable to new conditions, at the beginning of the century that was to see him degenerate.

In 1800, with *Harlequin Amulet or the Magic of Mona*, pantomime entered upon a new phase. Harlequin was played by James Byrne, dancer, ballet master, and choreographer, who had begun his theatrical career as a member of the *corps de ballet* at Drury Lane. Byrne was a dancing Harlequin in the tradition established by Rich, and, because of his long training and experience in ballet, he brought new beauty to the dancing of Harlequin, and insensibly reduced his acrobatics to a minimum. With Byrne, Harlequin's leap through the window became an exceptionally extended *jeté*.

Whether because of the demands of ballet or because Grimaldi as Clown was already stealing Harlequin's thunder, Byrne radically changed the traditional costume, which, with minor alterations, had been worn from the earliest days of commedia dell'arte until then. He replaced the loose jacket and trousers by silk fleshings, fitting like a second skin, entirely covered with over three hundred pieces of cloth sewn with nearly 50,000 spangles. The spangles alone weighed three pounds, and were all carefully sewn on by hand. The black vizard was replaced by an eye-mask. The Bergamask yokel was now a very fine gentleman indeed, as he flashed about the stage, a glittering quicksilver figure that caught every eye.

Byrne added other elements to Harlequin's tradition. He gave significance to the colours he wore in his sequinned patches: yellow stood for jealousy, blue for love, scarlet for anger, mauve for fidelity, and black for invisibility. When he struck his 'attitudes', his bat pointed always towards the colour signifying the emotion or quality he was expressing. He gave new life to the 'attitudes', which, since Woodward's time, had been taken over by lesser players and become rigidly formalised. In some cases Harlequin seemed to be continually in one or other of the five recognised positions, passing from one to another with scarcely any pause. Byrne abolished this convention, using the attitudes more dramatically, adding many others to the original five, and always pointing to the relevant colour among his spangles to support his pose. He made it abundantly clear that when Harlequin pointed to his black patches and wore his mask down he was invisible; and that whenever his magic slapstick was filched from his grasp he fell immediately into the power of his inveterate enemies, Clown and Pantaloon.

During the Regency, further small costume changes became apparent: for once Harlequin became sartorially a fine gentleman, he took care to follow the normal trends of fashion, without abandoning his spangled tights. In the Regency period, then, he sometimes sported a two-cornered hat like that made famous by Napoleon: sometimes a high cocked hat with a chin-strap, in both following the example of the dandies, the bucks, the beaux, and the *merveilleux* who devoted their lives to *bon ton*. Occasionally he appeared wearing only his skull-cap, to which he had always remained faithful, in honour maybe of his distant forebears, for whom the *rasus capitus* was an occupational mode. When he became a Regency buck his patches were neatly disposed in regular triangular shapes, his belt was made of black velvet, and the neck opening of his tightly fitting costume became V-shaped, finally taking elegant ruffles. A strip of black velvet—the line of invisibility—outlined his spine, and continued forward to meet the white ruffles at his neck. He wore black dancing shoes on his feet, and was, every inch of him, an elegant and handsome figure.

The outstanding factor in all these changes is their sterility. Harlequin exchanged his peasant clothes for emasculate fleshings: he gave up acrobatics for dancing, wit for 'attitudes', *lazzi* for a few stereotyped tricks. The paradox was that Harlequin had never looked so young or so beautiful as when he was old and failing, declining in power and activity, bolstered up only by a few magical effects. There was one other significant change. Arlecchino had been a great amorist:

and there was no doubt at all in the mind of his audiences as to the purpose of his approaches, and their result. Arlequin, too, from his early to his most polished period in France, slid neatly into Colombine's bed. But Harlequin reached English pantomime in his extreme old age. His courtship of Columbine was ideal, etherealised to the plane of magic and symbol, in which was nothing of the flesh. Arlecchino's coarse desires, Arlequin's sophisticated love-making, were in Harlequin subdued to an idyllic courtship without consummation.

In the course of the century changes came also to the pantomimes in which he still played lead.

Delpini, the comic French Pierrot, was responsible for the major change destined to mark the particular character of Regency pantomime. Garrick had engaged him to stage the Drury Lane pantomimes. In due course he came upon Sheridan's *Robinson Crusoe*. Delpini rearranged it as a dumbshow, and gave it in 1781 under the title of *Robinson Crusoe or Harlequin Friday*, with Grimaldi senior as Friday. As in Sheridan's original text, the Harlequinade characters were part and parcel of the action throughout.

In the first part of the pantomime, Pantaloon and Pierrot were discovered and captured by the savages on the island. They were rescued by Crusoe and Friday, after which they were all involved in adventures in Spain. Here Harlequin Friday pursued his magic tricks until, ill-treated by Pantaloon, he decided to commit suicide. In the nick of time there entered a Magician who, upon waving his wand, caused clouds to open and reveal Cupid in a chariot of gold, attended by the sun. Cupid then addresses Harlequin Friday in the following couplet:

> Here, take this purse, this sword, this cap of fame
> Friday no more! Be Harlequin thy name!

after which the Harlequinade pursued its normal course in the second part, the company switching from Spain to amazing topography, ending in a magnificent temple dedicated to Venus.

Until Delpini's version of *Robinson Crusoe*, the turning point in the story had been the bestowal of magic upon Harlequin when he appeared at some point unconnected with the main theme. After 1781, Harlequin was formed out of another hero, who appeared in the 'opening', so that a transformation scene became a necessary part of pantomime.

By the end of the eighteenth century the short 'opening' of a fairy tale, or nursery rhyme had replaced the traditional 'dark opening' which Rich had taken from the Italian players and kept in his own spectacles. This fairy tale opening was very brief and indifferently performed, with dialogue of a very elementary kind. The characters wore huge masks or heads, of much grosser form than those worn by the Masks of commedia dell'arte, and more nearly resembling the gigantic heads carried in carnivals; they were wrapped in voluminous robes. At the end of the banal little opening they were touched with the Fairy Queen's Wand, and in full view of the audience they cast off robe and mask, to emerge as Harlequin, Columbine, Pantaloon, and Clown. It is interesting to note that at this stage the transformation was invariably effected before a 'dark scene', the new position of the traditional 'dark opening'.

Then, for twenty charming, comic, romantic, farcical, and magical scenes, the Harlequinade took pride of place, with Harlequin and Columbine eternally pursued by Pantaloon and Clown, eternally saved at the end by the Fairy Queen or some other beneficent person, in a final scene of unparalleled splendour. In the course of the twenty scenes, Harlequin would perform his magic tricks. At the clap of his slapstick, doors would revolve, shop-fronts collapse, houses change into sentry boxes, goods and people disappear, others become paralysed, while watchmen and officers of the law would find themselves perched on church steeples, or securely locked in a prison that descended from the skies. Throughout was the excitement of the chase, with Harlequin leaping through clock faces, through windows and walls, with Clown for ever at his heels.

On December 26th, 1806, Thomas Dibdin's pantomime *Harlequin Mother Goose: or the Golden Egg*[1] was presented at Covent Garden. With this show Dibdin achieved fame, Grimaldi became the leading comic actor of the day: and Harlequin fell into decline.

Dibdin, born in 1771, was a member of a family well known in the theatre. His father, Charles Dibdin, had written and composed an opera staged at Covent Garden. His brother Charles was a playwright: and he himself, at the age of four, had appeared as Cupid, to

[1] For text see Appendix B, p. 207-218.

Above—Pierre Brasseur as the actor Lemaitre playing Arlequin in Marcel Carné's film *Les Enfants du Paradis*, 1944. Jean-Louis Barrault is seen as Deburau playing Pierrot. The statue is Arletty

Below—André Eglevsky as Harlequin in the ballet *Death of Columbine*, given in Chaplin's film *Limelight*, 1952

The actress Camilla (Anna Magnani) dressed as Arlequina in Renoir's film *La Carozza d'Oro*, 1952. The Arlequin is wearing an interesting film version of his eighteenth-century costume

A scene from M.G.M.'s film version of Rafael Sabatini's famous novel, *Scaramouche*, 1952. Stewart Granger played the name part and is here shown taking part in a show put on by strolling players in the commedia dell 'arte tradition

the Venus of Mrs. Siddons, in a revival of *Shakespeare's Jubilee* at
Drury Lane. By 1800, Thomas had written one or two pantomimes
for Covent Garden, while his brother was writing for the Sadler's
Wells Theatre.

Mother Goose became his most successful pantomime. On its first
presentation it was given an enthusiastic reception by audience and
critics alike. It ran until the end of the season, and then was given in
the next four consecutive years: yet Dibdin himself received very
little for it, in cash or in appreciation. His name did not appear on the
playbill advertising the opening night; the only name missing in a
long list of persons responsible for the piece.

The pantomime was typical of the period; and of particular interest
here. It showed the persistence of the 'dark opening'—in this case a
storm raging over the village in which the play was set: and one of
the variations on the old theme, worn threadbare by the Italians, of
the guardian who forces an unwanted suitor upon his ward. Here the
Young Lovers are not Lelio and Isabella, but Colin and Colinette,
later to be transformed into Harlequin and Columbine: so that in effect
the rôles of gallant and lady of Italian comedy are taken over by their
valet and serving maid in English pantomime. There is a suggestion of
Italo-French influence in the name Avaro, given to the guardian, who
will be changed into Pantaloon.

Mother Goose contains also an interesting flash-back to the technique
employed by Arlequin in France, when legitimate drama had driven
him to the fairs. The pantomime had no spoken dialogue. The action
was expressed in mime, and by the exhibition of written signs, similar
to those held by fairground players at St. Laurent or St. Germain nearly a
century before: or by choral singing. After the four short scenes of the
opening, the Harlequinade began. Mother Goose transformed the
characters, who quite openly removed the clothes worn as Avaro,
Squire Bugle, Colin, and Colinette to stand revealed as Pantaloon,
Clown, Harlequin, and Columbine. The fourteen scenes of the
Harlequinade gave ample scope to Clown, with the Harlequin
behaviour pattern closely following the Italian: so closely that the
episode in scene seven of the ascending chairs and tables is twin to one
played by Carlin in *Arlequin Esprit Follet*; then one of the living statues
appeared in several scenari, among them *Festin de Pierre*, with
Thomassin playing Arlequin; while the submarine part following

the throwing of the egg into the sea is reminiscent of scenari like *Arlequin Roi de la Mer*. The text of *Mother Goose* shows clearly how vivid was the imprint of Italian comedy as late as the nineteenth century.

Thomas Dibdin alone would not greatly have affected the fortunes of Harlequin: but he provided, with *Mother Goose*, the vehicle in which Clown ousted Harlequin from the leading rôle he had played and kept for three hundred years.

The man who rang Harlequin's knell was Joseph Grimaldi; from whom was derived the affectionate name 'Joey' for the type of clown he created. Grimaldi was born in 1778 of an English mother and Italian father in the Parish of St. Clement Dane's. His father Guiseppe, after earning his livelihood as a dancer and tumbler at fairs in Italy and France, came to England and settled there for the rest of his life. He made his first appearance as Pantaloon, to the Harlequin of Rich, at Covent Garden in 1739, in *Orpheus and Eurydice*. He next obtained employment with Garrick at Drury Lane, playing Harlequin and Clown alternately; and was soon appointed *maître de ballet* to Drury Lane and Sadler's Wells. He brought something of Harlequin's technique and tricks to the minor rôle of Clown, so unconsciously preparing the way for his son Joseph. It was he who lengthened the pantomimes by adding comic scenes to them in which Clown was given ample opportunity to hold the centre of the stage.

Joseph had a hard upbringing under a stern father; and from babyhood was familiar with grease paint. At the age of three he had already appeared in *Robinson Crusoe* at Drury Lane; and as a miniature Clown with his father in *Harlequin Junior or the Magic Cestus*. A veteran aged five, he fell forty feet through a trap, severely damaging his arm, while he was appearing in pantomime as a cat. His father died when he was ten, leaving the family destitute. From that time on Grimaldi worked harder even than before, a child who knew no childhood. He appeared at Drury Lane and Sadler's Wells on the same days, going from one rehearsal to another, leaving one performance to renew or replace his make-up in a carriage that transported him to his second show that night. By the time he was twenty he was well known to London theatre audiences; and in 1800 made a name for himself in *Harlequin Amulet; or the Magic of Mona*: indeed, there were many who believed that James Byrne, the Harlequin of the piece, devised his spangled costume to catch the eye of the audience that seemed wholly concentrated upon the antics of Clown.

Following a dispute that may well have had its origins in the professional jealousy of the company, he left Drury Lane for Covent Garden, where in due course he enjoyed his greatest success in Dibdin's *Mother Goose*. He was in any case well cast as the rustic Squire Bugle, for in private life he had the appearance of a jovial John Bull, the hale and hearty squire of fiction. Adversity and privation had not soured him: nor did success turn his head. He remained a modest unassuming man, sincere and loyal, filled with a golden-hearted sentimentality common to all the great clowns.

Once he was fully accepted—and he was well established in the theatre at seventeen—he concentrated his vitality and his talent on building the minor Clown into a character of prime importance. The genesis of Clown is confused. He does not specifically belong to commedia dell'arte: nor yet particularly to the mediæval tradition in England, but draws something of himself from several sources. He first appeared as Pantaloon's ragged servant, as, centuries before, Arlecchino made his first bow as Pantalone's ragged valet. He was originally played in Rich's pantomime by Jemmy Spiller, a crony of Hogarth. Grimaldi took over the character from his father, who had already enlarged its scope, creating from it a subtle and broadly comic figure the very reverse of his own personality, a Clown practising every imaginable vice. Indeed, Grimaldi's Clown was blood-brother to that long-ago Arlecchino from Bergama—thieving, cowardly, treacherous, greedy, lying, and hypocritical.

Underlying his buffoonery was a satirical quality that delighted his audience, a defiance of law and order, a comic anarchy that made mock of all established institutions. Yet through it all glowed the golden heart of Grimaldi, so that in spite of Clown's shocking depravities, the public loved him as much as they laughed at him. He brought to the rôle he created a wealth of tricks that became traditional. In one scene he constructed a figure from vegetables, and then nearly died of terror when Harlequin's bat brought the figure to life. The filching of sausages, eggs, fish, and legs of mutton, the practical jokes on tradesmen, the brandishing of the red-hot poker, were all his invention. The song he sang in *The Talking Bird* at Sadler's Wells in 1819 became Clown's traditional song:

A little old woman her living she got
By selling hot codlins, hot, hot, hot.
Now this little woman who codlins sold,
Though her codlins were hot she was very cold,
    So to keep herself warm she thought it no sin
    To fetch herself a quartern of—gin,
    Ri-tol-id-dy, id-dy,
    Ri-tol-id-dy, ri tol-lay.

The song had numerous verses: and the gallery much enjoyed shouting the last word of the last line of each verse. Throughout his career, whatever else he sang, the public clamoured for 'Hot Codlins' (toffee apples): and after Grimaldi's death, Clown sang at least a verse of it and a refrain, until there was no more Clown.

It was Clown then who accelerated the decline of Harlequin. At the end of his long life, he was brought into rivalry with the young lusty, newly-created Clown, brimful with invention and energy. The ageing Harlequin recognised kinship, saw in Clown the recrudescence of his own vital youth, albeit he wore a different costume, and his mask was only a painted one.

Harlequin was worn out. He had no more tricks up his sleeve, no more cards to play. He had assumed magic, but lost vitality. As early as 1814, when the comedian Liston was asked to play Harlequin in Dibdin's *Harlequin Hoax* at Drury Lane, he wrote, 'I have been too long on the stage not to know that Harlequin is the worst part in a pantomime—a thing of shreds and patches, without a single point to get applause except when he jumps, and *that* is always done by someone else.' Harlequin, too old now to do his own tumbling, was forced to step back into the shadows and to watch the young and lively Clown enjoy the limelight.

CHAPTER SIX

The Fall

LIKE the hero of the opera *I Pagliacci*, Grimaldi concealed tragedy and sorrow beneath his Clown's mask. His happy marriage lasted only a year, ending abruptly with the death of his young wife in childbirth. Their son inherited his father's talents and even, in Grimaldi's own opinion, exceeded them; but he drank himself to death in early manhood, without fulfilling the promise he had shown. These tragedies, together with the privation and strain of his childhood and adolescence, and the demands of his professional life, brought him to premature old age. At a time when most men are in their prime, Grimaldi was broken beyond recovery, and forced to retire at the early age of forty-eight.

A few months after his last appearance as Clown at Sadler's Wells, came his farewell at Drury Lane, on June 27th, 1828, when he was carried on to the stage in a chair. There are contemporary records of the occasion, among them a harrowing account from *The Times*: 'He was much affected (by the shouts of applause, etc.). But although labouring under great bodily infirmity, he bore up safely against it, and went through the scene with so much humour that the audience laughed lustily as of old; and they were so delighted with that funny song of his about "blue ruin" and "hot codlins" that there was a general call for repetition. But he was much too exhausted to obey the call immediately, and eventually he was allowed to retire without repeating it.'

He had, from his chair, acted a scene from a pantomime before speaking the farewell written for him by Thomas Hood, and containing phrases that moved his audience to the point of tears: 'Like vaulting ambition, I have overleaped myself, and pay the penalty in advanced old age. . . . It is four months since I jumped my last jump, filched my last oyster, boiled my last sausage, and set in for retirement.'

Grimaldi was nine years in retirement before he died, poverty-stricken, in 1837. He had won his place among the immortals: for his successor, Tom Mathews, continued to play Clown in the Grimaldi manner, wearing the great Clown's costume, and painting his face with the well-known scarlet smears. Even when Clown disappeared from pantomime, the Joey clown of the Circus ring kept Grimaldi's memory alive.

By the time of Grimaldi's death, Clown was established as the leading character in Harlequinade, with Harlequin reduced to the level of Columbine, an embellishment to a traditional scene. The English Harlequin demanded few, therefore, of the qualities required from his Italian and French prototypes, Once Lun had set his inimitable pattern, Harlequin was best played by a trained ballet-dancer.

Grimaldi played Clown to the Harlequin of James Byrne, and of John Bologna, junior, one of his closest friends. Bologna was a member of an Italian family of mimes, well known in the theatre, circus, and fairgrounds of Europe. It is possible that he was a descendant or collateral of Simone de Bologna, who played Arlecchino in the sixteenth century for the *Gelosi*. John Bologna first appeared at the Royal Circus, then for many years was with Grimaldi at Covent Garden and Sadler's Wells. It would seem that he was more than adequate as Harlequin, and not to be ranked with those who simply engaged in mechanical posturing, for Kemble is reputed to have said of him: 'If that man could speak as well as he acts pantomime, I would never again appear on the stage.' Like so many pantomime artists of the nineteenth century, Bologna died in extreme poverty. He was then seventy-one.

Tom Ellar, born in 1780, is perhaps the last of the notable Harlequins, though there were others after him who filled the dwindling rôle. Having begun his stage career in Dublin, he first played Harlequin at the Royalty Theatre, Goodman's Fields, on Easter Monday in the year 1808. He was so graceful in the rôle, and attracted such notice that by 1813 he was well established at Covent Garden and Sadler's Wells, following in Bologna's footsteps, playing Harlequin to the Clown of Grimaldi, and then of Tom Mathews. From Bologna he had acquired a curious trick. He would finish his series of 'attitudes' by spinning his head round like a top at a truly remarkable speed. Bologna had originally performed this feat in a drunken scene set in Vauxhall Gardens, being cured of it by Columbine who, taking up his magic bat, tapped him on the head with it, causing him to spin his head in the opposite direction until it stopped. It was a difficult feat to perform, and always brought a round of applause.

Leigh Hunt has left a memorable picture of this Harlequin: 'In comes Harlequin, demi-masked, parti-coloured, nimble-toed, lithe, agile; bending himself now this way, now that way; bridling up like a pigeon; tipping out his toe like a dancer; then taking a fantastic skip; then standing ready at all points, and at right angles with his omnipotent lath-sword, the emblem of the converting power of fancy and lightheartedness. Giddy as we think him, he is resolved to show us that his head can bear more giddiness than we fancy; and lo! beginning with it by degrees, he whirls it round into a very spin, with no more remorse than if it were a button. Then he draws his sword, slaps his enemy, who has just come upon him, into a settee; and springing upon him, dashes through the window like a swallow.'

Ellar earned the enthusiasm of his audiences with his magnificent leapings and vaultings over and through obstacles. An old Covent Garden playbill of 1815 advertises that: 'Mr. Ellar will positively, for this night only, fly from the back of the gallery to the extremity of the stage, a descent of upwards of two hundred feet, in a most surprising manner, never before attempted by any other person'—a feat that reminds us irresistibly of Carlin's dangerous walk around the rim of the circle. There is a vivid description of Ellar at fifty-six, recorded by a fellow actor, and giving a painful impression of the rigours of Harlequin's profession: 'When he came to the prompter's box, where I was standing, he looked a decrepit old man. He raised his mask to cool his face as he came off the stage after his first trip with Columbine, and tears mingled with the beads of perspiration trickling down his cheeks. I noticed with surprise that his features were strangely discoloured, and that his skin had a bluish tint, which even stage cosmetics could not subdue. Afterwards, I learned that the cast-off mistress of a chemist had a year previously administered to him, in one of her jealous moods, a mercurial poison which had thus changed his complexion, while enfeebling his frame. As he moistened his parched lips from the bottle of barley water which the call boy held in readiness, he dropped the bat, immediately wanted to change a trick already brought onto the stage. . . . During the run of the pantomime it was painful to note the physical exhaustion which followed even the slightest exertion of his powers: and one evening in the following February, he smote his wand upon a scene intended to represent the enlargement of every newspaper consequent upon the removal of the stamp duty; and fainted in my arms before the stage carpenters could reveal the size of the tremendous broadsheets supposed to be the result of the potential bat.'

His last years were spent in misery and destitution, struggling with ill-health and earning a precarious living playing the guitar in the streets, or dancing in fifth-rate music halls. Thackeray, a great lover of pantomime, was roused to indignant anger over Ellar's sorry plight, and wrote in an article dated 1840: 'Our Harlequin Ellar, prince of many enchanting islands, was he not at Bow Street the other day, in his dirty, faded, battered motley seized as a lawbreaker for acting at a penny theatre, after having well-nigh starved in the streets, where nobody would listen to his guitar? No one gave him a shilling to bless him, not one of us, who owe him so much. So passes the glory of Harlequin.' He died at the age of sixty-two, in 1842, at his lodgings in Lambeth, 'leaving a wife and child totally unprovided for', as a newspaper paragraph recorded.

The glory of Harlequin was passing in every sense. In the period following the death of Grimaldi, writers cast their net far and wide in their desire to titillate public curiosity; and very strange fish they had brought to shore. A brief list of titles current in the 'forties will serve to show the frenzy with which scriptwriters sought their themes in every possible or impossible place: *Harlequin and William Tell; or the Genius of the Ribston Pippin*: *Little Jack Horner; or Harlequin A.B.C.*: *Lindley Murray's Grammar; or Harlequin A.E.I.O.U.*: *King Alfred the Great; or Harlequin History and the Enchanted Raven*: *Harlequin and the Steam Engine; or Pervonte's Wishes and the Fairy Fog*: *Harlequin and the Tyrant of Gobblemupandshrunkthemdowno*: *Nell Gwynne; or Harlequin Merry Monarch*: *Tit Tat Toe, My First Go; or Harlequin N.E.W.S. and the Fairy Elves of the Fourth Estate*. These are only a few of the extraordinary titles given to the curious pantomimes in strange settings that flourished before E. L. Blanchard, who wrote some of them, established a new tradition.

The success of Dibdin's *Mother Goose* had brought about a number of pantomimes based upon fairy tales, in which the 'opening' tended to become increasingly important, requiring more than the four brief scenes in which it had hitherto been contained. Then, in 1843, the passing of the Statute for the Regulation of Theatres broke the monopoly of Drury Lane, Covent Garden, and the others under royal patent. New theatres were established: and pantomime, that most popular entertainment, found a home in all of them. The ancient rivalry between Drury Lane and Covent Garden was submerged in the highly competitive spirit emanating from the new theatres. Insensibly pantomime improved in plot, dialogue, and drama: acquiring in these processes considerable literary merit.

Among many who contributed to the establishment of pantomime in its improved form, the name of E. L. Blanchard deserves particular honour. He was one of the most prolific scriptwriters ever born; he wrote every pantomime for Drury Lane Theatre from 1852 until 1888, at a time when four or five were given in the course of the year. Under successive managements, he provided charming scripts in rhymed couplets, treated with delicacy and humour, and lacking all coarseness or vulgarity. His fairy tale opening was well written, well constructed, and conveyed in dramatic form the full savour and atmosphere of its source.

For Blanchard, as for Thomas Dibdin before him, fairy tale and legend became an exclusive source of inspiration. By 1870, authors of pantomime had not only abandoned extravaganza, they were beginning to restrict themselves to a few only of the many themes of fairy mythology. To this repertoire England contributed *Dick Whittington*, *The Babes in the Wood*, *Robinson Crusoe*, *St. George and the Dragon*, *Gulliver's Travels*, and *Goody Two Shoes*, based on a nursery tale by Oliver Goldsmith. From France via Perrault came *Cinderella*, *The Sleeping Beauty*, *Red Riding Hood*, *Bluebeard*, and *Puss in Boots*. *The Arabian Nights' Tales*, first translated into English at the beginning of the eighteenth century, yielded *Aladdin*, *Sinbad the Sailor* and *Ali Baba and the Forty Thieves*.

As the 'opening' of the pantomime became longer and more literate, it was attended with increasing magnificence. The transformation scene, formerly the crude casting-off of robe and head in full view of the audience, to reveal the quartet of the ensuing Harlequinade, became complicated and lavish.

Harlequin's transformation was attended by fairies hovering in the air with gauzy wings and jewelled diadems, or revealed by the opening of gigantic flowers, or mighty sea-shells in the Kingdom of Neptune. As the century progressed, and under the stimulus of Beverley and Planché, notable scenic artists of their day, the transformation scene became the climax of the pantomime. In 1860, in *Queen Ladybird*, the hero was transformed into Harlequin, and magical gifts bestowed upon him in an enchanted landscape, in which real fountains sent glittering spray high in the air; and still pools mirrored the rainbow skirts of myriad fairies. It was by now customary for every pantomime to contain an exotic transformation scene. These bear enchanting names that conjure up vistas of tinselled delight: The Bower of Fairy Coral 'neath the Silvery Sea; The Rainbow Glade of the King of the Silver Valley; The Coralline Columnar Palace of Queen Star; The Magic Fountain by the Golden Wishing Well. A contemporary description gives some impression of these magnificent scenes: 'The front scene being disclosed to strains of voluptuous music, curtains of gauze would rise and fall, each time to reveal fresh and more elaborate wonders, sparkling with tinsel under ever-changing limelight. Giant lilies, flowers, orchids of wonderful size and colour, outrivalling nature in design and magnificence, vast sea-shells, and fairy bowers would open and expand, disclosing nymphs. Fairies would hover over these splendours. Then, when the final gorgeous tableau was effected, the transformation of the characters would take place.'

Through all these changes, Harlequin kept his precarious footing. He had fallen so low that as early as 1855 he was played by a woman, Madame Celeste, at the Adelphi Theatre: so successfully that she played him again in the following year. From that time onwards he was frequently played by a female dancer, often accompanied by another in a feminine version of his costume, and billed as Harlequina.

It is possible, but not certain, that the 'principal boy' of pantomime —the hero played by an actress—was associated with the playing of Harlequin by a woman. Madame Celeste is the earliest recorded female Harlequin: but in 1852, three years before her first appearance in motley, Miss Ellington had appeared at the Lyceum as the Prince in *The Good Woman in the Wood*. By 1870, the 'principal boy' was a feature of pantomime. Towards the end of the century, the custom was abandoned, to be revived when the 1914–1918 War caused a shortage of young men. From then onwards until the present day, the 'principal boy' has been feminine, and the 'dame' played by a man.

Another innovation, and one that affected Harlequin more closely, was introduced in the seventies. The characters of the Harlequinade were no longer played by the characters of the 'opening', as they had been when Grimaldi played *Squire Bugle, afterwards Clown*, in Dibdin's *Mother Goose*. The 'opening', now the major part of the pantomime, made greater histrionic demands upon the players: while Harlequin and Columbine were required only to dance, and Clown and Pantaloon to play the fool. It became customary therefore to engage two sets of artistes: and the extravagant spectacle of the transformation scene now served to mark the moment at which the fairy-tale actors withdrew, and Harlequin and his fellows took over from them.

Since the Harlequinade quartet now played only vestigial parts of their formerly difficult rôles, producers were no longer restricted to dancers and clowns of experience and ability. Very soon actors engaged to take part in the 'opening' swallowed most of the pay-roll: while minimum salary and prestige were given to the Harlequinade players, with a consequent falling-off of standard and appeal.

The end of the nineteenth century saw Harlequin beautiful, sterile, a magician with a banal box of tricks, popular still, but almost lost in a welter of effects that surrounded his sparkling shape, and threatened to overwhelm it. He danced, he clapped his magic bat, and he leapt through a window; but there was no humanity in him any more, and his coarse virility had become a glittering neuter.

Certain managements, in order to revitalise pantomime, began to introduce music hall comedians into the plot, engaging them to play the Robber Uncles in *Babes in the Wood*, or the Baron in *Cinderella*. These comedians brought their music hall technique and repertoire to the parts they played, delighting the audience with their novelty, their topical gags, and their knockabout farce. Their introduction into pantomime made Clown's humour seem heavy and old-fashioned, and the public began to find the Harlequinade tedious.

From the moment they entered pantomime, the music hall comedians took over the best parts of the show, and rapidly made themselves the central figures in it, introducing their 'speciality acts', songs of the moment, and the ribald mirth and coarseness previously expunged by E. L. Blanchard. The 'opening' now took in all but the full length of the show, for the length of time required for this special playing was stolen from the already diminished Harlequinade. Few among the audience minded. Harlequin was now irrelevant, for the 'principal boy' was the new hero of pantomime, with a 'principal girl' to replace Columbine. Clown and Pantaloon were unnecessary. Their rôle was played now by the 'dame' and the funny men, who had usurped their place and taken their best tricks.

There were certainly some who mourned the passing of ancient tradition; and none more sorrowfully than Blanchard. He, who for over thirty years had supplied Drury Lane and other leading theatres with scores of delightful scripts, intensely disliked pantomime in its new form. After seeing *Aladdin*, in 1885, he recorded his view of it in his diary, published after his death: 'It is more dazzling than funny, and I get very weary of the gagging of the music hall people, and with eyes dazzled with gas and glitter cannot stay until midnight, when the Harlequinade only commences, and which few now care about. Oh! The change from one's boyhood. Left to be rattled through as rapidly as possible, and without, I fear, any adequate rehearsal.' He suffered still more intensely when, in 1888, *The Babes in the Wood*, the last pantomime bearing his name, was presented in the new manner. Just before he died, he sadly recorded how little of what he had written had been allowed to remain: 'My smooth and pointed lines are turned into ragged prose and arrant nonsense.'

Towards the end of the century, the Harlequinade was merely a few scenes of traditional business perfunctorily gone through in front of a row of shops, an unwanted addendum to a show that was complete without it. 'There were still babies to kidnap, butter slides to make in front of the grocer's shop, geese and sausages and fish to be stolen, and the red-hot poker to be applied to Pantaloon's backside. Policemen were still flattened through the mangle, and now and again

Harlequin with a slap of the bat would transform a bed into a horse-trough, and so forth.'

Only he no longer performed such magic as he had at Drury Lane in 1840, when Clown and Pantaloon took refuge in furnished lodgings, which, at the touch of Harlequin's magic bat, emptied themselves of all their furniture. They watched in bewilderment and terror, as chairs slipped through the windows or the walls, the fire irons flew up the chimney together with the table-cloth, lighted candles floated away, curtains dissolved into nothingness, tables and sofas rose and walked off, while ornaments hurled themselves at Clown's head, and a mirror fell, and broke over him.

Now, the few brief scenes of Harlequinade became one scene only, played in front of a backcloth painted with a row of shops. Harlequin, who had survived the vicissitudes of a life over four hundred years long, packed with hardship, triumph and disaster, adventure and peril, and three separate careers in Italy, France, and England, was fast approaching the time when his glittering, enigmatic figure would be seen no more.

The great Augustus Harris of Drury Lane had no liking for Harlequinade, and an obsession with magnificent spectacle and pageantry. Under his autocratic rule, Harlequin became more shadowy. When, after Harris's death in 1896, Arthur Collins took over the management of the theatre, Harlequin dwindled to vanishing point. It was Arthur Collins who gave Harlequinade its *coup de grâce*, as far as the big theatres of central London were concerned. While he was in power at Drury Lane, pantomime ended with a ten-minute solo by Clown, heralded with an unmeaning 'Here we are again!' salvaged from the opening of true Harlequinade, and followed by the distribution of bonbons and crackers to a few lucky members of the audience. Then even this was curtailed, taking place not against the painted shops of the back cloth but before the closed crimson velvet curtains of the stage.

With Harlequin, much else disappeared from pantomime. There were no longer appearances through the trap-door. Since trap-work requires a special training not now in fashion it is unlikely that it will ever be reintroduced into pantomime. There was no more pursuit of the lovers; there were no more acrobatic displays by demons and spirits, no more fabulous transformation scenes to cover the entrance of Harlequin. Very often the Fairy Queen forgot to enter from the right of the stage, leaving the left for the Witch or the Demon King: and when she changed her wand from the right hand to the left whenever her enemies were on stage, no one remembered that she did so 'to protect her heart with good magic'.

Henceforward pantomime shaped itself differently. The shortest, least important part had become the whole. He who had been its hero disappeared from the form he had engendered. The transformation scene, which once had marked his changing from ordinary mortal to magical Harlequin became the Grand Finale. Occasionally it was kept, appearing somewhere in the pantomime without rhyme or reason, save that it was beautiful to look upon: and sometimes its purpose was misunderstood, because the origins of pantomime were forgotten. A snow-covered wintry wood would be 'transformed' into a summer's glade, its leafy trees and blossoming bush lit by a limelight sun. Even the ghost of Harlequin was absent from these.

CHAPTER SEVEN

The Persistence of Harlequin

THERE is a prophetic strain in Harlequin. In 1716, the curtain that rose upon Lelio's company in the Hôtel de Bourgogne, nineteen years after the Italian Players had been driven from Paris by an irate King, bore the device of a Phoenix emerging from the flames, and the words *I am Reborn*. In 1803, *Wizard's Wake: or Harlequin and Merlin*, a pantomime by Dibdin, was given at Sadler's Wells, with James Byrne as Harlequin, and Grimaldi playing Clown. The first scene showed Merlin, absorbed in occult studies, being interrupted by an assembly of wizards come to celebrate their wake. Merlin invoked them in the following terms:

> Wizards, our wake you know's the fav'rite hour
> We meet to exercise our special power;
> My books inform me that our fav'rite son,
> Gay Harlequin, his motley race has run.
> His sword has lost its virtue and himself, grown old
> And feeble, thrown upon the shelf.

Harlequin then made his entry 'tottering with age', bowed and bent. Merlin ordered him to ascend a funeral pyre, that he might be consumed, and born anew from his own ashes, like the Phoenix. The elderly Harlequin then disappeared in red and green flames, to emerge young, vital, and ready for adventure in France, where his search for Columbine successfully took place.

These prophecies in due course came to pass. The Harlequin known to us since his childhood in Bergama died at Drury Lane, and was reborn in diverse places. His ghost so wonderfully described by Lamb, 'like the apparition of a dead rainbow', lingered on. No one remembered much about his origins or his career, or wondered why he had been masked and in motley: yet he was never wholly forgotten.

Driven from Drury Lane by the invasion of the music hall element, his ghost found shelter at the Lyceum, where the Melville Brothers established the new home of pantomime. They had both loved the old tradition: so much so that, in spite of changing fashion, and new demands from the public, they snatched ten minutes for Harlequin from the ever-lengthening shows, and kept his ghost leaping through clock faces and over walls as long as they possibly could, long after he had been abandoned by all other leading London managements.

He wandered also in the provinces, where old customs died harder. One of the very last of these ghost Harlequins was Fred Leoville, of the Old Britannia, whose end in 1922 was as pathetic as that of many who had preceded him. He was playing Harlequin at the end of the Christmas pantomime *Aladdin*, at the Olympia, Liverpool, when one morning his wife collapsed across the breakfast table, and died before he could rise from his chair to reach her. The shock was a terrible one. Leoville tried to perform each night as usual, collapsed, rallied, then died only a few days after his wife.

Harlequin's rebirth in the theatre in recent years is a curious phenomenon. In 1944, Eleanor and Herbert Farjeon collaborated to write *The Glass Slipper*, a play based on the Cinderella theme, which Robert Donat presented at the St. James's Theatre. The production was, in effect, a protest against the modern music-hall type of pantomime evolved from the pattern set by Augustus Harris, and in which the fairy-tale element was increasingly distorted to make room for speciality acts and cross-talk comedy not suitable for children, and very often extremely tedious for them. *The Glass Slipper* was a charming fantasy, keeping close to the well-known story, appealing to both children and adults. Its comedy was simple and derived from farce, without vulgarity. It ended, in the proper manner, with a Transformation and a Harlequinade: *Harlequin in Search of his Heart*,[1] given in mime and dancing, with a tenor, bass, and chorus singing the dialogue.

In 1951, The Intimate Theatre Group, then playing in the Library Theatre, Manchester, gave *Pinnocchio* as their Christmas show. The

[1] For text see Appendix B, p. 233–239.

Professionals in Denmark. Lisa Kaergaard as Columbine, with Erik Bidsted as Harlequin, at the pantomime of the Tivoli Gardens, Copenhagen

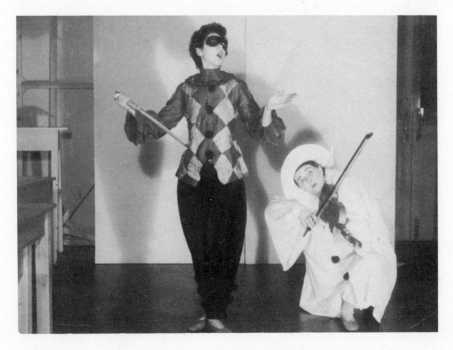

Amateurs in Devon. Mair Staniland as Harlequin, with Hilda Hallowell as Pierrot

ARLEQUIN

From the painting by Picasso

play was ingeniously adapted from Collodi by Brian Way and Warren Jenkins, and produced by the latter. The puppets of the beginning of the play, moving on strings and manipulated by the Puppeteer, were in the form of Harlequin, Columbine, Clown, and Pantaloon. At the end of the play, the puppets cast off their strings to perform a Harlequinade, in which Pinnocchio took part as a butcher boy. The method of building this Harlequinade, danced and mimed to music from Le Coq's *Mam'zelle Angot*, was curiously close to the methods of the original Italian Players. It was evolved from the improvisation of the actors, upon a 'scenario' suggested by Rosalie Williams. The improvisation was then timed, and developed by choreographer and producer into a traditional Harlequinade.

In the year following, at least two London pantomimes included the ancient quartet: *Babes in the Wood* presented at the little Player's Theatre: and Val Parnell's *Dick Whittington* at the Palladium. Here the Harlequinade was placed in the finale of the first half of the show, exactly where, in the nineteenth century, the Transformation Scene properly took place.

In the spring of 1955, the ancient Arlecchino, with his fellow Masks, trod the boards of the Vieux-Colombier in Paris. A young Franco-Italian company, directed by Jacques Fabbri, was responsible for this astonishing and exciting resurrection. The company spent over a year rediscovering commedia dell'arte, with the expert advice and assistance of Monsieur Léon Chancerel, who offered them all the resources of his extensive library, and of his unique collection of *lazzi*. Monsieur Lecoq, director of mime at the Piccolo Theatre in Milan, instructed them in the presentation of the Masks, and the special technique required to play them; and Sylvio Walter, after months of patient experiment, was able to make leather masks identical with those worn by the sixteenth-century players. From this careful research, allied to the genuine enthusiasm of the members of the company, and their excellence in mime, came *La Famille Arlequin*, the story of a troupe of Italian comedians travelling through the centuries until the present one found them bankrupt. Pantalone and Il Dottore flapped across the stage as they had done four hundred years before, Colombina flirted, Isabella murmured sweet nothings to Leandrino, Brighella fought Il Capitano, Pagliaccio and Pulcinella caused trouble whenever they appeared. It was as if dusty scenari, together with half-forgotten theatre prints and costume designs, had been touched with Harlequin's magic bat, and brought to vivid life, as the long-dead Masks surged from their museums back to the boards on which they were born, as extraordinary and as elemental as when they first appeared.

Yet perhaps the most notable Harlequin Phoenix is the one reborn from the flames of the Mime Theatre Company founded in 1949 by Alison Malcolm and Clifford Williams, with Greta Douglas and A. V. Coton as Directors. Their history to date is vividly reminiscent of that of the original nomads who played commedia dell'arte wherever they could find a pitch: 'We cut expenditure to the minimum. For scenery and lighting we relied on the facilities offered wherever we happened to play. Similarly, we only travelled half a dozen unusual props. Everything else—chairs, tables, jugs, boxes, rostrums, teapots, cups, flowers—we borrowed on the spot. We carried a few cloths and coverings to throw over chairs, etc., in order to brighten things when necessary. We cut our costumes to the minimum, devising a basic costume which could be modified by simple additions to be used in a number of plays. Our total costumes, scenery, and props went in one tremendous case which promptly burst its seams, in spite of which we still use it. Another case contained our make-up, programmes, and office gear, and we carried a gramophone and records. These, with personal cases, comprised our load, and we travelled exclusively by bus and coach (having devised a technique of persuading the driver or conductor to look the other way whilst we smuggled our gear aboard). No group could have been more mobile or flexible. Although we took great pains to dress our stage (which might be one end of a classroom in a village school, or the draughty expanse of a town hall platform) we were able, when necessary, to arrive at 6.30 p.m., press the costumes, set the stage, put out the props, rig up the gram, make up, and ring up by 7.15 p.m. Then—end of performance 9.30 p.m., dismantle, pack, catch bus to next town 9.45 p.m.; find digs, sleep, and next morning perform to an audience of school children.' In spirit and in kind, Clifford Williams's account of the early days of his company is one with that of the Italian strolling players who packed their trestles on a cart and set off on foot or on horseback to bring Arlecchino and his fellow Masks to the nearest fair or market place.

The Mime Theatre Company, improvising as they went, experimented with all the potentials of mime—traditional, stylised, abstract, folk art, Elizabethan dumbshow, French pantomime, satire, farce, parody, comedy, tragedy. Into their six years of existence they have crowded a recapitulation of the history of commedia dell'arte, transforming *La Cantarina* into a gramophone; and choosing those Masks most familiar to an English public—Pierrot, Harlequin, Columbine, and Pantaloon to take part in some of their improvised themes,[1] while others are built upon clowns and characters of their own devising. Part of the originality of the Company arises from their presentation of Harlequin and his fellows in the traditional dress and manner, but in modern settings. Clifford Williams's Pierrot, with his white foolish face, his gaucherie, his stupidity, comes straight from the Italian Mask, with just a tinge of the later wistful clown of Watteau. The Harlequin and Pantaloon of Norman Rose and Antony Harling, the Columbine of Barbara Brown revive the characters created before English pantomime transformed them. Only, they wander now in a surrealist Heaven that is essentially twentieth century: or hover round the camp where Pierrot is a sad and silly conscript in his loose white blouse and a tin hat, with Harlequin his bullying sergeant, in motley still.

The Bergamask clown, and the glittering neuter of pantomime are with us still, a recapitulation of the past. Yet there is a third aspect that represents, in some measure, the only progress left to Harlequin Phoenix. Harlequin was a dancer at the fairs, in Italy, almost as soon as he was created. He danced at the great fairs in France and England and through all his vicissitudes in the theatre: and then Lun made the dancing Harlequin the core of his pantomimes. This unbroken tradition paved the way for Harlequin's entry into ballet, where his magical beauty and his mystery so properly belonged.

The demand for ballet, fostered and fed by the Russians, and by Diaghilev who broke away from Russia, became so great in the course of this century that it has not yet been assuaged: and Harlequin, catching the imagination of choreographers in widely different parts of the globe, found a new sphere of living in this specialised form of theatre. In 1900 Anna Pavlova and Michel Fokine, dancing in *Arlequinade* at the Maryinsky Theatre, St. Petersburg, restored him to beauty: and ten years later Fokine created *Carnaval*, a delightful

[1] See Appendix B, pp. 239–250.

Romantic ballet set to music by Robert Schumann, in which Columbine, Harlequin, Pierrot, and Pantaloon presented yet another version
of their eternal story. This ballet has several times been given by
Sadler's Wells, with Robert Helpmann playing Harlequin in 1934
and Pierrot in 1935 and in 1944.

Every decade since has seen Harlequin flash across the stage in a
ballet suited to his special talents, interpreted by Russians, Americans,
Frenchmen, Englishmen, Lithuanians, and Germans, for Harlequin in
ballet has proved as universally exciting as Harlequin in drama. In
1922, *Les Millions d'Arlequin*, with choreography by Boris Romanoff,
was given by the Russian Romantic Theatre in Berlin; in 1928 the
Society of Chamber Music in Washington presented *Arlecchinata*, the
choreographer being Adolph Bolm; and in 1934 Lithuanian Ballet at
the State Theatre in Kovno mounted *Arlequinade*. One of the most
interesting of these Harlequin-ballets was given in New York in 1936
by American Ballet Caravan. Entitled *Harlequin*, it was described as:
'A ballet-pantomime in the spirit of the Italian popular comedy, with
music by Domenico Scarlatti, and choreography by Eugene Loring.'

Since then there have been three English ballets of interest. The first,
in 1938, was *Harlequin in the Street*, with book and choreography by
Frederick Ashton, and presented by Sadler's Wells. Then in 1950 came
Harlequinade, given by Festival Ballet, the Markova-Dolin company.
While Ashton's ballet was in the spirit of Italian comedy, *Harlequinade*
was exactly like a Victorian theatre-print come to life, and drew its
theme from nineteenth-century pantomime. The music was by
Richard Drigo, written for the Lithuanian *Arlequinade* of 1934.

The most recent of the three was *Harlequin in April*, a ballet commissioned for the Festival of Britain, and devised by Johnny Cranko,
choreographer of the Sadler's Wells Theatre Company, and presented
by that junior company attached to our national ballet. The theme,
based on the well-known lines from *The Waste Land*, was a complicated one for ballet. Harlequin, Columbine, and Pierrot, recognisably
the Masks of commedia dell'arte, symbolised Man, Man's Ideal, and
the Destroyer in Man. The genesis of Harlequin in the ballet had
something in common with Rich's *lazzi* of man hatched from an egg.
For in *Harlequin in April* Pierrot sprinkles two groups of plants with a
watering can 'and gradually their tentative shoots reach upwards to
the light and air. Then from their midst emerges Harlequin, naked,

blind, helpless, but groping out towards life. Pierrot gives him his coat and lath, and he springs into full manhood.' Such heavy symbolism as the ballet contains sits oddly upon the flashing Harlequin and his wanton Columbine, while Pierrot as the Destroyer, however well meaning, is outside the idiom of his rôle in commedia dell'arte. There is nevertheless a precedent set, since in the eighteenth century Fielding and his fellow wits used Harlequin in their satires and parodies regardless of his own personality or rôle, and as a symbol for politics, institutions, figures in the public eye, or whatsoever best served the purpose of their pamphlet or play.

It must not be supposed that Harlequin, after his centuries of experience, should fail to make his entry into any form of entertainment, however modern. He has appeared (in the Mime Theatre Company, under the aegis of Clifford Williams) on the radio and television. Had he been born later he could, like Shakespeare, have enjoyed a brilliant career in films. His rare appearances in this medium have been of peculiar interest, partly due to the quality of the films in which he figures. Jean Renoir's *La Carrozza d'Oro* (*The Golden Coach*) is concerned with the story of Camilla (Anna Magnani), the leading actress of a troupe of players touring Spanish America during the last century, and of the three men who loved her. The film was made in Italy, with Italian and English versions, and filmed in Technicolor. The Harlequin of the company is a Regency Harlequin; and Camilla, playing with him, wears the Harlequina costume, with an unusually low-cut neck.

A recent version of *Scaramouche*, Rafael Sabatini's famous book, whose eighteenth-century hero joins a company of strolling players in France, also shows a Harlequin of the period: while Charlie Chaplin, in his nostalgic film *Limelight*, introduces a ballet, *The Death of Columbine*, in which nineteenth-century Harlequinade is transmuted by Chaplin's romanticism into something rare and strange, that is perfectly attuned to the theme and atmosphere of the film.

It is beyond the scope of this present book to enter into Harlequin's persistence in literature and in art, where he has inspired poets, painters, and sculptors of more than one nationality, through his enigma. Sacheverell Sitwell touches upon Harlequin in painting in his preface to C. W. Beaumont's *History of Harlequin*; and makes it abundantly clear in his few pages that there is material enough for a study devoted wholly to Harlequin in Art. Among the paintings, that are legion and universal, are varied representations of the first Mask that catch certain aspects of his being without ever presenting the whole: for Harlequin is all things to all men. Contemporary canvases bear witness to the enchantment Harlequin continues to cast over modern artists—Picasso's sad and thoughtful *Arlequin*, now in the Museum of Modern Art in Barcelona; Doris Zinkeisen's richly theatrical Harlequinade; and Duncan Grant's magnificently architectural *The Arrival of the Italian Comedians*, painted for an exhibition that toured the country in connection with the Festival of Britain in 1951, the Festival for which *Harlequin in April* was the commissioned ballet —examples taken at random to prove how fecund a source of inspiration still exists in Harlequin.

In the eighteenth century in Europe, porcelain figurines of the Italian Masks abounded, sometimes copied from contemporary theatre engravings, or from the illustrations to the works of Riccoboni, or, less often, from the vivid and grotesque designs of Callot. Harlequin was a favourite subject for Johann Joachim Kändler, the first modeller of the exquisite Meissen ware. Since then, many lesser artists have formed Harlequin in porcelain, catching something of his mobility and his poetic presence, some with considerable success.

Two hundred years ago, Covent Garden presented a pantomime with the title *Harlequin Everywhere*, which offered its audience a panorama of the British Isles in addition to the courtship of Harlequin and Columbine, and the intervention of a galaxy of gods and goddesses. The title aptly expresses Harlequin's position today, where he persists even in most curious and unlikely places. Buses have been placarded with his stylised form, advertising a jam sponge roll; a football team bears his name, and its members, I trust, wear motley shirts and give every evidence of their patron's inexhaustible vigour and agility. Glassware, biscuits, sweets, and table-mats are known by his name; Christmas cards and crackers bear his imprint, writing paper is sold under his sign; and he still appears in children's books. In South Devon, Hilda Hallowell and Mair Staniland, playing respectively Pierrot and Harlequin, visit remote hamlets and scattered branches of the Women's Institutes to demonstrate mime, reviving ancient *lazzi* and the lusty farce of commedia dell'arte; while in London, the Art of Movement Studio directed by Rudolf Laban and

Lisa Ullmann includes scenes from commedia dell'arte in its syllabus. The fairs of Barcelona still have a dancing Harlequin in a gaily decked booth; and the little open air theatre in the Tivoli Gardens at Copenhagen gives a pantomime every evening during the May-September season, featuring Harlequin and Columbine in shows reminiscent of late commedia dell'arte. Marcel Marceau, when he brought his programme of mime to the Arts Theatre in 1953, was described by Richard Buckle, with exact truth, as 'portraying the Adventures of a modern Harlequin called Bip'.

It is a pleasure to recall that G. K. Chesterton's immortal Flambeau played Harlequin for the purposes of his 'most beautiful crime, which was also, by a singular coincidence, his last'. For it was while he was perched in a tree, wearing Harlequin's motley, that Father Brown persuaded him to enter upon the paths of righteousness, for the sake of his immortal soul. Harlequin-Flambeau appears in *The Flying Stars*, a story contained in the collection published under the title *The Innocence of Father Brown*. Not the least interesting factor in Flambeau's metamorphosis is the transmutation of a rogue into a poetic symbol, in true Harlequin tradition: 'The Harlequin danced slowly backwards out of the door into the garden, which was full of moonlight and stillness. The vamped dress of silver paper and paste (jewels) which had been too glaring in the footlights, looked more and more magical and silvery as it danced away under a brilliant moon. . . . The green gaiety of the waving laurels, the rich purple indigo of the night, the moon like a monstrous crystal, make an almost irresponsibly romantic picture; and among the top branches of the garden trees a strange figure is climbing, who looks not so much romantic as impossible. He sparkles from head to heel, as if clad in ten million moons; the real moon catches him at every movement and sets a new inch of him on fire as he swings, flashing and successful, from the short tree in this garden to the tall, rambling tree in the other.'

Harlequin's second entry into the world of crime and detection was more complete. As a child, Agatha Christie was fascinated by a set of Dresden *Commedia dell'arte* figurines in her mother's room. She has recorded the fact that an early series of poems she wrote included 'Harlequin's Song', which, when published in *Poetry Review*, marked her first appearance in print. When she turned from poetry to crime stories, the haunting shadow of Harlequin went with her: and over the years she wrote those stories which, collected under the title *The Mysterious Mr. Quin*, are unique among the many detective tales and novels from her most able pen for their mystical and magical atmosphere. So completely has Harlequin exerted his fascination over Miss Christie that, in her own words: 'Though each story about him is quite separate, yet the collection written over a considerable period of years outlines in the end the story of Harlequin himself.'[1]

The first number of *The Model Stage*, a quarterly launched by Sir Ralph Richardson, George Speaight, and others, to resuscitate the Toy Theatre tradition unhappily lost at the beginning of this century, contained a Harlequinade play in the old 'penny plain, tuppence coloured' manner, Pollock's nineteenth-century prints being reproduced for that purpose. There could have been no happier choice. *The Model Stage* brought back nostalgic memories of juvenile drama and toy theatres, derived from eighteenth-century prints of actors and actresses. In 1800, Robert Dighton had the happy inspiration of printing full-length portraits of players in dramatic costume and pose. Then several were printed on the same sheet, until, by natural extension of the idea, happy children of the nineteenth century could buy their penny (plain) or twopenny (coloured) sheets of characters and scenery for any given play, and mount their shows in toy theatres with lilliputian cardboard characters and authentic décor. J. K. Green, Skelt, Redington, and Pollock are the memorable names of those who issued the prints, now becoming rare collector's pieces, and giving valuable clues to much that is mysterious in the theatre of the eighteen-forties and 'fifties. Scenery was copied from actual backcloths, the figures show a wealth of costume detail. Pantomime was a popular part of juvenile drama, and prints still extant show Harlequin 'in the five attitudes'; characters wearing robes and 'heads' before the transformation; and sheets of 'magical tricks'. To mount the Harlequinade given in the first issue of *The Model Stage* was to gaze upon a lost but familiar world.

The history of drama, like any other history, evolves through tradition handed down by people and circumstances long since dead and forgotten. The very names given to parts of the theatre—the

[1] It should be recorded that Dorothy L. Sayers' egregious Lord Peter Wimsey attended a fancy-dress dance as Harlequin in *Murder Must Advertise*, and there performed the *lazzi* of diving into a shallow pool.

ARLEQUIN
Gargallo

Photo Rigal, Paris   *Courtesy Jean Cocteau*

Photo Rigal, Paris   *Courtesy Jean*

ARLEQUIN

Pastels by Jean Cocteau

gods, the circle, boxes, pit, proscenium—arise from the evolution of theatre buildings from the earliest days of drama. Harlequin became a tradition, and created new genres. He gave *opéra comique* to France and pantomime to England. He is, moreover, the only traditional figure who escaped into the wider world beyond the proscenium arch, and in his own person roamed the universe.

His persistence is due perhaps to his own evolution from a realistic Bergamask yokel to a figure as legendary and poetic as the Phoenix he so much resembles within the esoteric mythology into which he was incorporated. In the beginning he was a mischievous child, undisciplined, uneducated, bursting with unusual vitality, and exerting the inexperienced but fundamentally true judgment of childhood. Not a nice child, Arlecchino: a greedy, cowardly, dirty-minded little boy: yet one who nevertheless promised to develop an original talent. In his manhood, spent mainly in France and Italy, with travels of less importance throughout the European countries, his young potentialities were developed. He acquired wit, polish, culture, and discipline, and became a great artist in the theatre, his brilliant intelligence stimulated, his acrobatic dexterity freed from the shackles of his peasant origins. His vigorous manhood was succeeded by his senility. Wit and vitality departed from him, and only the glimmer of his former glory lingered on in his swift grace. The lusty appetites of his youth, disciplined and mastered in his prime, fell from him in his old age. His loutish pursuit of Colombina became the witty courtship of Colombine, and then degenerated into a relationship purged of all desire. His greed became a gourmet's appreciation that dwindled into complete indifference to food. In nineteenth-century pantomime Harlequin neither ate nor drank throughout the rigours of the pursuit. Like an old beau, he decked his withered carcase with spangles and frills: but he was by then a simulacrum, not a personality. The fundamental difference between Harlequin and Everyman is the difference between four hundred years of living and three score years and ten.

Beyond what was normal and known, Harlequin became the symbol of life in its mysterious essence. His plebian origins and magical power blended to make of him the *élan vital* that lifts mankind into a sphere of living beyond that of the animals: and his last metamorphosis, the scintillating shape that glowed upon the stage, is a direct presentation of this element in him. He represents the sublime, the unattainable, towards which mankind for ever aspires. His final costume was the most beautiful and the most theatrically effective ever to be devised. His mystery derives from many sources. In part, it lies in his great age and extraordinary endurance, in the battles he waged, the triumphs he enjoyed, in the evolution of a symbolic life force from a peasant clown. It lies in part in his enigma, which has nowhere I think been better expressed than in the superb *Arlequin* by Gargallo, a figure nearly three feet high, to be found in the Musée d'Art Moderne in Paris. Many artists, working in many media, have illuminated some facet of Harlequin's personality: I know of nothing else which, by explaining everything and giving nothing away, so captures the enigma of the haunting figure that remains mysterious even when we know his origins, his career, and the probable reasons for his motley, mask, and slapstick.

Another factor in his mystery is his capacity to annihilate material things. The world had no bounds for him, time no limits. Mercury had tapped his heels while the mists of antiquity swirled round him. In his most loutish days he bore the godlike sign upon him, and was greater than the limitations of man. His magic bat made him master of the universe.

His bat is highly significant. It unifies the elements of magic and mystery, and expresses Harlequin in terms of the *élan vital*. In his background, as in that of all European clowns, lurk the Fescennine farces and the Dionysian revels, a blending of religion and drama based upon phallic worship. The phallophores are among his remote ancestors: and he himself wore the phallus in his earliest days in Italy. When such crudity became outmoded, he no longer wore the ancient sign of the phallophores, but carried instead a small stick, and then a wooden dagger, both passive symbols. Then, as he came into his decline, he acquired his magic bat or slapstick, actively endowed with magical properties, among them the giving and taking of life, a clear transference from person to symbol. For when he was most virile, he carried a small stick; in his prime the wooden dagger; and only when he was senile, the magic bat, symbol of the life impulse.

In addition to this magic, rooted in primitive human truth, Harlequin was dowered with another, the magic of fantasy, that lifts our hearts whenever we meet with it. At every twist and turn of malevolent fate, a benevolent deity or magician stepped in to protect Harlequin, the darling of the gods. In his service the Heavens opened, the Earth trembled and was torn asunder. The elements were released to work on his behalf. Through however many scenes Harlequin might run, his enemies at his heels, it was certain that immortal powers would snatch him from them at the end. Harlequin was invincible. He defied even the judgment of history, that pronounced him dead in the early years of the present century. Harlequin Phoenix not only arose from the ashes of his dead self: bored with the tedium of four hundred years of living on this earth, he pulled down his mask of · invisibility and slipped off, with a final slap of his magic bat, to join the immortals, leaving behind his legend and his poetic fantasy.

Appendix A

SOME CELEBRATED PLAYERS OF HARLEQUIN

(a) ITALIAN

GANASSA, Alberto. Early years unknown. Name first appears in Mantua in 1568. Directed a company that travelled widely in Italy and France. Merged with rival troupe in 1570 to form *Il Comici Gelosi*. Four years later the company divided. Ganassa went to London, then joined the rest of his original company in Madrid. Played in Spain until imprisoned in 1582. All record of him ceases after December 1583.

BOLOGNA, Simone de. Early years unknown. Played for the *Gelosi* under the direction of Flaminio Scala 1574–1578. Few records of his career, none of his date of birth or death.

MARTINELLI, Tristano. 1553–1630. Native of Mantua. In 1600 made Director of the *Accesi*, the Duke of Mantua's company. Greatly in favour at the court of Henry IV of France. Author of the *Compositions de Rhétorique de M. Don Arlequin*. When become famous, signed himself *Arlechinus*: at the height of his career called himself *Dominus Arlecchinorum*.

ANDREINI, Giovanni Battista. 1578–1650. Born in Florence, son of Francesco and Isabella Andreini. After beginning his career playing Lelio, probably in his father's company (*Gelosi*), he became the Arlecchino for the *Fedeli*. He wrote poems and plays. His mystery play *Adamo* (1613) was said to have inspired Milton, who saw a performance of it while travelling in Italy, and from it derived the theme of his *Paradise Lost*. Andreini retired at the age of seventy-three, with the title of Grand Huntsman to the Duke of Mantua.

LOCATELLI, Domenico. 1613–1671. In 1639 came to Paris with a company directed by Guiseppe Branchi, upon the invitation of Louis XIII. Created Harlequin variant *Trivelino*. Composed in French the scenario of *Rosaure, Impératrice de Constantinople* given at the Théâtre du Petit Bourbon in 1658. The company to which he belonged was the first to settle in Paris, under the patronage of Mazarin.

BIANCOLELLI, Domenico. 1640–1688. Known as Dominique. Born in Bologna. Parents both members of a troup established in that town. In 1659 invited by Mazarin to join the latter's company in France as second Harlequin, which rôle he played until the death of Locatelli in 1671. Biancolelli then took over his place with great success; established himself in the affections of the King, the court and the people. Once, when he was suffering from a liver complaint which gave him an exceptionally jaundiced outlook, he consulted a doctor who advised him to go to see Dominique, the famous Harlequin who made everyone laugh. 'Alas!' replied Dominique. 'Then I am a lost man indeed! For I *am* Dominique!' He died as the result of a chill contracted when he performed a burlesque of a dance given by Beauchamp, the King's maître de ballet, before a private and royal audience. Pneumonia developed, and after an illness lasting eight days, he died at the age of forty-eight.

GHERARDI, Evaristo. 1666–1700. Born at Prato in Tuscany. Son of Giovanni, a well-known player of the *Flautino* rôle, and member of the company established in the Théâtre Italien in Paris. His son, educated in Paris, became bilingual. Gherardi was about twenty-three when he first played Harlequin, with immediate success, in *Le Divorce Forcé*. He was Biancolelli's successor. Member of the company expelled from the Hôtel de Bourgogne after the affair of *La Fausse Prude*. Spent three years of exile in collecting, editing, and publishing, under the title *Théâtre Italien*, the best scenari played by his company.

THOMASSO, Antonio Vicentini. 1683–1739. Known as Thomassin. Born at Vicenza. Joined travelling company at early age. Became Harlequin of company formed by Luigi Riccoboni in 1716, upon the invitation of the Regent of France. Was the Harlequin therefore of Marivaux's plays. When he died, after a long illness, he was buried at St. Laurent, and was allowed to receive the last unction, that had been refused to Molière.

SACCHI, Gennaro. 1708–1788. Parents natives of Ferrara: son born in Vienna. Became Director of company under patronage of the Duke of Modena, established in the Teatro San Samuele. Carlo Gozzi wrote scripts in the traditional manner for the company. Sacchi played the Harlequin variant *Truffaldino*, and enjoyed in Italy fame equal to that of Carlin in France.

BERTINAZZI, Carlo Antonio. 1710–1783. Known as Carlin. Born in Turin, son of an army officer in the service of the King of Sardinia. Father died when Carlin was three years old. At fourteen he became an ensign. After his mother's death, he resigned his commission in order to become an actor. Played Harlequin successfully in Bologna and Venice. Upon the death of Thomassin, Riccoboni invited Carlin to join his company in

Paris. In 1741 he made his first appearance with the company in *Arlecchino muto per forza*. Author of a three-act comedy, *Les Métamorphoses d'Arlequin*, in which Arlequin assumed manifold disguises. Goldoni wrote of him: 'He is an upright man of excellent character, famous as Harlequin, and enjoys a reputation equal to that of Dominique and Thomassin in France, and Sacchi in Italy.'

(b) ENGLISH

HAINES, Joseph. Early years unknown. In 1667 gave first performance of Harlequin in a public theatre, in Ravenscroft's *Scaramouche a Philosopher, Harlequin a Schoolboy Bravo, Merchant, and Magician: a comedy after the Italian manner.*

JEVONS, Tom. 1652–1688. Excellent dancer. Actor in low comedy parts. Appeared as Harlequin in Mrs. Aphra Behn's *The Emperor of the Moon*, given at the Duke's Theatre, Dorset Gardens, in 1687. In 1702, Pinkethman played a Harlequin based on Tom Jevons's in a revival at Drury Lane.

RICH, John. 1692–1761. Known as Lun. Son of Christopher Rich, an attorney who in 1688 bought a share in the patent of Drury Lane Theatre. From the interludes in which dancing Harlequins appeared Lun created pantomime, and himself set the pattern for the English Harlequin. Built Covent Garden Theatre in 1732. Died at his house in Covent Garden Piazza, and was buried in Hillindon Churchyard.

WOODWARD, Henry. 1714–1777. Eldest son of a tallow chandler of Southwark. Trained in boyhood by Rich, who engaged him as junior Harlequin when he opened Covent Garden in 1732. He first appeared in the rôle in 1734 in *The Tavern Bilkers*. Sometimes called himself Lun junior. Joined Garrick's company at Drury Lane. Became known as 'the attitude Harlequin'. In 1747 left Drury Lane to appear in Dublin. Then accepted engagement at Covent Garden. Produced and acted in many of own scripts. Buried in vaults of St. George's, Hanover Square.

BYRNE, James. (Unrecorded.) Ballet master at Drury Lane. In 1800 produced *Harlequin Amulet: or The Magic of Mona* in which he played Harlequin. Radical costume changes—innovator of the spangled tights. Also introduced changes in the 'business' of the rôle. Played with Grimaldi.

BOLOGNA, John. 1795–1802 was playing Harlequin at the Royal Circus. Came of a family of pantomimists. Left the Circus to join Sadler's Wells company. Played with Grimaldi there and at Covent Garden. Married sister of Grimaldi's second wife. The Clown and the Harlequin were close friends in private life. One of Bologna's sons was playing Harlequin in the fifties.

ELLAR, Tom. 1780–1842. Began career as dancer at the Crow Street Theatre,

Dublin. Came to London. First played Harlequin at the Royalty Theatre, Goodman's Fields, in 1808. Made his first appearance at Covent Garden in 1813. Highly successful Harlequin: but died at his lodgings in Lambeth, destitute.

LEOVILLE, Fred. ? –1922. Played Harlequin at the Old Britannia. Died while engaged for pantomime in Liverpool.

Among famous actors who at some time in their career played Harlequin are David Garrick, Edmund Kean, and Wilson Barrett.

Several members of the famous Lupino family have also taken the rôle. Georgius Lupino (1710–1787) was apprenticed to John Rich, and made his first appearance as a child Harlequin in *The Two Harlequins* at Lincoln's Inn Fields in 1718. When Rich opened Covent Garden Theatre, Georgius was in his company. The cast of a Harlequinade given at the Old Britannia in 1880 shows Arthur Lupino as Pantaloon, George Lupino as Harlequin, Harry Lupino as Ally Sloper, and George Lupino, jun., as Clown. Another George Lupino, who died in 1932, arranged his last Harlequinade shortly before his death, in which he played Clown, and his son Barry Harlequin.

Appendix B

SCENARI AND EARLY PANTOMIME BOOKS, WITH EXAMPLES OF MODERN HARLEQUINADE

(A) Extracts from scenari of *commedia dell'arte*. Taken from the collections of Scala, Biancolelli, Gherardi, and Sacchi.

From Act III. LA CACCIA. *Scala. Sixteenth Century*

Pantalone, Grattiano, Claudio, Burattino, and Arlecchino return from the hunt with much game, in high spirits, and sounding the horn. Each takes leave of the others, and goes into his house.

Pantalone remains on stage, and knocks several times at his door.

Pedrolino opens, tells Pantalone to be quiet because Isabella feels unwell and is retiring.

Isabella pretends to be stricken with a fever. Pantalone and Pedrolino decide to take her to Burattino's house, so that she can be with Flaminia.

Isabella says she is willing. They call.

Franceschina, weeping, says that Flaminia has a fever.

Burattino says that his daughter feels ill, and they enter to visit her.

The Capitan announces his willingness to suffer anything to avoid the threat of the gallows.

Arlecchino sees him without a sword and makes a terrible din behind him, blowing the horn in his ears. The Capitan cries out that he does not wish to be hanged, and goes out. Arlecchino pursues him, sounding the horn.

Oratio and Flavio look for Pedrolino, to send him about their business.

Pedrolino arrives, in tears, and tells the lovers that Isabella and Flaminia have become ill of a severe fever. The young men are in despair.

Isabella (*at the window*) tells them it is not true, and that they must do whatever they are told to do. Arlecchino withdraws to one side and listens. Pedrolino sends Oratio and Flavio to disguise themselves as doctors. They go out gaily.

Arlecchino, who has understood, says he is going to play a trick. He goes, Pedrolino stays.

Pantalone begs Pedrolino to find two doctors. Pedrolino goes out, Pantalone remains.

Grattiano learns of the illness of the young ladies, he gives numerous remedies from the stables, all entirely beside the point, and they all go out.

Pedrolino is amazed that the doctors have not yet arrived.

Oratio and Flavio come in, disguised as doctors; Pedrolino knocks at the door of the young ladies, and sees to it that each receives her lover. Pedrolino remains.

Arlecchino, disguised as a doctor, enters Flaminia's house. Pedrolino supposes him to be the doctor called by Burattino.

Claudio, father of Oratio, learns from Pedrolino about the young men and their disguise, and that at the moment they are enjoying themselves with their mistresses. He asks Claudio to secure for him a pardon from Pantalone.

Grattiano learns from Claudio the success of Oratio and Flavio, and promises to intercede for Pedrolino.

Pantalone and Burattino learn from Pedrolino that the doctors are in the house, then, turning to Burattino, he says that he must pay the two doctors in the house. Pantalone and Burattino enter their house, the others stay with Pedrolino. They hear a noise. Pantalone asks the doctor to show his face. Oratio with signs refuses. Claudio, his father, makes him known as his son, Oratio. He soothes Pantalone, who consents to allow him to wed with Isabella, but insists that Pedrolino must be sent to the galleys, and Franceschina whipped. Pedrolino flees. Burattino begs them all to make less noise, so that the doctor can give all his attention to his daughter Flaminia. All laugh, Burattino, irritated, goes into his house, and comes back with Flavinia and Flaminia. Flavio refuses to uncover his face. Grattiano recognises his son, to whom Flaminia is given in marriage. Learning that all this is the work of Pedrolino, he agrees with Pantalone to send him to the galleys. Burattino goes into his house. A noise is heard.

Burattino brings out the doctor he has found with Franceschina, discovers his identity and gives him Franceschina for wife. Then all plead for Pedrolino, and obtain his pardon. Pedrolino says that for his part he will forgive them all, they all laugh, and the comedy ends.

From I MORTI VIVI. *Biancolelli. Seventeenth Century*

Doctor and Trivelino on stage.

Arlecchino comes in a huge black cloak and a large black hat. He begins to weep. They perform the *lazzi* of replying only by monosyllables.

Arlecchino tells them he is looking for a dyer who will dye him black;
and that in future he will only eat black bread, black chickens and
truffles; will only drink black wine. Tells them of the death of Eularia,
Mario, and Aurelia. They all heave great sighs, knock against each other,
fall down, and go out together.

Lazzi of terror by Arlecchino. Sits to mourn death of master. Mario
enters backstage, put his hands beside Arlecchino's, and his foot between
Arlecchino's feet. Arlecchino counts his hands and feet, finds too many.
Seized with terror. After several *lazzi* of terror, sees Mario, runs off
screaming for help.

Doctor, Pantalone, and Trivelino on stage, trembling. Arlecchino joins
them, each clutching another. *Lazzi* of terror together. Mario comes in.
Redoubled terror. He explains that he was dragged from the river by
some fishermen . . .

From ARLEQUIN MERCURE GALANT. *Gherardi. Presented at the Hôtel de
Bourgogne on January 22nd, 1682, by His Majesty's Italian
Players*

Arlequin, dressed as Mercury, appears in mid-air, mounted on
Jupiter's eagle, and seeing the God himself on earth disguised as a
shepherd he says to him: 'Addio, Signor Giove.'

JUPITER   How does it happen that Mercury is mounted on my eagle?
           Hasn't he got wings on his heels to fly with?

ARLEQUIN   Alas! Lord Jupiter, my wings are no good to me any more,
           perchè passando per una strada, una servanta emptied a chamber
           pot over them, and drowned them so completely that *se non
           fossi* fallen *per bonhor* on a dunghill, *Mercurio si sara rotto il
           collo; e cosi ho trova la vostra Aquila* in the stable, tied to the
           rack, and so I made use of it *per far tutte le commissioni* I'm
           burdened with.

JUPITER   Now, I've something to say to you. Come down, and assume
           the form of a shepherd.
                   *The machine disappears, and Arlequin comes in in his
                   ordinary costume, mounted on a donkey.*
           Leave your ass there, and give me all the news from above.

ARLEQUIN   (*dismounting, and approaching Jupiter*) Well, now, I can tell
           you, there've been terrific scenes up there since you left.
           Vulcano, come Vosignoria sà, è malizioso come un diavolo. He
           had the brilliant idea of making nets *per atrapar Marte con
           Venere; e con questa scusa promenandosi nel Zodiaco, il* drew
           near the Sign of Pisces and caught them in his net, and went

to sell them to a fishwife at the Market. *Marte che hà visto sta furbaria, a tira la spada* and ran after Vulcan. Unfortunately, as he ran by he trod on Scorpio, who immediately stung him in the leg *che gli è diventa grossa come la testa; é come l'hà poura ch'el poison non penetra, el m'ho ordina* to buy him a chest of quack medicines and bring it to him. . . . (Following detailed news of a similar kind, Jupiter announces himself enamoured of Rosalba, and tells Arlequin to seek her out and discover whether she would be likely to welcome his advances.)

Jupiter goes off, and Pan comes in. Seeing Arlequin, he caresses him, and tells him he is in love with Rosalba.

ARLEQUIN   You in love with Rosalba? Listen, I speak from the heart. *Rosalba è bella*; and you, you are wonderfully hideous. *Rosalba ha una bella* face; and you, you've a gallows look. *Rosalba è ben fatta*; and you, you're made like a maggot.

Pan replies that he is handsome, and the God Pan.

ARLEQUIN   That's true enough. *Vosignoria è il Dio Pane, ma un pane* very dark, *un pane bruno*, fit only to make hard tack for convicts, and not for the appetites of honest men.

Pan, seeing the donkey on which Arlequin was mounted, asks Arlequin if it belongs to him. Arlequin replies that it does, that it is a virtuoso donkey that knows how to do tricks, can walk on its hind legs, and plays the harpsichord excellently well. Pan asks if he may borrow it. Arlequin consents. Pan climbs on to the donkey, which takes a few steps, and then splits into two pieces, so that Pan crashes to the ground. Arlequin jeers at him, and goes off.

From ARLEQUIN EMPEREUR DANS LA LUNE. *Gherardi. Presented March 5th,* 1684

THE DESPAIR SCENE

ARLEQUIN (*alone*)   Ah! Unhappy that I am! The Doctor is going to marry Columbine to a Farmer, and I must live without her! No, I would rather die. Ah! Ignorant Doctor! Ah! Wanton Columbine! Ah! Knavish farmer! Ah! Most unhappy Arlequin! Let us hasten towards death. It shall be written, in both ancient and modern history, that Arlequin died for Columbine. I shall go into my room, I shall fix a rope to the ceiling, I shall climb on to a chair, I shall put the rope round my neck, I shall kick the chair away, and there I am—hung. (*He assumes the posture of a hanged man.*) That's done then, nothing can stop me, let's rush to the Gallows. . . .

To the Gallows? Fie, sir, you mustn't think of it. Kill yourself for a wench? That would be an incredible folly. . . . Of course, sir; but for a wench to betray an honest man, why, that's a knavish trick. . . . Agreed: but when you're hung, will you be any better off? . . . No, I'll be worse off, but that suits me well, so what have you to say now? If you want to join in, you've only to come along with me. . . . Ho, no, thanks, but don't you go away. . . . Ho, yes, I'm going. . . . Ho, no, you're not going. . . . I am going, I tell you. (*He draws his knife out of its sheath, and taps himself with, then says:*) Ah! That's driven that bothersome fellow away! Now that there's no one to stop us, let's be off to get hung. (*He pretends to hurry, then suddenly stops short.*) No. To hang is an ordinary death, an everyday sort of affair. I'll get no honour from it. Let's find some extraordinary death, heroic death, Arlequinian death. (*He ponders.*) I've got it. I'll stop up my mouth and my nose, my breath won't be able to escape, and so I shall die. It's as good as done. (*He stops up his mouth and his nose with both hands, and after staying like that for some time, he says:*) No, that's no good either, it just comes out elsewhere. Alas! How difficult it is to die! (*To the audience:*) Gentlemen, if anyone would be good enough to die, just to show me how it's done, I would be very much obliged to him. . . . Ah! Now I really have got it. History has recorded that people have died of laughing. If I could die laughing, that would be a risible death. . . . I'm wonderfully ticklish. If someone tickled me long enough, I should die of laughing. I'm going to tickle myself to death. (*He tickles himself, laughs, and falls to the ground. Pasquariel arrives, and seeing him in this state believes him to be drunk, calls to him, lifts him up, consoles him, and leads him off.*)

NOTE that in this scene, wherever the words are followed by . . . these are put to show that in those places Arlequin changes his voice and his gestures, moving from one part to the other. The meaning of the words makes this fairly clear, which is why these instructions were not given in each place. Those who have seen this scene will agree that it is one of the most amusing ever given at the Italian Theatre.

From LES FÉES OU LES CONTES DE MA MÈRE L'OYE. *Gherardi. Presented March 2nd, 1697*

   Scene III. Arlequin, The Ogre, Ismenie, A Fairy.

ARLEQUIN   Oh, woe is me! I don't know where I am. I've just fallen down a mountain. Where shall I find my master?

OGRE   Good, good, here's some more fresh meat. Quick, seize him and put him on the spit with the other one.

> *As the Ogres fall upon Arlequin, a Fairy appears, and they desist.*

FAIRY   Stop, wretches, stop!

ARLEQUIN   Yes, stop, go on, stop!

OGRE (*exit*) Kick up a shindy, mistress, if you must, but remember your power is ended today. (*The Ogres and Ismenie go off.*)

ARLEQUIN   Ah, mistress fairy, I am deeply grateful to you. Had you not arrived, I should have been turned upon the spit. But could you not give me news of he whom I am seeking?

FAIRY   And whom do you seek?

ARLEQUIN   I seek my friend, whom I lost in mid-air.

FAIRY   And who is your friend?

ARLEQUIN   A Prince, who is a friend of mine, and whose colours I wear.

FAIRY   I understand. But what are you seeking in this region?

ARLEQUIN   Alas! I am seeking my Mistress's lost treasure,
            I cry out in vain to these sweet woodland echoes,
            That nary a whisper will ever disclose:
            Has she then been prudent, discreet in full measure
            And given her honour in silent ill-fame
            For fear lest the echo should cry out her shame?
              But you, madame, who are you?

FAIRY   I am a Fairy by vocation. I travel everywhere without moving from one place; I empty treasure chests without opening them; I make debtors lose their shame, and creditors their memory; I sleep wide awake, and I feed upon air: but my primary occupation is to fly ceaselessly to safeguard the honour of maidens.

ARLEQUIN   And you sometimes arrive just a trifle late, don't you? For my part, I'm chasing after my Mistress's virtue—she's been carried off by an Ogre.

FAIRY   Tell me about it.

ARLEQUIN   Most certainly, I'll tell you the whole story. There was once a Prince about a foot and a half high, who was known as Little Flick, because of the number of battles he had won by bowling the enemy over with a flick of his fingers. He married the Infanta Bichette, known as Black Eye, because of a punch in the eye he gave her the first day of the honeymoon. The Infanta was the heiress apparent of a kingdom her father would have liked to conquer. Little Flick had a daughter of the Infanta, a child fair as the dawn: and he was so enchanted with her that he spent his days and his nights rocking her in

his arms, singing, 'Sleep, sleep, the baby sleeps.' For he was
the first Prince in the world and had a wonderful gift for
sending children to sleep.

FAIRY   Continue, I have heard people speak of this story.

ARLEQUIN   It happened one day that Little Flick went on a turkey hunt.
He grasped one of them by the beard; but was enormously
surprised to find in its place a Fairy on a horse, who addressed
these words to him:

> *Great Prince Whippersnap*
> *Let me announce a sad mishap.*
> *I vow and swear by That Turkey,*
> *That never now shall spitted be,*
> *Soon will come the fatal hour*
> *That an Ogre shall deflower*
> *Your fair child, unless you haste*
> *To find a Prince who's to her taste.*
> *She must have, at sweet fifteen*
> *An able man to free his queen.*

FAIRY (*looking at Arlequin*)   An able man?

ARLEQUIN   Yes, an able man. Little Flick, appalled at the Fairy's prophecy,
shut his daughter up in a vast iron Tower; but an Ogre, who
had fallen madly in love with her, discovered this, made himself a ring with lodestone, and so magnetised the Tower, and
drew it after him like a little spaniel. He had put on his
seven league boots so that he could not be caught. Seven
league boots are a very great assistance to an abductor of
young maidens. We've been following the trail five years
now, for the honour of my Mistress. But I do assure you,
Madame, that an honour moving in seven league boots for
five years puts even greyhounds to shame.

FAIRY   I have already told you that I protect the honour of young
maidens: but my power is limited. I can preserve it for them
up to the age of fifteen years and six minutes, and that is the
utmost limit of my power.

ARLEQUIN (*looking at his watch*)   Fifteen and six minutes! Alas! In half an
hour my Mistress will have reached that age! My Mistress's
honour has only half an hour to go! And time rushes by!
Ah, unhappy Ismenie!

FAIRY   What! You are seeking the Princess Ismenie?

ARLEQUIN   Yes, Madame.

FAIRY	I can inform you that she is in that cave, that I will save her honour, and that you are the able man who will deliver her.
ARLEQUIN	Do you really mean that?
FAIRY	I am quite able to do it, since I have already saved the life of Prince Octavius. I changed him into a Mountain just in time to save him from being devoured by an Ogre.
ARLEQUIN	Ah, Madame, you have ruined me! He'll be deaf when I ask him for my wages.
FAIRY	I am going to take you to a Fairy more powerful than I am. I will give you a magic cloak and an enchanted wand to help you free your Princess. You must change her into a Mountain when the Ogre is about to wed her, and you will restore her to her former shape when you see a golden urn brought in. But here is the Fairy.

Scenario of THE BROKEN CONTRACTS, *in the repertoire of Sacchi's Company. Eighteenth Century*

ACT ONE, LIVOURNE

Brighella enters, looks round the stage, finds it empty, and shouts for someone.

Pantalone (*miming fear*) enters.

Brighella wants to leave his service, etc.

Pantalone throws himself on his mercy.

Brighella weakens, and promises to help him.

Pantalone says that his creditors are dunning him, Truffaldino worst of all, and that his bills are due that very day, etc.

Brighella calms him down.

At that moment:

Truffaldino (*scene of dunning*).

Brighella finds means of sending him off.

Pantalone and Brighella on stage.

At that moment:

Tartaglia, at the window, listens.

Brighella sees him. He does the riches scene with Pantalone.

Tartaglia comes into the street. Plays the begging *lazzi* with Pantalone.

Finally they agree that Tartaglia's daughter shall marry Pantalone's son.

At that moment:

Truffaldino comes to demand his money.

Brighella makes it look as though Pantalone is giving it to him.

Having done this three times, they all go off.

Florindo speaks of his love for Rosaure, and of the hunger that is tormenting him. He knocks at the door.

Rosaure listens to his declaration of love, wishes to put it to the test, and demands a love-token.

Florindo says that it is not the right moment, and that he has nothing with which to buy one.

Rosaure tells him to wait; she will give him one; and goes off.

At that moment:

Smeraldina, with a basket, gives it to Florindo, and goes off.

Florindo stays.

At that moment:

Brighella, having heard that Rosaure gave him the basket, steals it from him, and makes off.

Florindo goes after him.

Leander speaks of his love for Rosaure.

He tries to deceive Pantalone.

At that moment:

Tartaglia comes out, talking to himself about Pantalone's wealth.

Leander asks for his daughter in marriage.

Tartaglia tells him she is betrothed to Pantalone's son.

Leander is astonished, makes a scene, etc.

(B) Some early Pantomime Books, showing the influence of *commedia dell'arte* on English Pantomime

1741

HARLEQUIN STUDENT OR THE FALL OF PANTOMIME, WITH THE RESTORATION OF THE DRAMA, *an Entertainment as it is now performing, with great Applause, by Persons for their diversion between the two parts of the Concert at the late Theatre in 'Goodman's Fields'.*

With the Scenes of Action and Tricks as they are variously introduced.

Also, a Description of the Scenes and Machines painted by Mr. Devoto particularly of Shakespeare's Monument as lately erected in Westminster Abbey.

And the Words of the Songs and Chorus's, as set to music, by Mr. Prellem.

London

Printed for Thomas Harris; at the Looking-Glass and Bible on London Bridge.

1741. Price 6d.

The Characters Represented:

Harlequin Student	1st Countryman
M. Ventrebleau, the Beau	2nd Countryman
Mynheer van Grub, the Miser	3rd Countryman
Tenebroso, a Magician	4th Countryman
Pierrot	1st Watchman
John Trot	2nd Watchman
Old Shepherd	Columbine

In the last grand Scene

Jupiter	Minerva
Mars	Melpomene
Mercury	Thalia
Cupid	Hebe

After the overture the Curtain rises to Solemn Musick and discovers SCENE ONE: *Tenebroso the Magician's cave.* Harlequin sitting as a Student in a Hollow of the Rock. Tenebroso leans upon part of the Rock. After a pause, he comes forward and sings.

Recitativo

TENEBROSO My care is past, nor are my precepts lost
For Harlequin a Lettered mind can boast
He now shall Study Quit, and this Retreat
Well versed in Arts and grown a Man compleat.
What still my *Harlequin* on Wisdom bent
Wrapt up in thought, and on the book intent?

(*Enter Harlequin dressed like a student with a book and pen in hand, makes a bow to Tenebroso his Tutor.*)

Recitat

TENEBROSO Pursue my boy these studious Toils no more
From Labour cease, and Pleasure's Path explore;
Shut up your Volumes, lay aside your Pen,
You now must read the World, and study Men;
Taste other Joys, contemplate Beauty's Charms,
And yet more happy take 'em to your Arms.

Air

Cupid wing a thrilling dart
Pierce my Pupil's youthful Heart,
Fill his Soul with soft Desires
Pleasing Pains and glowing Fires,
Man tho' deeply read will prove
Still unlearned, till taught by Love.

Recitat
Be gone—but first your Orders to attend
Behold a Guide, a Servant and a Friend.
(*Here part of the Rock breaks asunder, and discovers Pierrot Asleep, who
wakes surprised, Tenebroso joins his and Harlequin's hands, and then proceeds.*)

Recitat
Pierrot awake—I thus your Hearts unite
Together go and revel in Delight,
Accept this ring, with this you'll ne'er complain
Wish what you want, nor shall you wish in vain.
(*Harlequin and Pierrot take their leave of Tenebroso, who, shewing a great
Reluctance at parting with his Pupil, retires into a cave.*)

SCENE TWO : *Covent Garden.*

Enter Harlequin and Pierrot, who seem surprised at the Town. They
welcome each other to the Town. The Miser and his Daughter enter; she
sorrowful, he angry, pointing to the Beau's house, and expresses he shall
have money for her, she seems still more sorrowful, and he is approaching to knock at the door, she holds him upon her knees and sings:

Air
Oh, cease your vain Entreaties, cease;
Nor thus my guiltless Youth intice.
Still bless your Child with humble Peace,
Nor curse her Days with splendid Vice.
My Beauty you should keep like Gold,
Locked up by Men of honest Fame,
Who guard it safe from Ruffians bold,
But pay with joy a lawful Claim.

The Miser is still resolute, Harlequin and Pierrot down upon knees to
entreat him not to be cruel to her. The Miser goes to strike, they open
Right and Left and he falls between them. Harlequin and Pierrot get up,
as if they had thought some scheme and go off, eyeing Columbine. The
Miser knocks at the door and John Trot opens the door and introduces
'em. Harlequin and Pierrot stand in suspense how to get in, and spying a
Counsellor and his Clerk Prevail on them to lend them their dresses and
thus disguised they knock at the door, and are admitted by John Trot.

SCENE THREE : *A Handsome Chamber with a Settee, etc.*

Miser, Columbine, and Beau in nightgown sitting on a Settee, the Miser
threatening, Beau entreating, and Columbine crying. John Trot introduces Harlequin and Pierrot, the Beau orders Harlequin to make a
Settlement. They sit and write; then he sends Trot for wine; after that

Harlequin goes to show the Beau the Settlement, and Pierrot the Miser, and changes the Settee into a Den of Wild Beasts. The Miser and Beau pop up their Heads and are beat down again by Harlequin and Pierrot. They carry off Columbine. John Trot comes in with wine and laughs to see 'em in the Den, offers 'em wine in that Portion, and after more sport with 'em drags 'em out at the bottom. Beau and Miser, enraged, resolve to pursue Harlequin and stripping to dress, the Scene closes with Covent Garden as before.

SCENE FOUR : *Covent Garden*

Enter Harlequin, Pierrot, and Columbine. Sword on awkwardly. Harlequin sends Pierrot and Columbine on before and stays behind to watch the motions of Beau and Miser. Enter Beau dressed with Miser and Trot. He sends Trot before to find 'em out and as Beau and Miser are walking out, Harlequin strikes Beau and turns him, then Miser and turns and whilst both are looking whence it came, Harlequin strikes Miser again and slips between 'em. They both draw and lunge at him at once. Harlequin flips 'em, the Beau wounds the Miser and Harlequin escapes ; the Beau takes Miser in his house.

SCENE FIVE : *The Tower. A Water Plug on the Stage.*

Enter Pierrot and Trot struggling for Columbine. Harlequin comes behind and strikes Trot on the fingers. Trot lets go and falls. Harlequin sends Pierrot off with Columbine and Trot gets up to call his master. Harlequin lies behind the Cock. As Trot is pursuing he falls at Harlequin's legs and Beau with him. They immediately get up. Harlequin leaps over the Cock. They run at him again, he leaps again and it changes into a Hot Codlin Woman's Stall. After a little Scene of Humour, the Old Woman steals his Snuff box and puts Hot Codlins in the Room. They, Beau and Trot, go after Columbine.

SCENE SIX : *A Wood*

Enter Harlequin, Columbine and Pierrot very joyful. Pierrot discovers the Beau coming. They get up into the Side Wings and Beau enters in a Passion looking for his Snuff box and finds Codlins in his pocket. Trot laughs. Beau throws them in his face and sends him to look for his Snuff box. Harlequin and Beau and Pierrot fight. At last Pierrot takes Columbine. Beau sees her and makes for her, Harlequin strikes him, he returns. Harlequin goes off after Columbine, Beau follows.

SCENE SEVEN : *A View of the Hermitage in Richmond Gardens.*

Beau enters quite tired, as he sits the Bench sinks, he is turned into a Rolling Stone. John Trot enters and being pleased with the place, to divert himself rolls the stone till, frightened at the noise in the rolling stone, he calls on the Gardeners who release *Beau* and carry him off.

SCENE EIGHT: *A Distant View of a Country with Hedges and Hillocks on which are Cattle grazing, etc.*

Harlequin and Columbine enter, rejoiced that they are got into so delightful a place but are disturbed at Pierrot's being pursued by John Trot, etc., Pierrot to get clear leaps through the hedge and Trot following him to it, immediately changes into a hovel and encloses him. Harlequin being closely pursued by the Constable, etc., and finding no other way to escape leaps quite over the Hovel, the old Shepherd and his Men enter and looking into the Hovel, find Trot and take him out to duck him as a Thief.

SCENE NINE: *A Street.*

The Countrymen bring on Trot wet and stript as from ducking and are going to punish him further, but the Beau enters and releases him and goes off to visit the old Miser to carry him to his daughter.

SCENE TEN: *The Miser's Chamber*

A Table set out with Juleps, Slops, etc.

Miser ill of his wounds in an Elbow chair. Harlequin as the Nurse. The Miser wakens, rouses Harlequin who pretends to sleep and sends him to the door. Enter Beau with Columbine and Trot. Harlequin as a nurse mixes something out of all the things on the table and gives it to the Miser, John Trot discovers Harlequin attempting to lay hold of him. He leaps into corner Cupboard. Beau and Miser, who finds himself much better, resolve to follow.

SCENE ELEVEN: *The Tower*

Pierrot and Harlequin pursued. The Lemon Woman enters, Pierrot is changed into a Lamp upon a stone pyramid. Beau and Trot surprised at the change and in disappointment resolve to pursue him no farther.

SCENE TWELVE: *Covent Garden.*

Harlequin enters with dark Lanthorn and Ladder to get into the house. Watch is heard crying Past 12 o'clock, Harlequin hides but is seen. Gets into house by bribing Watch. Noise within, Watch is called but Harlequin and Columbine pass 'em. They lay hold on Beau and Trot who comes out in his Nightcap and unbuttoned. Released by the Miser who go in pursuit of Harlequin and send Trot to take care of the house, but as are going off are met by Tenebroso the Magician.

Recitat

TENEBROSO Mistaken Men! Your fruitless Search forbear
You'll ne'er again molest the happy Pair
No more enraged your senseless scheme pursue
Behold them safe from mortal power and you.

(*Tenebroso waves his wand, and it changes to:*)

SCENE THIRTEEN: *The Court of Cupid.*

(Being a view of Elysium, with bowers of roses and other flowers. Cupid standing in middle attended by several other Cupids rang'd in order on each side of the stage, drives off the Miser, the Beau and John Trot. Cupid to entertain Harlequin sings:)

Recitat

Behold, your Pantomimic Friends arise
To Pay their homage and encrease your joys.

(At which Scaramouch, Pierrot, and Punch arise in the middle of the stage and perform a dance in character. After the dance, Cupid comes forward.)

Recitat

Cease, cease your sports, and now ye happy Pair
To Hymen's Temple, let us all repair,
There will I give into thy longing arms
Fair Columbine and all her matchless charms
                    (*It thunders*)

Mercury descends

Forbear the Rites, Mistaken God of Love;
Such is the Mandate of your Father Jove
The Sister Muses urge their just Complaint
The Nine petition, and the God will grant,
Genius and Taste to *Britain* He'll restore,
And Farce and *Harlequin* shall be no more
                    (*It thunders again*)

(The Court of Cupid disappears, and a Stage descends, representing the Heaven of the Heathen Gods on which are Jupiter with Mars and Minerva, Melpomene presiding over Tragedy; and Thalia the Muse presiding over Comedy; and Hebe, with other Gods and Goddesses. They all come forward and Cupid kneels.)

Recitativo

Dread Sire! Behold your Son and Subject kneel;
Oh, let not *Harlequin* your Vengeance feel.

JUPITER Cupid no more, your suit is urged in vain,
Thalia and *Melpomene* must reign;
In Pity to their just complaints I come
To fire their Empire, and pronounce his doom.
Too long *Britannia* hast thou blindly erred,
And Foreign Mimes to English wit preferred!
Eunuchs to Sloth your senses have betrayed

And British Spirits (as they sung) decayed.
But see, behold, a Better Time returns
Each Bosom now with nobler Rapture burns,
Immortal Shakespeare's matchless Wit revives,
And now the Bard in speaking Marble lives
Numbers each Night, his endless Beauties praise,
Each Day with Rapture on his statue gaze;
For ever thus th'unequall'd Bard adore.
Let Mimes and Eunuchs lull their Sense no more
But with his Muse, your own lost Fame restore.

(It thunders, Harlequin trembles, and immediately Incantation Sounds are Heard. Mercury sings.)

1

Rise! Rise! Thou Honour to the Age,
Support and Glory of the Stage;
Immortal Shakespeare rise!
While Folly's Clouds over Britain hung
No tuneful Bird of Phoebus sung;
Each Warbler to his Covert fled,
Untuned his Throat and droop'd his Head,
Till you sung forth and filled the Skies.

2

Sink, sink Dishonour of the Age
Disgrace and Scandal of the Stage,
Ye worthless Crew, away!
Down, down, to Hell, from whence ye rose,
Minerva's and the Muses' Foes,
Shine forth, thou Sun, great Bard appears,
The Mists disperse, the Darkness clears
And Britons bless with endless Day.

(The Scene draws and discovers the Monument of Shakespeare, exactly as lately erected in Westminster Abbey.)
Minerva sings   While Britons bow at Shakespeare's Shrine,
                 Briton's Sons are Sons of Mine.

Mars sings the same

Minerva 1
Banish Foreign Songsters hence,
Doat on Shakespeare's manly sense
Send th' invading Triflers home.

To lull the Fools of France and Rome
Study well this Bard Divine,
Britons then, you're Sons of Mine.

Mars 2

Eunuchs taint the soundest Part,
Weaken Man in every part.
Shakespeare's soul—exalting Muse
Will raise your Thoughts to noble views.
Read but o'er his matchless Verse.
Soon you'll prove the Sons of Mars.

Chorus

Britains rouse your wonted Spirit !
Nought approve but real merit.
Senseless sounds and Show despise.
Let immortal Shakespeare charm ye,
Let his noble Ardour warm ye.
    And evermore
    As heretofore
Be counted Brave and Wise.

The Christmas Pantomime HARLEQUIN MOTHER GOOSE OR THE GOLDEN EGG *by Thomas Dibdin.* As given at *Covent Garden*, December 26th, 1806.

Characters of the Pantomime:

Mother Goose	Mr. Simmons
Colin (afterwards Harlequin)	{ Mr. King { Mr. Bologna, jun.
Avaro (afterwards Pantaloon)	Mr. L. Bologna
Squire Bugle (afterwards Clown)	Mr. Grimaldi
Beadle	Mr. Denman
Landlord	Mr. Bologna
Woodcutter	Mr. Truman
Cabin Boy	Master Smalley
Sergeant	Mr. Banks
Odd Fish (or Water Sprite)	Mr. Menage
Gardeners	Messrs. Daris, Dick, Morelli
Waiters	Messrs. Baker, Banks, Griffiths

Villagers, etc., by Messrs. Abbott, Atkins, T. Blanchard, Brown, Burden, Everard, Fairbrothers, Fairclough, Goodwin, Lee, Linton,

Meyers, Monk, Oldwell, W. Murray, Platt, Powers, Reeves,
Rimsdyck, Serjant, Street, Tett, S. Tett, Thomas, Treby,
Wilde.

Fairies .... Masters Benson, Goodwin, Morelli, Searle
Colinette (afterwards Columbine) .... Miss Searle
Woodcutter's Wife .... Mrs. Whitmore
Villagers, Fairies, etc., by Mesdames Benson, Bologna, L. Bologna,
Bristow, Findlay, Follett, Grimaldi, Cliff, Lesewe, Masters, Price,
Slader, Watts.

SCENE ONE. A VILLAGE WITH STORM AND SUNRISE (painted by Hollogan).

On the P.S. (or prompter's side) are the entrance gates to Squire Bugle's
mansion; on the O.P. (or opposite prompter) a Church and Cottage,
with the churchyard in front. The Perspective is rendered beautifully
interesting by a distant view of the river, and a bridge over it, which is
heightened considerably in effect by moving objects both on the river
and bridge. After the Storm the clouds disperse, and a rainbow is seen;
the sun rises gradually, and its golden beams are finely reflected on the
windows of the church. A crowd of male and female peasants assemble
decorated with favours, to celebrate the nuptials of the Squire and Colinette. They dance, and afterwards sing the following:

Chorus

Neighbours, we're met on a very merry morning,
Lads and lasses dressed in all their pride so gay
To celebrate the happy hour, when maiden Shyness scorning,
Sweet Colinette is married to the Squire today.
Old and Young
Join the throng
 Cutting nimble capers;
Haste to the church,
In the lurch
 Leaving care and vapours.
No one sad
Hey, go mad
 Man and maiden seem to say,
'If I know who,
Prove but true,
 The next may be my wedding day.'

THE SQUIRE now enters from the mansion, preceded by huntsmen,
jockies, grooms, servants, etc., from the opposite side *Avaro, Colinette,*

Colin, etc. Colinette is presented to the Squire; she appears to turn from him and welcomes Colin; the Guardian interferes, etc. The tomb of the Squire's late wife is seen in the centre of the churchyard, bearing the inscription:

In Memory of
Xantippe,
wife of
BULFACE BUGLE
Esquire

THE SQUIRE sings the old air of:

'First wife's dead,
There let her lie,
She's at rest
And so am I.'

MOTHER GOOSE now crosses the stage, mounted on a Gander. COLIN, THE SQUIRE, AVARO, COLINETTE, etc., sing the following:

Sestetto and Chorus

COLIN	When guardians break a promise due,
SQUIRE	Who dares our progress stop;
AVARO	When richer suitors come to woo
SQUIRE	Such folks as you may hop.
COLINETTE	Yet listen to the inspired Youth
AVARO (*to Squire*)	Your dignity he mocks,
COLIN	I claim her hand,
SQUIRE	Indeed! Forsooth
	I'll put him in the stocks,
	Then merrily, merrily march away,
	For this shall be my wedding-day.
CHORUS	Then merrily, merrily, march away,
	It is the Squire's wedding-day.
COLIN	This should have been my wedding-day.

Mother Goose is brought before the Squire by the beadle and country-men, as a reputed witch, to be punished. Colin intercedes for her, desiring them to pity her age. The Squire orders her to the ducking stool, Colin cries, shame on them, and the Squire says:

Don't list to him,
But try if she chance to sink or swim;
Meantime we'll merrily march away
Because this is my wedding-day.

14

CHORUS   Merrily, merrily, march away
             And keep the Squire's wedding-day.

While they sing the Chorus, Colin rescues Mother Goose from the beadle and countrymen, who makes her exit. The Squire approaches his late wife's tomb, and strikes it with a stick; the tomb opens and her ghost appears, clad in white satin and poppy ribands, follows the Squire, shakes her stick at him, and descends through a trap. The Squire runs off terrified and the scene now presents to view

SCENE TWO: MOTHER GOOSE'S HABITATION (painted by Phillips).

The front a thick wood; on one side an entrance, on the other thick foliage, and an owl seated on a branch very prominent; in the perspective a clear blue sky, with moon and stars beautiful in effect, Mother Goose enters, followed by urchin Spirits, most fantastically habited, they dance round her and sing this:

Air and Chorus
The grasshopper chirrups, listen! listen!
The cricket chimes in with the sound;
On water and windows the moonbeams glisten
And dewdrops bespangle the ground.

Then haste from dogrose, briar, and bell!
From dingle, brake, or daisied dell,
Collect each potent fairy spell,
        Our magic can produce;
To plague you, Squire, and to aid
Young Colin to obtain the maid,
And when my orders are obeyed
        You'll laugh with Mother Goose.

CHORUS   Ha! Ha! Ha!   Ha! Ha! Ha!
               We'll laugh with Mother Goose.
MOTHER GOOSE   Now softly! see, Auroras blush
               Birds cease your revels, hush! hush! hush!
CHORUS   Hush! Hush! Hush!

The wood on the O.P. side opens and presents Mother Goose's Dwelling. Colin enters in a very desponding state. Mother Goose approaches, followed by her favourite or Golden Goose, and addresses Colin in these lines, with action appropriate:

MOTHER GOOSE   Youth, why despair? The girl thou shalt obtain,
               This present shall her guardian's Sanction gain
               Nay, doubt not. While she's Kindly used, she'll lay

A golden egg on each succeeding day.
You serv'd me—no reply—there lies your way.
(*They exit, and the Scene shows:*)

SCENE THREE: A HALL IN AVARO'S HOUSE (painted by Hollogan).

Avaro and Colinette enter, and are followed by Colin and Goose. Avaro endeavours to turn Colin out, when Colin shows him the Goose and Golden Egg, and explains what wealth he may possess; avarice gets the better of Avaro's promise to the Squire, and he joins Colin and Colinette's hands, but presuming he shall gain all the gold at once by destroying the Goose, he draws his Knife, and is preparing to murder her, which Colin prevents. The Squire enters, when Colin, fearful of losing his prize, consents rashly to the Sacrifice of the bird. The Goose now makes her exit through a panel in the back scene, which turns round and presents Mother Goose, who addresses Avaro as follows :

Thou avaricious, selfish ingrate elf,
Like other fools, too cunning for thyself;
Thy ward shall still perplex thee by her flight
Lo! Thus I change the lovers

(*Colinette is changed to Columbine, and Colin to Harlequin.*)
Motley wight! (*To Harlequin:*)
Thou too shall wander, till this egg of gold
Which in the sea I cast, you once again behold.

The Scene opens and discovers

SCENE FOUR: THE SEA.

Mother Goose throws in the Golden Egg; and the Scene changes again to Avaro's Hall, Mother Goose retires and sings as follows:

MOTHER GOOSE   Stop, fool! Some recompense is yet thy due! (*To the Squire:*) Take that——
(*Changes him to the Clown.*)
While thou (*to Avaro*) shalt wear my liv'ry too.
(*Changes him to Pantaloon.*)

Air

For slighted Kindness take your due,
Yet mirth shall with your toils entwine
Be Harlequin—While you pursue
Not Colinette, but Columbine.
This gift receive (gives Harlequin the Sword),
    Amend what's past
And guard it better than the last,
Regain the Egg, and happy be,
    'Till then, farewell, remember me.

SCENE FIVE: AVARO'S HALL.

Mother Goose retires, and is seen to ascend mounted on a Gander. A bustle ensues, they endeavour to secure Harlequin, who eludes their grasp, and leaps through the face of the clock, which immediately presents a sportsman with his gun cocked, the Clown opens the Clock door, and Harlequin appears as the pendulum, the Clown saying, 'Shoot, Present, fire!' The Sportsman lets off his piece and the Clown falls down, during which period Columbine and Harlequin escape (who had previously entered through the panel). Pantaloon and the Clown run off in pursuit and the scene presents

SCENE SIX: A COUNTRY INN (painted by Phillips).

In the front of which is a sign-post with chequers, and on it a large puncheon with the word RUM, a garden seat is on one side of the door, and seated on it are a recruiting-sergeant, a drummer, and fifer; they beat up for recruits, and various characters enter, amongst which is the Clown, who runs off terrified at drum. A drunken Cobbler is the only recruit gained, who, with the recruiting party, enter the inn. Pantaloon and the Clown enter, place themselves on each end of the garden seat, and imperceptibly are thrown against each other, and off the seat, they change situations and the like again takes place, which is productive of much whim and laughter. The Clown now Knocks smartly at the door, the landlord appears with a full jug, and Pantaloon and the Clown receive the contents in their faces; a fracas ensues, and they exit into the house. Harlequin leaps from the window, smacks his sword, and the rum puncheon descends from the sign-post, which he transforms into a fruit barrow, and a painted puncheon with a Bacchus astride ascends in its place; the Landlord comes out of the house, and is struck with the change, but wishing for his puncheon again, Harlequin changes the painted one into a rum puncheon as before. He now throws off his Harlequin's dress and appears *a complete St. Gile's Fruit Girl*, the Clown is seen at the window and wants to buy fruit.

Harlequin beckons him down, the Clown obeys, and endeavours to steal the fruit. Harlequin prepares to treat him roughly, Pantaloon enters, he makes his complaint, the Clown appears sorry for his conduct, and makes love to the nymph, a reconciliation takes place; a dance is proposed, and a mock opera one is excellently executed by the Clown and Harlequin; they exit and the scene shows

SCENE SEVEN: THE INSIDE OF THE INN (painted by Phillips).

The Landlord enters, followed by servants, who place chairs and a table covered; Harlequin and Columbine enter and seat themselves; they are surprised by the Clown, on whom Harlequin plays tricks and he runs off, which opportunity Harlequin and Columbine embrace to disappear; the Clown enters, followed by Pantaloon, they seat themselves, and are thrown off their chairs; they seat themselves again at the table, the Clown drinks wine, and Pantaloon prepares to cut up a pie, when a live duck flies out of it and walks forward on the stage, crying, 'Quack! Quack!' Pantaloon retires and the Clown sits down to regale. Harlequin enters from the door, waves his Sword, and the magic table ascends; the Clown walks under it and again seats himself; the table now descends, and the Clown and chair go up; he bellows lustily; the Landlord comes in, wonders and comes back with a saw to cut him down, during which time the Clown has been let down. Pantaloon enters, the Clown is still seated, when the table ascends gradually, and presents first a second, and then a third table, covered with Cloths, and furnished exactly as the first, with two wax lights to each; the Clown and Landlord separate them, when Pantaloon, Landlord, and Clown place themselves at the respective tables (the Clown in the centre). And all three tables, with Pantaloon, Clown, and Landlord ascend together to a height of Six or Seven feet, the Clown, forgetful of his own situation, is laughing at his neighbours, when another table, to represent a small dining one, is brought on, Harlequin touches it, and a complete supper appears on it, lit up with six candles; Harlequin and Columbine seat themselves and enjoy the elevated situation of their exalted friends. Harlequin and Columbine exit, when a humorous scene ensues by the Clown pelting the servants with plates, etc. The scene now shifts to

SCENE EIGHT: A VIEW IN A MARKET TOWN (painted by Phillips).

A crowd of villagers enter singing Dibdin's Chorus of the Country Fair.

> 'While pipes and tabors rend the air,
> Neighbours—neighbours, haste to the fair.'

Morris dancers now enter and exhibit.

Harlequin and Columbine enter, pursued; they claim protection of the Morris dancers, which they accede to. Pantaloon and the Clown enter, they hustle the Clown, a hurly-burly follows, and grotesque figures walking on their heads conclude this Scene, which is followed by

SCENE NINE: A WOOD-CUTTER'S COTTAGE (painted by Grieve).

A sailor boy comes forward and sings the following Song.

> *The sea was rough, the clouds were dark,*
> *Far distant every joy,*
> *When forced by fortune to embark*
> *I went a cabin-boy.*

My purse soon filled with Frenchmen's gold
I hastened home with joy;
But, wrecked in sight of port, behold
A hapless cabin-boy.

The boy knocks at the Cottage-door, his mother appears, and shortly afterward the woodcutter returning from labour; Harlequin and Columbine enter, pursued, entreat a concealment, and their wish is gratified. Shortly after, an Officer and Constable come to distrain the Woodcutter's goods for rent; they lament their hard fate, and Harlequin condoles with them; finds he has no money about him, but suddenly recollecting his power, he changes a wheel, that is seen on the stage, to Fortune moving on her axis, who dispenses out her golden favours from her cornucopia, to the gratification and relief of the poor woodcutter and family. The Clown enters, and, as usual, plunders from the woodcutter's wife; they retire, the pursuit continues, and the scene presents

SCENE TEN: A PAVILION BY MOONLIGHT (painted by Grieve).

In the grounds of which appear steel traps and spring guns; the Clown is caught by the trap, the gun goes off and frightens the Pantaloon, who leads off the Clown, when the pavilion is changed by Harlequin to

SCENE ELEVEN: A FLOWER GARDEN (painted by Grieve).

Gardeners bring in three large tubs with trees, the centre one which is changed by Harlequin to a sunflower unfolding its brilliant lustre, with beautiful effect, and Columbine dances a graceful *pas Seul*. Harlequin (on the Clown and Pantaloon's appearing) changes the other two trees to the Statues of himself and Columbine, behind which they conceal themselves, and the scene presents

SCENE TWELVE: A VIEW OF GOLDEN SQUARE (painted by Hollogan).

The Clown and Pantaloon appear, a house with lodgings to let attracts their attention; Pantaloon enters it, and here a number of whimsical tricks between the Clown and Pantaloon are displayed, which to be enjoyed must be seen, as all description would fall short in effect. The scene again changes and presents

SCENE THIRTEEN: ST. DUNSTAN'S CHURCH (painted by Whitmore).

Harlequin and Columbine are still pursued; he waves his wand, the clock-face descends, they place themselves on it, and are conveyed to the recess, when the two figures with clubs give place to them. The Clown and Pantaloon view them with wonder, Harlequin and Columbine retire, and the two figures with clubs take their original situation; the Clown and Pantaloon appear entranced, and while they are lost in thought, the dial again descends with the two figures, who beat time with their Clubs, terrify Pantaloon and Clown, whose hats are changed by Harlequin into two bells; the figures keep close to them, Pantaloon mounts the dial, and the Clown clings round it. The scene shuts and presents

SCENE FOURTEEN: ENTRANCE TO VAUXHALL GARDENS (painted by Whitmore).

Various characters now enter, beaux, belles, and a great variety of mixed company, attended by watermen, hackney-coachmen, link boys, etc. The Clown enters and puts in practice his old tricks, pilfers a gentleman of his hat, and a light horseman of his Sword, when the following catch is sung:

VISITORS	Here we are, will all be merry
	Vauxhall galas banish care,
WATERMEN	Hope you'll please to pay the Wherry,
COACHMAN	Hope you'll pay poor coachy's fare.
FIRST VISITOR	Hang your nasty Skulls and oars,
SECOND VISITOR	Come, let's in, and see the fun.
FIRST VISITOR	What's to Pay—what monstrous bores!
	What's your number?
COACHMAN	Three and sixpence.
A VISITOR	I'll take care of number *one*.
COACHMAN	I'll summons you all,
WATERMAN	To Watermans' hall.
COACHMAN	To Somerset House.
CHORUS	Oh, rare Vauxhall!

The scene draws, and discovers the

SCENE FIFTEEN: ORCHESTRA IN VAUXHALL GARDENS (painted by Whitmore).

This enchanted view must forcibly remind every frequenter of Vauxhall with the perfect facsimile of the place; the orchestra is fully illuminated as on a gala night; the musicians appear in motion; the company consists of great variety, and the illusion is completed by the entrance of the pandean minstrels playing the favourite air; the Clown enters and excites much laughter by playing on a large tin fish-kettle (which is hung round his neck), with a ladle and whisk, his chin resting on a hair broom, which he supports between his feet; his action is perfectly correspondent to the pandeans', and is perhaps one of Grimaldi's happiest efforts in the pantomime; the air as played last season at the gardens strikes up, and the company form a country dance after which the Clown throws the waiters and company into confusion by stealing tablecloth, etc., and a scene ensues, full of merriment and fun. Plates thrown in all directions, fowls fly away off the dishes, etc., when the scene closes, and presents the Spectators with the outside of:

SCENE SIXTEEN: A GROCER'S SHOP AND POST OFFICE (painted by Whitmore).

The Clown enters and steals the letters out of the box ,he opens one and secretes some of the notes, then another, and reads, 'Sir, I'll trouble you with a line'—and exhibits a small cord, which is enclosed in the letter. Harlequin enters, changes the letter box into a lions' head, the Clown advances, puts his hand in, to get letters, and is caught fast in the mouth of the lion; he endeavours to extricate himself, and draws out of the box a little postman, who annoys the Clown with his bell. A baker comes on, sets down a loaf, throws it to the Pantaloon, and covers the postman with the basket. While Pantaloon and the Clown are endeavouring to keep the basket over the postman, the top opens, and a blackamoor's head appears and recedes; they are both terrified; the Clown goes in and returns with a board, Pantaloon pops up on one side of the basket, when the Clown breaks the board in two on his head. They exit. Two porters then bring in a chair-man's horse, on which are two chests of tea. Harlequin and Columbine enter, pursued, he changes the chest into an elegant sideboard, furnished complete, behind which he and Columbine hide themselves. The scene is here changed to the

SCENE SEVENTEEN: THE GROCER'S PARLOUR (painted by Phillips).

The Clown and Pantaloon enter, and drink wine, and a very clever trick is played off the Clown, with the magic bottle; the Clown and Pantaloon go off, and Harlequin changes the sideboard into a beehive stand; the whole of this scene, as if by magic, in one second presents the interior of

SCENE EIGHTEEN: A FARM YARD (painted by Richards).

Harlequin with Columbine are concealed behind the bee-stand, when Pantaloon and the Clown enter, each one takes up a bee-hive, the bees swarm about their heads, and they exit bellowing. The scene now changes to

SCENE NINETEEN: THE MERMAID'S CAVE (painted by Whitmore).

This scene is very beautiful, the perspective shows the sea through the opening of the cavern; Mother Goose enters, attended by her four fairies, whom she addresses in these lines:

> Your task concludes; your mistress's rage is o'er;
> These wand'ring mortals I'll perplex no more.
> Go, wake the fav'rite of my sprites, who sleep,
> Within the briny bosom of the deep;
> The spell-bound Egg from bondage to redeem,
> Reward true love, and end our magic dream.

Mother Goose and fairies exit, when Odd Fish (and a very odd fish it is) rises out of the sea, comes forward, smacking the serpents that twine around his legs, and takes up two shells and devours the fish, he then exits, Harlequin with Columbine enters, as also, soon after, Odd Fish; they are terrified, and Harlequin strikes out of his Sword a trident, with which he charms Odd Fish, and pours wine into his mouth from his Sword. Harlequin now commands him to dive into the sea for the Golden Egg; he obeys, and returns with a seaweed, which Columbine receives; he goes a second time and comes forward with the *Golden Egg*. Harlequin receives it from him. Pantaloon and the Clown enter; Harlequin and Columbine take shelter behind Odd Fish, who keeps each at bay with his serpents. Mother Goose enters; Harlequin presents to her the Golden Egg, and she reconciles all parties with these lines:

> The egg returned, receive thy lovely choice,
> The gift is sanctioned by her guardians' voice;
> You, soon restored to person, house, and lands,
> Shall, like a hearty English Squire, shake hands;
> Meanwhile his magic dwelling you shall view
> Furnished by fairy hands to pleasure you.

Mother Goose waves her stick, and the Spectator is presented with a view of the last scene, representing

SCENE TWENTY: A SUBMARINE PALACE (painted by Hollogan).

The wings or sides of which are dolphins; in the perspective a tripod of them; and two recesses or alcoves, in each of which is seen a mermaid, busily employed in combing their hair and the whole terminated by a distant view of the sea; dancers approach, habited to correspond with the scene, and the finale is sung by Mother Goose, Squire and Chorus.

Finale

MOTHER GOOSE	*Ye patrons kind, who deign to view* *The sport our scenes produce,* *Accept our wish to pleasure you* *And laugh with Mother Goose.*
CHORUS	*Ye patrons kind, etc.*
SQUIRE	*And let no critic stern reject* *What our petition begs,* *That we may from your smiles collect* *Each night some golden eggs.*
FULL CHORUS	*Ye patrons kind, who deign to view* *The sport we'd fair produce,* *Accept our wish to pleasure you* *And laugh with Mother Goose*

MOTHER GOOSE *Who humbly begs*
On bended legs
That you, good lack,
Her cause will back,
And scorn to crack
Her Golden Eggs.
CHORUS   *Who humbly begs, etc.*

DIBDIN'S HARLEQUIN IN HIS ELEMENT OR FIRE, WATER, EARTH, AND AIR, 1810

SCENE ONE: *Grand Pleasure Garden painted by Whitmore.*

Is preceded by excellent overture. Curtain rising unfolds to view a Spacious garden on which every luxury of art and nature expended. In middle elegant fountain, erected and ornamented according to the Egyptian architecture.

Genie of the Air, portrayed with great exactness descends in a cloud-formed car, she comes forward and speaks some words expressive of the nature and power of the element over which she presides.

She is then joined by the Genie of the Water, who rises from the Cascade and invokes the appearance of a third element—a subterranean noise is heard and Terrana the Goddess of the Earth ascends, her head tastefully and emblematically adorned with ears of Corn and field flowers, her wand is twined with the choicest productions of Flora, her figure striking and majestic.

Again the Earth is agitated and Ignoso the God of Fire ascends on his flaming throne, canopied by fiery clouds embodied by sulphur. He comes forward in an infuriated rage, derides the Sister elements, and boasts his own importance, exclaiming that he will give them a sample of the mischief he can produce. With his flaming brand he endeavours to set the surrounding scenery in a blaze, but his efforts prove abortive—Earth, Air, and Water counteract his intention and a jarring of the four elements takes place.

Tired of this contention, they agree to form a bond of amity, and mutually assist each other and Fire, Water, Earth, and Air become friends.

The Genie of the Air then informs her companions that the rich old owner of the Garden, Sir Feeble Sordid, keeps his lovely ward Columbine in Captivity, to force her to accept his hand.

They resolve to free her and give her a more suitable Lover, whom they combine to form.

Earth strikes ground with her wand, a mound opens and Harlequin, the motley hero, is discovered as a Corpse. By united efforts of Water and Air he receives life and animation. Fire then performs his part, and endows Harlequin with Spirit and Energy.

Harlequin then receives Sword and instructions from four patrons who return to native elements. *This part forms one of the chief ornaments of the Pantomime.* Earth descends to slow music, Fire to his Subterranean abode enclosed in his flaming envelope, and Air ascends in her celestial Car. Water returns to her fountain, which instantly begins to play with *real Water* from every point, particularly from the mouth of the Sphynxes which form Corners of this magnificent fountain, further embellished by ornament of Gold and Silver fish at intervals seen descending amid pellucid Streams.

Sir Feeble Sordid now makes his entrée, preceded by four men servants in elegant liveries, black attendant habited in Indian fashion, with his parasol, and the Clown (Grimaldi).

He hands Sir Feeble his Snuff box, mirror, etc., and attends with great promptitude to his Commands, till the harmony of the Scene is interrupted by the tricks of Harlequin who inflicts a Stroke with his wooden Sword on the person of the antiquated beau which he mistakes as coming from the Clown, whom he pursues with his cane and a laughable confusion ensues.

Fountain continues playing through whole of this Scene. Columbine now appears, with a bouquet of flowers in her hand. Harlequin enters, takes the nosegay from her and begins his addresses. She receives his advances at first with extreme coolness and some symptom of disdain. At length she becomes more favourable. He presents her the nosegay, on his Knees, she accepts it, and receives him as her Lover.

They are now interrupted by the return of Sir Feeble and his servants. He perceives his motley rival and becomes friends with the Clown upon condition of latter joining in pursuit of Harlequin who has retired with the lovely Columbine: which gives rise to the second scene.

SCENE TWO: *Pavilion and Bridge* (Whitmore).

A beautiful rivulet appears with a Chinese bridge in the background— on the right a spacious tree surrounded by a spiral staircase terminated by platform and railing: on left isolated ivy tower.

Harlequin and Columbine enter, the former plays some pastoral tunes on his flageolet, and latter dances to his music, in a manner expressive of the softer passions.

Interrupted by the entrance of the Clown who, perceiving the lovers, is about to retire and inform his master, which they prevent, and force him

back. He artfully professes his friendship and joins their diversions—
when a reel is commenced, he again endeavours to steal off. Harlequin
pursues and pulls him in backwards, and their dance recommences; he
again runs off and is pulled in by one ear, at which he makes a most
ludicrous face which, joined to the whimsicality of his dress, excites
much mirth—his curious habit is surmounted by a large hat bordered
with fur, as a satire on the present mode of female fashion.

Sir Feeble now enters on one side and his servants on the other; the
former drags off his Ward and the latter bar the progress of her lover, and
make themselves sure of taking him in their toils, when by a surprising
leap over their heads he obtains his freedom—this is followed by the
imitations of the Clown.

SCENE THREE: *Columbine's Saloon.*

A splendid Saloon in Sir Feeble Sordid's house—preparations appear
making for company and a cold collation is set out. Sir Feeble, after
giving his orders, retires, and leaves Columbine and the Clown; the
latter is wholly absorbed by the dainties around him, and tastes every
dish—he then seats himself at one of the tables, and whimsically tucks
one napkin under his chin, and spreads the other before him. He then
attacks the wine and fills the glasses on each side of him. Harlequin, who
has entered unperceived by him, and holds a conversation with Columbine, charms the glasses with his wand, and the wine disappears as fast
as the Clown fills it, till at length rising in a passion, he exclaims, 'The
devil is in the wine!' Harlequin after a struggle with the Clown, effects
his escape with Columbine.

SCENE FOUR: *Evening View, near London* (Grieve).

Evening, and a distant prospect of the Metropolis in which the west
towers of the Abbey are most perceptible. A watch box is in the middle
—on the right a hotel—and on the left an oil shop over which is written
'Thump, Oilman'. Harlequin and Columbine enter, but perceiving
themselves pursued take refuge in latter place.

Sir Feeble Sordid enters with the Clown, and being fatigued, the former
resolves to pass that night at the hotel—he knocks at the door, the waiter
comes out, and in obedience to his Commands presents him with a bill of
fare. He orders dinner and retires into the interior of the house. Sir
Feeble is now seen through a window, in a room on the first floor,
attended by the Clown.

The watchman enters with, 'Past six o'clock and a cloudy evening'.
Sir Feeble comes and gives him money, with orders to call him at an
early hour, and to alarm him if Harlequin and Columbine appear, whom
he dislikes. He then returns to his dinner and sends some wine to the

watchman by the hands of the Clown, who enters with a bottle and glass. The Guardian of the night is now fast asleep in his box and the Clown makes free with the wine himself, till being quite inebriated he determines on a frolic, which commences by stripping the watchman and clothing himself in the great-coat and hat. Wishing to take another sup of his wine, he, after many fruitless attempts, at last gets hold of the bottle but not being able to guide it to his mouth, he with the other hand feels for his mouth and tries again in vain to put the neck of the bottle into it. Vexed, he takes up the lantern and holding it to his cheek, effects his wished-for purpose. He then shuts the sleeper into his box and with the lantern and rattle parades the stage, crying the hour in a ludicrous tone. Harlequin and Columbine enter from the oil shop and the former mistakes the Clown for the watchman, shows him where they reside, gives him money and makes signs for him to call them in the morning. The Clown now discovers himself, Columbine retreats, and a struggle ensues between former and Harlequin. The mock Watchman springs his rattle in a most furious manner, and awakes his master, who issues from the hotel and pursues Harlequin who runs off. At that instant the door of the watchman's box flies open and the Watchman, transformed to an old woman, with a mob cap, tumbles out and flings down the Clown who was following Sir Feeble.

SCENE FIVE: *Dyer's Shop* (Hollogan).

A Street with shops of various trades, among which the most conspicuous is a Dyer's, kept by Indigo and Green—a pole is fixed in the front, on which is suspended some great coats which have been Scoured.

The Lovers find a friend in the Dyer—they take each a wrapping coat from the pole and disguise themselves. The Guardian and his Valet the Clown enter and after a little time discover the supposed Strangers to be Harlequin and Columbine. But at that moment the Dyer's men fasten the two pursuers to the pole which is raised to the height of the second floor and places them in a ridiculous position. The Clown is extricated from his perilous exaltation by the aid of a ladder, but breaking it in his descent the master still remains suspended till his valet devises the following means of liberating him.

The Dyer's men stand to receive him in a blanket and the Clown enters the house, but reappears at the window and cuts the cord—the Dyer's men give the aged lover a hearty toss in the blanket, and then hurry him off the stage.

SCENE SIX: *Moonlight View, on the Thames* (Hollogan).

A timber Yard on the banks of the Thames affords a pleasing view to the Spectator: among the scenery is the exterior of a glass house.

Columbine appears fatigued, Harlequin strikes some poles, which turn into a green awning, beneath which they seat themselves, till the entrance of her Guardian and Clown. Former seats himself on a bench, which is converted into a railing and encloses him, while a block of wood on which the Clown was seated extends itself upwards to a pole of an amazing height, diversified with a variety of colours and exalts him into the air. While this is acting in the front of the stage, some sailing boats appear on the Thames, which have a most beautiful and picturesque appearance. Leaving their enemies in durance, the Lovers quit the stage and an immediate transformation takes place.

SCENE SEVEN: *Glass House, inside* (Hollogan).

In middle stage appears the furnace: on each side are shelves on which are arranged various articles of glass. One of the men shows Columbine method of blowing glass through tube. The Clown snatches one of them from the furnace and begins to imitate the man, when two globes of red-hot glass rise from the end next his mouth and fasten one on each cheek, to his great terror and the amusement of the spectators. Harlequin, closely pursued by Sir Feeble, leaps into the furnace: the Clown takes the circuit of the stage and follows his example but not with same fate. Harlequin under protection of Genius of the Fire escapes but Clown is dragged out by amazed Glassmen with clothes in flames, which they appear to extinguish with difficulty.

A crate now brought on the stage containing some glass and a large plate or mirror. Harlequin re-enters, strikes it with his Sword, on which the most beautiful transformation in the pantomime takes place.

SCENE EIGHT: *Hancock and Shepherd's Cut Glass Manufactory* (Hollogan).

Middle stage superb and curious temple of cut glass—on each side are hung Girandoles, Chandeliers, lustres, etc., of various dimensions, richly ornamented, one of the proprietors enters with an attendant, each bearing lights, to conduct Sir Feeble, Columbine, etc., in viewing this.

Clown so much engaged in viewing surrounding objects, does not perceive departure of rest, left in darkness. While in this perplexity, Harlequin enters and raises two bronze statues each representing boys, they are animated and one enters on either side of the terrified Clown, bearing three lustres with lighted candles, they torment him as he turns by touching him behind, till enraged, he extinguishes the candles with breath, and leaves himself in darkness: not knowing where to go he gropes his way out and returns with lighted candle, tries to re-light the lustres borne by the bronze figures. Efforts rendered abortive by the power of Harlequin. Candlesticks undergo a variety of changes in his hands and at last put out by violent explosion. Clown in darkness. As he creeps out Sir Feeble enters and Clown unconscious of what he is doing, catches hold of his master's leg and flings him down, people enter with lights, bronze figures disappear.

SCENE NINE: *Masquerade Warehouse* (Hollogan).

On left a Masquerade, on right dwelling of Counsellor Grumpy.

Sir Feeble enters with Columbine and knocks at Counsellor's door. Opened by spruce cleark. Sir Feeble explains that he wants the marriage settlements drawn up between himself and youthful Ward. Counsellor (a little decrepit man) appears and invites them into his house which Columbine enters with reluctance.

Harlequin, watching, appears and by the aid of a pile of hats, enters one of the windows but is detected and turned out. Grumpy goes out on business, briefs in one hand, green bag in the other. Harlequin takes advantage of this circumstance. Enter publican lad with gallon of beer which Harlequin converts into Counsellor's wig and bag. So attired, gains admittance. While this is transacting, people are seen going to Masquerade Warehouse, from whence return in various characters, exit.

Real Counseller now returns, treated by Cleark as impostor. Violent altercation, enter Sir Feeble, Columbine and Clown with Harlequin disguised. Clown discovers Harlequin, retreats into Masquerade Warehouse followed by Columbine.

Clown enters in character of Punch and is followed by Harlequin as Joan. Whimsical *pas de deux*. Change into rightful characters again—lovers renew flight, are again pursued.

SCENE TEN: *Dodd's Paper Mill at Cheyney near Rickmansworth* (Hollogan).

Mill surrounded by picturesque scenery. On right a wood. Lovers cross stage, Sir Feeble and Clown follow. Smart Milliner meets him and enquires the way—he makes love to her but is rejected with much contempt. He succeeds in stealing her band box and hides with it among trees. Girl runs off. Bootmaker next appears with several pair of boots on a stick. Enquires his road of the Clown who while directing him, purloins the best pair of boots. A woman with a basket of vegetables comes next on the stage. Met by Fishmonger, they drink together. Clown steals from woman's basket, filches Salmon from man. They go, Milliner returns with Beadle to look for thief, who eludes them.

Cross-stage Clown comes behind beadle, steals his large hat, clapping bunch of turnips instead on his bushy wig.

Clown places boots erect, puts box stolen from Milliner on top. Attaches long Glove on each side for arms, piece of Salmon for head, the whole surmounted by Beadle's hat. Harlequin enters, strikes figure with wand. Salmon transformed into face and figure nods at Clown who is terrified.

SCENE ELEVEN: *Interior of Paper Mill* (Hollogan).

Harlequin and Columbine find friends among paper makers who favour their escape. Clown dipped in their soaking tub, and Sir Feeble in pursuit of rival, crosses the stage and steps on wheels of mill. Harlequin strikes it and it is converted into the village round house with the adage 'Live and Repent'. Encloses Sir Feeble.

SCENE TWELVE: *A Village* (Hollogan).

Round-house in middle, romantic Scenery on each side, among which Cottages and distant view of the church. Scene enlivened entrance old blind Soldier, drawing hand organ, attended by Son. Boy sings, villagers bestow charitable benefaction upon old Soldier. Three sailors among group.

Harlequin enters and transforms organ into model man o'war. Music strikes up Rule Britannia and sailors give three cheers. Sir Feeble and Clown draw near to examine Ship when two guns discharge and terrify them. Ship drawn off. Three Savoyard girls enter, Irish air played and trio entertains audience with pleasing dance. Sir Feeble now released by Beadle who goes off with him.

SCENE THIRTEEN: *Bookseller's, Trunk Maker's, and Pastry Cook's Shops* (Hollogan).

Bookshop kept by *Title-page*, pastry cook's by *Puff*, Trunkmaker in corner, view of St. Paul's at the back.

Bookseller accosted by poet of wretched appearance with a manuscript. Former refuses it, refers him to Trunkmaker. Poet will not line trunks, but at length gives it to Puff, in return for dish of pastry. While eating voraciously, Clown creeps behind him and steals part of his food.

Puff sits down in front of house, begins to read manuscript, yawning frequently. Meanwhile Clown feasting on dainties of deserted shops. Lovers cross stage enter Puffs. Sir Feeble goes into Title-page.

SCENE FOURTEEN: *Bookseller's Parlour* (Grieve).

In middle, bookcase: on left, printing press. Sir Feeble, Columbine and Clown enter. While Title-page is busy, giving orders to his men, newsboy enters, receives papers, Sir Feeble has large bill printed offering reward £500 for head of Harlequin. One stuck on wall.

Harlequin appears from behind bookcase, they chase him, he leaps through bill, where large playbill appears instead with FIVE MILES OFF and CATCH HIM WHO CAN.

SCENE FIFTEEN: *Equestrian Statue and Square* (Grieve).

Beautiful statue on pedestal with railing. In background a square.

Harlequin and Columbine cross stage, pursued by Clown who catches hold of Harlequin who gets away clear after struggle.

SCENE SIXTEEN: *Nursery Garden* (Grieve).

A garden. Gardners place full bloom rose tree in front and on other side an evergreen in a large tub.

Harlequin and Columbine enter. Latter exhausted, lover strikes rose tree, in their stead appears beautiful passion flowers. Transforms evergreen into Chairs for himself and Columbine to rest upon. Harlequin buys fruit off Peter Plant the nurseryman, is invited into grounds.

Sir Feeble appears followed by Clown. Sir Feeble goes into grounds, Clown sits on chair, Harlequin appears and changes tree and evergreens back so Clown falls.

SCENE SEVENTEEN: *Code's Artificial Stone Manufactory* (Whitmore).

Mason at work on accurate décor. Busts, effigies, etc., scattered. In front two pedestals. On each an Egyptian Sphynx. Harlequin and Columbine retreat here, tell principal stone mason of their distress. He becomes their friend and influences men to favour their concealment.

They perceive Sir Feeble and Clown. Envelop themselves in mantles of slate colour. Harlequin strikes pedestal and Sphynxes vanish. He ascends one and Columbine the other.

Sir Feeble and Clown enquire after lovers. Mason shows them round, Sir Feeble goes. Clown stands between pedestals terrified, sees statues nodding heads and making faces at him. Realises truth, goes to tell his master. Harlequin and Columbine descend, go into mason's house. Sir Feeble and Clown return. Seeing empty pedestals Sir Feeble believes that Clown is fooling. But Clown protests, mounts pedestal to show how it was done, persuading Sir Feeble to mount other. Stone vase springs up on each pedestal enclosing them. Heads just perceived above summit.

SCENE EIGHTEEN: *Interior Exhibition Code's Artificial Stonework* (Whitmore).

Extremely beautiful. Statues heathen deities ranged on either side, among them White bull of Europa.

Stonemason enters with Harlequin and Columbine to view exhibition.

Sir Feeble and Clown appear, from whom lovers find it impossible to escape without help of elemental Genii.

SCENE NINETEEN: *Rendezvous of the Geniis* (Whitmore).

Rendezvous of the Geniis, a retreat among rocks interspersed with emblematical insignia.

Aurino, Genie of the air, descends in her cloud-formed car. Invokes presence of Aquino, Terrano.

Aquino comes forward and Terrano ascends. Lovely trio join in invocation to Ignoso, who appears.

They consult together. By their influence Sir Feeble brought there with Columbine and Clown, summon Harlequin also. Lovers express by signs great transport at this meeting. Sir Feeble looks upon rival with rage, going to lead Columbine off.

Genii interfere, he is forced to listen and convinced by them, joins hands of the faithful lovers, whose patrons offer them future protection for which suitably thanked.

SCENE TWENTY: *Grand Temple of the Elements* (Whitmore).

Last scene truly magnificent and superbly decorated, Temple divided into partitions, respectively appropriated to each presiding Genius: *Ignoso*, A Hall of Fire. Arches seem to emit burning lava and the basis resembles a sulphurous lake, while background has a volcanic appearance: *Aurino*, Beautiful Doric pillars skirted by pedestals on which placed birds who seem to be living. Places assigned to Earth and Water on left Emblematical of elements, appearance not so striking as former.

Four Elements stand on front of stage, surrounded by attendants, in the most splendid attire. Those of Air interesting with wings and light spangled robes. Each of the Genii chants some lines expressive of power and influence over mankind.

Retire gracefully back stage, curtain falls.

HARLEQUIN MUNCHAUSEN: OR THE FOUNTAIN OF LOVE
1818

In which those REAL FACTS, recorded by that celebrated Traveller, *Baron Munchausen*, have been varied and expanded, according to the admitted Privileges of the Pantomime.

Baron Munchausen .... Mr. Simmons
Sir Hilaro Frostico (afterwards Pantaloon) .... Mr. Norman
My Lord Humpy Dandy (afterwards Clown) .... Mr. Grimaldi
Signora Fragrantia (afterwards Columbine) .... Miss F. Dennet
    Attendants: Mesdames Wells, Louis, Chipp, Twamley, Robinson
Harlequin .... Mr. Ellar
Vulcan .... Mr. Comer
Cyclops .... Messrs. Norris, George, Crumpton, Heath, etc.
Venus .... Miss Shaw
Cupid .... Miss R. Boden
The Graces .... Mesdames Vedy, Mori, Newton
Moon-King .... Miss Ryals
His Ministers .... Hornet, Moonshine, and Orbit Crescent

Tube of the Dog-Stars ....Bow-wow, Howl, Bay, Bark, and Bite
Man in the Moon ....Mr. Louis
Dame Full-Face, his wife ....Mad. Collette
Post-boy ....Mr. Grant
Mameluke Chief ....Mr. Vedy

The Overture and Music selected and composed by Mr. Ware.

The Scenery by Messrs. Phillips, Whitmore, Pugh, Grieve, Hollogan, Hodgins, I. Grieve, Carrol, and Assistants.

The Tricks, Changes and Transformations by Messrs. Bradwell, Saul, jun., W. Bradwell, and Norman.

The Machinery by Messrs. Saul and Bradwell.

The Dresses by Mr. Palmer and Miss Egan.

The whole arranged and produced under the direction of Mr. Farley at Covent Garden, 1818.

SCENE ONE: *Mountains of Snow, near Mount Aetna; the Burning Lava Running Down, the Snow wastes gradually and discovers a Village at the base of the Mountain* (Grieve).

    Baron Munchausen laying on the Ground and his Horse hanging to the Steeple Top of the Village Church.

    Villagers enter

Chorus

No more we view the hills of Snow,
No more we hear the North wind blow;
Smiling Spring's bright tints appear,
Summer's treasures open here.
   In scenes so gay
    Joying in this glorious day,
Warm to love each bosom glows
Melting like the melting snows.

FIRST VILLAGER (*seeing Baron Munchausen*)
    Neighbours, behold! Lo! what lies here?
    A frozen Traveller—dead, I fear!
    He stirs—He yawns—He opes his eyes,
    Ho! Master, ho! arise! arise!

MUNCHAUSEN (*rising*) I am not dead.

FIRST VILLAGER (*to others*) I think he lies.

MUNCHAUSEN Ya-aw! I've had a chilly nap!

FIRST VILLAGER Your nightcap wasn't air'd, mayhap.

MUNCHAUSEN To me all nightcaps are the same
    And seasons too.

FIRST VILLAGER Pray, what's your name?

MUNCHAUSEN Baron Munchausen stands before thee, Youth,
Fam'd for his travels, wond'rous for his truth.

CHORUS T'is he, t'is he! hail! great Munchausen, hail!

MUNCHAUSEN But have you seen my jet black steed
Who far outstrips the arrow's speed?

FIRST VILLAGER No, great Munchausen, we have not, indeed.

MUNCHAUSEN Hark! well I know his cheering neigh
He hangs on yonder steeple's top;
Don't be alarm'd, good people, pray
I'll bring it down, e'en with a pop.

The Horse drops from the church, sound wind and limbs; the Baron
mounts him, to the great wonder of the villagers.

Chorus

Baron Munchausen—what a swell,
Baron Munchausen—fare thee well!
Bim-bom-Bell! Bim-bom-bell!
Baron Munchausen, fare thee—well!

The Baron gallops off in a most horseman-like attitude.

SCENE TWO: *An Apartment in Sir Hilaro Frostico's House* (Grieve).

His ward, the Signora Fragrantia, and her attendants, busily employed,
are interrupted by Sir Hilaro, to whom a servant enters, to inform him
that

SERVANT Sir, my Lord Humpy Dandy waits below. And sends his compliments to great Sir Hilaro.

HILARO What is today?

SERVANT T'is Saturday you know.

HILARO Saturdays I'm at home; admit him—So!

Lord Humpy Dandy, one of the exquisite order of Dandyism, is proposed as a lover to the Signora, but a more favoured one defeats their
projects and carries off the fair Italian.

SCENE THREE: *A Subterraneous Cavern in Mount Aetna.*

With the Forges of Vulcan—Thunderbolts, with the Armour of Mars,
etc., distributed about the Scene; on one side is a brazen door, leading to
the apartment of Venus (Grieve).

Vulcan and his One-eyed Cyclops hard at work. Yet, like all good
workmen, full of mirth.

Chorus (*Vulcan and his Cyclops*)
Strike! Strike!
Let the hammer resound

> *While we take the stroke round*
> *Tan-tan-tan-tan!*
> *Hark! The echo replies, replies*
> *Tan-tan-tan-tan!*

The Baron and the Signora fly for refuge into the cavern.

VULCAN (*to Munchausen and Lady Fragrantia*)
> Now, mortal, what do you desire
> Within this smithy of the God of Fire?

MUNCHAUSEN Protection for this lovely fair, I crave.

VULCAN Sir, to a fair one, Vulcan is a slave.

Vulcan strikes the Brazen doors, which fly open.
> There is my wife's boudoir; to Venus go.

The Signora enters, but the Baron is stopt by Vulcan.
> Hold! man, don't enter there—no, Baron, no!
> You stay with me, and bravely face your foe.

The Baron is too deep for Vulcan, who steals into Venus' Apartment, which Vulcan perceiving, is in a flaming rage.

VULCAN
> Sulphur and Fire! where has that caitiff been?
> What! dare approach the couch of Beauty's queen?
> (*To Lord Humpy Dandy, etc.*)
> My friends! and Cyclops, with your pincers hot,
> Drag this Munchausen to the cloud-capt spot,
> Where, headlong plunge him, till at once he's hurl'd
> Down Aetna's crater, to the nether world.

(*They pursue the Baron into the abode of Venus.*)

SCENE FOUR: *The Boudoir of the Venus, beautifully and fancifully decorated* (Grieve).

Venus surrounded by the Loves and Graces receives the Baron and Signora and vows to protect them against the power of Vulcan and her Guardian.

CUPID (*to Vulcan, etc.*) Who dares the power of my love defy?

VULCAN I dare!

HILARO And I dare!

LORD And so do I!

VENUS T'is well! But first, Munchausen, since thou'rt mine
> Be Harlequin! (*Munchausen is changed to Harlequin*).
> Fragrantia, be thou Columbine.
> (*She is changed to Columbine.*)

VULCAN Hammer and tongs! thus do you scoff me? Soon
> I'll spoil your sport! Hilaro Frostico, be Pantaloon.
> (*Hilaro is changed to Pantaloon.*)

Now, crooked Humpy Dandy, kneel down straight
And rise the Clown, our laughter to create.
             (*My Lord is changed to Clown.*)
VENUS (*to Harlequin and Columbine*)
Away! Such countries to explore,
As were never seen before,
Till at Egypt's famed Pyramids danger you'll prove.
VULCAN   Where I'll beat you to mummies, I'll do it, by Jove!
VENUS   Till restored to new life at the Fountain of Love.

Venus and the Graces conduct away Columbine, who ascends on a cloud, and passes through the Regions of the Moon, followed by Harlequin and Pursuers until they arrive at

SCENE FIVE: *A State Apartment in the Lunairian Palace* (Grieve).
      The way in which the Great Personages of the human Court carry their Heads—The Lovers are received with much condescension by the Moonshine King high Majesty—to whom a special Messenger arrives from his Majesty the

DOG-STAR CHIEF   Syrius the Dog-Star, to the Moonshine King,
Snarls a defiance, and by Saturn's ring
He swears—If Lunatics a veto clap
On yielding him the milky way to lap;
To prove how much the Moon he then despises
He'll howl at her, When e'er she sets or rises!

      A Battle; the King loses his Head; but picks up another that does not fit him quite so well.

KING OF THE LUNAIRIANS   Mine's a wrong head!
                            (*Pointing to one of his Chiefs.*)
                   And he no head doth wear!
CLOWN (*with the King's head under the arm*)
             And I've two heads—my own, and Mooncalf's, there!
                   (*Lunairians approach Clown.*)
             Keep off, ye Lunatics! I brave! I dare ye!
                   (*Head bites his fingers.*)
             Oh Lord! He bites! Let the right owner wear ye!
      The Whole Court is thrown into confusion, and everyone's head is—turned.

SCENE SIX: *The Inside of the Man in the Moon's Public House,* called 'The Lunar Packet-House" (Pugh).
      The Lovers take shelter here from the snow—Harlequin proves that terrestrial Dinners are better than Lunairian ones—the Horn thaw'd,

sound some melting notes; 'IN CASE' of an emergency, how to get on your journey—by a conveyance lately discovered at the NORTH POLE.

SCENE SEVEN: *A Picturesque View of the Bay of Constantinople,* a British Man of War lying at Anchor (Pugh).

The Lovers are nearly caught, but by the power of magic, Harlequin becomes a great personage and Columbine is arrayed in state.

An Equestrian Feat, never yet performed by any Horse dead or alive.

SCENE EIGHT: *A Road near Constantinople* (Pugh).

The Magic Dial, 'Or What's O'clock. Is it Night or is it Day?'

PUBLIC NOTICE

'Holla! Holla! Holla! All Good Mussulmen
Attend—the Grand Vizier's Bridal Procession
Will pass this way at the Sixth hour—Holla! Holla! Holla!'

SCENE NINE: *The Deck of an English Man of War at Anchor* (Whitmore).
All aboard. Clown and Pantaloon very ill. Sailors full of fun, etc.

GLEE

Push the grog to your left hand man,
Cares that are dry grow quicker and quicker;
The chaplain he tells us that life is a span,
So fill to the brim and tipple the quicker
Then clinkity clinkity clink goes the can,
When each jolly sailor has tossed off his liquor!

Clown and Pantaloon are sent to Davy's Locker.

SCENE TEN: *The Bottom of the Sea* (Whitmore)

The Clown in astonishment, never saw the like upon earth—the best fish market in the world—*The Diving Bell.*

SCENE ELEVEN: *Dublin Bay, with Ships lying in the Harbour* (Whitmore)

Clown caught in his own net.—The real and only sea serpent that ever 'was' caught.

SCENE TWELVE: *A View of College Green, Dublin* (Carrol).

Irish game—The quickest way to roast a duck-Venison, with cherry-tree sauce.

SCENE THIRTEEN: *The Exhibition Room of Monsieur Chaubert,* the Fire proof Phenomenon (Hodgins).

The Professor promises to perform more than most people can

'Swallow'.—But the Clown 'performs' What the professor has long *promised*—'When the body is too hot, how to cool it'.

SCENE FOURTEEN: *View of Waterloo Place* (Phillips).

Fashionable stick and parasol shop—A New French One-Horse Carriage, duty free.

SCENE FIFTEEN: *The River Thames*, with a distant View of the Dock Yard, at Woolwich (Whitmore).

The grand expedition to Egypt—The Clown gets there 'quicker' than he intended.

SCENE SIXTEEN: *A View near Alexandria*, with Pompey's Pillar (Hollogan).

Clown very 'high' in Egypt—His 'post' is too elevated—how to get down without loss of limbs—The thing has 'BEAN'—Columbine enamours the Mameluke Chief, who carries her away from Harlequin.

SCENE SEVENTEEN: *A Subterranean Chamber of the Pyramids at Gaza* (Hollogan).

The Lovers in thraldom—To them appears their old enemy, the Deity of Blacksmiths.

VULCAN: (*to Harlequin and Columbine*)

> Here have you enter'd in a luckless hour,
> These subterraneans own their master's power!
> (*To Pantaloon and Clown*)
> Ye daring foes to Vulcan! Hence! away
> To regions never blest by light of day
> As mummies for tedious ages to stay.

The Queen of Beauty appears and interposes.

VENUS   Vulcan, forbear, now let thy anger cease,
> Come join with me in Harmony and Peace
> Thy trials past (*to Harlequin and Columbine*)
> For those who constant prove,
> By Hymen shall be crowned, 'Here at the fount of Love'.

SCENE EIGHTEEN: *And Last.* *The Fountain of Love* (Whitmore)

Hymen, Cupid, and the Graces, surrounding the Fountain of Love. The Lovers hands are joined by Hymen, and the piece concludes with the

FINALE

> Now Munchausen's travels ended,
> Venus and her joys appear.

CLOWN (*to Audience*)   By your cheering smiles befriended,
> Love his fountain fixes here.

CHORUS   Now Munchausen's etc.

(C) Examples of Modern Harlequinade.

From THE GLASS SLIPPER *by Eleanor and Herbert Farjeon. Presented by Robert Donat at the St. James's Theatre on Friday, December 23rd, 1944.*
The Harlequinade

'HARLEQUIN IN SEARCH OF HIS HEART'

HARLEQUIN	Walter Gore
COLUMBINE	Sally Gilmour
THE TENOR SINGER	Geoffrey Dunn
THE BASS SINGER	John Oliver
THE DOCTOR	Michael Holmes
THE MERCHANT	Michael Bayston
THE CAPTAIN	Rex Reid
THE THREE GRACES { Truth	Brenda Hamlyn
Love	Jean Stokes
Beauty }	Joyce Graeme

Music by Clifton Parker
Production by William Armstrong
Décor by Hugh Stevenson
Ballet and Harlequinade by The Ballet Rambert
Choreography and Ensembles by Andrée Howard
Conductors: Ernest Irving and Gideon Fagan

Harlequin whirls in. Solo dance. He pulls his heart out of his breast and plays with it.

Columbine appears. Harlequin hides his heart behind his back. They coquette, she being the wooer. He tantalises her, responding to her blandishments at moments, then running away and playing with his heart out of her reach. She pursues him and attempts to locate it. The heart suddenly spreads wings and flies away.

Harlequin stands staring up into the flies. Columbine makes love to him. He is unmoved, even, to his own perplexity, when she kisses him. Columbine weeps. During this the following is sung:

TENOR   Poor Harlequin!
Away his heart has flown!
     Poor Columbine!
Her heart must beat alone!
Alas for his despair
    And her distress!
What remedy is there
    For heartlessness?

CHORUS   Poor Columbine!
                 Poor Harlequin!
          His heart has flown away!
                 Away, away!
          His heart has flown away!
                 Poor Harlequin!

Zany appears. He comes between Harlequin and Columbine, rallies them, and then offers them advice as the following is sung:

TENOR   The Doctor, the Doctor,
                 The healer of ills,
             Compounder of powders
                 And plasters and pills
             To the Doctor depart
             To see, if the art
                 He is fam'd for exploring
                 Will succeed in restoring
             Poor Harlequin's heart.

Harlequin and Columbine take hope. Preceded by the Zany they approach the first of the three compartments. Zany pulls bell-rope. Bell tinkles. Curtains part, revealing Doctor with the elaborately fantastic and decorative impedimenta of his trade. He comes forward and mimes and dances as the following is sung:

BASS   A cure, a cure
             I can ensure
             For all the ills
             That men endure.
             I have written a thesis,
             With full exegesis,
             On all the specifics
             For all the diseases—
                 Neuralgia,
                 Nostalgia,
             Climatic sciatic otalgia,
                 Neuritis,
                 Gastritis,
             And chronic bubonic bronchitis.
             I've physic for folk who are down in the dumps,
             For corns and carbuncles and similar lumps,
             For rabies, scabies, megrims and mumps,
             The itch and the stitch and the twitch and the jumps.

Doctor examines Harlequin with stethoscope, pummelling him and turning him upside down.

> I've nostrums and potions and balsams and lotions
> For blisters that burn and for cuts that are deep.
> I've tonic emulsions for cramp and convulsions,
> Exotic narcotics to send you to sleep,
> Cataplasms for spasms and smooth embrocations
> To brace up the face and encourage the hair.
> I've simples for pimples and worse inflammations,
> But—
>   but—
>   but—
>   but—
>   but—
>   but—
>   But—

I CAN'T CURE A HEART IF THE HEART ISN'T THERE!

Doctor throws down his stethoscope in disgust. Columbine entreats. Harlequin implores. He waves them away and storms back into his compartment, leaving them more dejected than before.

To them once more the Zany with advice.

TENOR   The Merchant, the Merchant,
         The seller of wares,
      Purveyor, provider
         For all our affairs,
      To the Merchant depart
      To see if his art
         Will succeed in supplying
         What they've come to be buying,
      A suitable heart.

With renewed hope, and led by the Zany, they approach the second compartment and pull the bell. Bells jangle, Merchant, oriental, disclosed, displaying his wares.

TENOR   For gold, for gold, for gleaming gold
      All things are bought, all things are sold.
      An ivory bracelet for the lady? Note
         The curious chasing.
      This coral necklace for her pretty throat
         Is past all praising.
      These feathers are pure phoenix—feel how gentle!

These bales of silk are rather oriental.
For gold, for gold, by all men sought,
All things are sold, all things are bought.
The gentleman desires a heart? I see—
    For presentation!
These, my dear sir, I guarantee to be
    Best imitation.
(*Harlequin buys one*)
    A clever choice, sagacious and judicial,
(*Harlequin tries to manipulate it in vain.*)
    But—
            but—
                    but—
                            but—
                                    but—
                                            but—
                                                    but—
                                                            But—
            HEARTS CANNOT BEAT WHEN THEY ARE ARTIFICIAL!

*Harlequin flings the heart away in disgust. Merchant retires. Zany returns,
reflects, advises.*

TENOR   The Captain, the Captain,
            The Captain's our man!
        A heart he will steal us
            If anyone can!
        To the Captain depart
        To see if the art
            Of robbing and thieving
            Will succeed in retrieving
        Poor Harlequin's heart.

*They approach the third compartment and ring the third bell. It clanks. The
Captain is discovered, very swashbuckling and lady-killing and Spanish.
During his offer of hearts Harlequin each time is attracted but dissuaded by
Columbine's imperative objections.*

BASS   Come sir! What's your pleasure?
            Ha, ha, ha, ha, ha, ha!
        I can steal at leisure
        Any heart you treasure—
        For a moment's pleasure—
            Ha, ha, ha, ha, ha, ha!
        Hearts? They're two-a-penny—
            Ha, ha, ha, ha, ha, ha!

I have twice too many!
If you fancy any
Hearts at two-a-penny—
  Ha, ha, ha, ha, ha, ha!
(*He produces handfuls of hearts.*)
        Here's a Spanish Lady's
        That I stole in Cadiz—
I myself am done with it.
      This one is Italian,
      Lured aboard a galleon—
You might have some fun with it!
      This one is Byzantine
      (Although adamantine,
I knew how to fondle her!)—
      Both of these are Grecian,
      This one is Venetian,
Picked up in a gondola!
        Here is a tender token,
        Rather badly broken
When I took my toll of it—
        This one's started cracking,
        This one's slightly lacking
I've not quite the whole of it.
(*He grows angry.*)
        Blood and thunder! Flood and fire!
        These are not what you desire?
Lungs and lights and liver too!
None of these will do for you?
Hearts of every sort I steal,
Noble, common and genteel,
Sweet and savage and refined,
I have hearts of every kind
In my varied clientèle,
But—
        but—
              but—
                    but—
                          but—
                                but—
                                      But—

THE HEARTS I STEAL ARE NEVER MALE!

The Captain retires. Harlequin and Columbine are more dejected than ever.

CHORUS   Poor Columbine!
              Poor Harlequin!
              His heart has flown away,
                  Away, away!
              His heart has flown away!
              Poor Harlequin!

TENOR   The Graces, the Graces,
              Olympian race,
          With flowers in their faces,
              Beseech them for grace.
          To the Graces appeal,
          Pay homage and kneel,
              Invoke them, adore them,
              And devoutly implore them
          Your heart to reveal.

The Zany leads Harlequin and Columbine once more to the compartments. Each pulls a bell-rope. Tuneful peals ring out as the curtains part and the three Graces are revealed.

TENOR   Where reposeth, ladies, say,
              The errant heart that flies away?

TRIO OF VOICES All such errants come to rest
              In the place that Love knows best.

TENOR   Shall we find it, ladies, speak,
              In a year or in a week?

TRIO   Nay, the search will last as long
              As the ending of a song.

The Graces move forward and, with formal and gracious movements, conduct Harlequin to the throne of the Prince and Cinderella.

TENOR AND CHORUS Sweet Fates, begin,
              Begin your thread to spin,
                  And weave the line
                  That nets our Columbine.
              Sweet Fate, draw fine
              The web of life's design,
                  And trap within
                  The mesh our Harlequin,
              Look not below, look not above,
              O Lovers, look upon the seat of Love.

At last Harlequin is standing before the throne. The Graces indicate the Prince's doublet. Harlequin, with deprecating gestures, feels timidly inside. He

*produces his own heart still winged. Cinderella claps her hands with delight.
Columbine moves forward. Harlequin looks from her to Cinderella, suddenly
kneels, and offers Cinderella the heart. The whole Court claps its hands.
Cinderella detaches the wings from the heart and gives one to Columbine and
one to Harlequin. They caper away waving their wings, and the Court follows
them, joined by the Doctor, the Merchant, and the Captain, the train being ended
by the Zany. A picture is formed by Cinderella and the Prince with the Graces
posed at their feet. The caperers fade out till only the Zany is left. He catches
the curtains, pulls them together, grins through them at the audience, and that is—*

THE END

THE DISGUISES OF ARLECCHINO

A COMEDY BY CLIFFORD WILLIAMS
BASED UPON AN EIGHTEENTH-CENTURY SCENARIO
OF THE ITALIAN PLAYERS

Pantalone ....an old and rich widower
Arlecchino ....his servant
Clarice ....an ugly widow
Colombina ....her maid

Given by the Mime Theatre Company, May, 1953

Stage l is the house of Pantalone, stage r the house of Clarice. U.S. centre
is a large box. When the curtain rises, Pantalone is dusting books in his
house. Colombina comes along the street—laden with parcels. She drops
some of these. The noise brings Pantalone to his window. He sees and
admires Colombina. She picks up her parcels, sees Pantalone and—
with a shudder—hurries into the house of Clarice where she disappears.

Pantalone calls for Arlecchino. Colombina is seen giving her parcels to
Clarice.

Arlecchino enters well laden and drops some parcels. Clarice looks out of
her window and admires Arlecchino. He sees her as he picks up his parcels
and hurries into his master's house muttering under his breath.

Music is heard throughout this action but now ceases.

Pantalone's house

ARLECCHINO Here, sir.

PANTALONE Where've you been, scoundrel Arlecchino?

ARL. Shopping, sir, shopping. Terrible town, this. High prices and short
measures everywhere you go, sir. Now, how's the master getting
on?

PAN.   I don't like this house-moving business. I'm getting too old . . .
       need a wife for all this sorting and dusting and what-not. By the
       way, Arlecchino, have you found out who our neighbour is over
       the way? A very handsome woman by the look of her!

ARL.   Very handsome? . . . (*He looks out of the window and sees Clarice who
       is also leaning out of her window. She smiles at him, he grimaces and with-
       draws from the window.*)

ARL.   Here, your glasses need a good polish, master.

Clarice's house

CLARICE   Colombina, have you noticed our new neighbour? Such a
       beautiful young gentleman. Don't look so surprised, girl. I'm not
       too old to feel partial to . . . besides, I do need a new husband.

COLOMBINA   But surely not that . . .

CLA.   Now, now, girl. You're too young to appreciate the finer points.
       Just you come and see him, though!

Pantalone's house

PAN.   Thank you, Arlecchino. Now let's see if she's there.

ARL.   But . . . (*he is propelled to the window.*)

PAN.   Come along . . . there!

Both houses

ARL. AND COL.   Oh! (*as they see each other.*)

PAN. AND CLA.   Gorgeous! (*not referring to each other.*)

PAN.   Isn't she a beauty. . . . Who's that dreadful old harridan standing
       behind her?

ARL.   Er, . . . probably her nurse.

PAN.   Of course.

CLA.   Isn't he lovely?

COL.   Yes! (*with real conviction as she regards Arlecchino*).

CLA.   Who's the old fossil with him, do you think?

COL.   Oh! . . . Probably his tutor.

CLA.   Ah! Yes!

PAN. AND CLA. (*turning away from their windows*)   I shan't rest till I have
       him/her for my very own.

       (Arlecchino and Colombina wave to each other and then leave the
       windows. Clarice sits—overcome with emotion—and is fanned by
       Colombina.)

Pantalone's house

ARL. You really mean you're in love, sir?

PAN. Absolutely. I must marry her. Is it possible, do you think?

ARL. Why not, indeed, sir? A romantic gentleman like yourself. Of course, it'll cost a tidy bit, sir. There's five pounds for the . . . vicar.

PAN. Exquisite!!

ART. Possibly, ten pounds for a good vicar!

PAN. Superb!!

ARL. And another five for his curate . . .

PAN. Magnificent!!

ARL. Say thirty pounds for vicar and curate combined . . .

PAN. Rapturous!!

ARL. Add to that . . . fifty?

PAN. Ravishing!!

ARL. About thirty for hire of the church . . .

PAN. Divine!!

ARL. And that makes one hundred . . .

PAN. She must be my . . .

ARL. Then you can definitely spare two hundred?

PAN. Goddess!!!

ARL. Two hundred and fifty will cover everything, master.

PAN. (*giving him bags of money*) Take it, my boy, take it. I rely on you, Arlecchino.

ARL. You may indeed, sir. I shan't waste a penny.

PAN. Excellent, excellent.

(Pantalone retires from view, and Arlecchino emerges from the house muttering 'Not a penny, not a farthing shall be wasted'. He hides the money in the box U.S. centre. He pauses and speaks: 'Now for a plan.' At this moment, Clarice looks out of her window. Arlecchino rushes forward and bows to her. She drops a handkerchief out of the window. Arlecchino picks it up and enters Clarice's house. She almost swoons with pleasure, Arlecchino winks at Colombina and restores the handkerchief —gallantly placing it in Clarice's bosom. She produces a portrait and presents it to Arlecchino. He bows deeply, kisses her hand and leaves. In the street, he turns and waves to Clarice. She retires. Colombina takes her place at the window. Arlecchino motions her to wave to Pantalone who now appears at his window. She does this and retires. Pantalone calls, 'Come here, quickly, boy', and returns to his room. 'Coming, sir,' replies Arlecchino. 'I'll give him "boy".' (He looks at the portrait.) · 'Fancy living with this. Still, the frame must be worth a bit.' He pushes the portrait into the box, and enters Pantalone's house.)

16

Pantalone's house

PAN. Ah! Have you fixed everything, Arlecchino?

ARL. Yes, sir. Everything in order, sir. Got the vicar, curate, organist, choir, and church. Very smart wedding, this will be, sir, . . . if you remember to ask the lady to marry you. You'll recall she doesn't yet know your intention.

PAN. That's a point, a very tricky point. She must be told, of course.

ARL. Persuaded, if necessary?

PAN. Persuaded? How?

ARL. Flowers, sir. Armfuls of rare exotic flowers—that's the way to a lady's heart.

PAN. Hah! The garden's full of them. Pluck them, my boy, arrange them tastefully and deliver them to . . . er . . . and find out her name while you're about it.

ARL. Begging your pardon, sir, but I fancy the garden flowers are a little too modest for the occasion. Consider, master. The more expensive the gifts you give her now the less she'll require in the future, and whilst the present moment is short, the future may seem endless.

PAN. Very true, Arlecchino. Good logic! What do you suggest?

ARL. Orchids, master.

PAN. Orchids they shall be *(he gives money to Arlecchino)* Orchids!

(Pantalone retires and Arlecchino runs out of the house counting the money. He puts it in his box. He looks around and runs off stage.)

Clarice's house

(Clarice and Colombina enter.)

CLA. Now remember, Colombina, you're to fetch his servant or tutor or whatever he is so that I can question him, for I must learn his master's name . . . and intention. Now hurry, girl.

COL. Yes, ma'am.

(Colombina leaves the house and runs into Arlecchino just as he returns with a bunch of weeds.)

In the street

COL. Arlecchino!

ARL. Yes, ma'am. Oh! it's you.

COL. What on earth are you doing with those weeds?

ARL. Weeds? These are expensive orchids specially purchased by my master for you . . . that is, your mistress.

COL. Arlecchino, will you please tell me what trick you're up to now? I thought I'd seen the last of you when you fell in that canal in

Venice, but here you are again with a new master. Well, I have a
new mistress also, and I don't want to lose her through one of your
stupid pranks.

ARL. Now steady on, Colombina. My one aim is to marry and make an
honest woman of you. All I need is a little capital behind me—and
I'm well on the way to that.

(He shows the contents of his box to Colombina. They sit on the box.)

COL. Now tell me what you plan.

ARL. Well—in brief—my new master thinks that you're your new
mistress and doesn't know that your new mistress isn't you, whilst
your new mistress thinks that I am my new master. This has
possibilities.

COL. But when your new master finds out that I am not my new mistress,
we'll be undone.

ARL. Don't be vulgar, Colombina, but listen.

> If he thinks that you are she
> And she thinks that I am he
> We'll play upon their idiocy
> And ourselves form the brand new family tree.

COL. Really?

ARL. You'll see!

COL. But I've been sent to fetch thee.

ARL. Me?

COL. For she thinks you are master . . .

ARL. And he is servant . . .

COL. As he thinks I am . . .

ARL. Mistress . . . and she is . . .

COL. Maid!

(They rise and go down front.)

ARL. Now take these flowers . . . to the old girl and say they're from
Signor Pantalone whose servant follows with an important message.
I'll dress in his clothes and come as me . . . that is him . . . oh . . .
hurry . . . Hey! what's your name?

COL. What?

ARL. Her name!

COL. Oh! Madame Clarice.

ARL. Good!

(Both enter their respective houses.)

Pantalone's house

ARL.   Signor Pantalone! Where are you, good sir? (*aside*) Old idiot!
PAN.   (*entering*)   Here, Arlecchino. What news? Speak up!
ARL.   The lady's name is Clarice.
PAN.   It is . . . Clarice!
ARL.   She thanks you for the lovely flowers.
PAN.   She does . . . my lovely flowers!
ARL.   She returns your love.
PAN.   She returns . . . my love!
ARL.   She will marry you.
PAN.   She will . . . marry me!
ARL.   But she says she would first like to have some personal token from
       you.
PAN.   She would . . . A ring? A book? What?
ARL.   Er, . . . Why not your cloak, sir? Such a fine present would surely
       content her.
PAN.   My cloak? Ah! well, take it to her. (*He disrobes and shivers.*)
ARL.   Never mind, sir. You've a warm heart, eh?
PAN.   Yes, my heart . . . very w-w-warm. (*He retires.*)
ARL.   Now!

   (He puts on the cloak and covers himself carefully. He crosses the street
and is admitted to Clarice's house by Colombina.)

Clarice's house

ARL.   How do I look?
COL.   Just like him!
ARL.   Oh!
CLA.   (*entering*) Ah! Signor Pantalone's servant. What's your name, fellow?
ARL.   Arlecchino, madam.
CLA.   (*to Colombina*) What an ugly fellow he is.
COL.   O, they're a terrible family these Arlecchinos! Awful liars too . . .
       (*Arlecchino writhes*) . . . I never have anything to do with them
       myself (*Arlecchino pinches her*).
CLA.   Your message quickly, please.
ARL.   Signor Pantalone sends his most felicitous regards to the most
       inspiring apple of his eye, his peach among all the plums, a veritable
       tangerine of blushes, a grapevine of virtue. . . .
CLA.   Oh!
ARL.   (*aside*)   The old banana!
       . . . and he offers you his hand in marriage.

CLA. Supreme honour! You may kiss my hand in token of my acceptance of your master's proposal.

ARL. *(aside)* Ugh! *(He kisses her hand.)*

CLA. And now return to your master and tell him I am ready . . . I am ready for the happy ceremony.

ARL. I will, madam. But here's a snag. My master being newly arrived in town regrets that all his baggage hasn't arrived yet. He finds himself—temporarily you understand—a little short of ready money. Of course, he's very anxious to give you the best of weddings, epicurean food, vintage wines, a noble reception, you understand, but . . .!

CLA. Signor Pantalone need have no worries. I will myself attend to all these things. He has, I am sure, arranged the ceremony itself?

ARL. Yes, indeed, madam. Cost him two hundred and fifty . . . er . . . that is . . . about . . . quite a lot of money. We're to have the Cardinal himself.

CLA. The Cardinal! Wonderful. Arlecchino, I cannot wait. I must see Signor Pantalone just once—dressed in his handsome shining tunic with all those pretty colours.

ARL. You must. *(aside)* Indeed, that's not so easy.
Very well, madam, I will try and prevail upon him to show himself if you will be patient a few moments. *(exits.)*

CLA. Colombina, run swiftly and fetch the Leader of the Town Band, the Master Pastry-Cook and the Captain of the local dancing girls— those will do for now.

COL. Yes, ma'am. *(She exits.)*

Street and the two houses

ARL. *(having discarded Pantalone's cloak and made certain that Pantalone is not watching calls up to Clarice's window)* Clarice, my Clarice.

CLA. *(at window)* Pantalone, my Pantalone. Oh you grow more handsome with every minute. Thank you for sending your servant. *(Pantalone enters his room and hears Clarice's voice. He listens with pleasure.)* Everything is arranged, my dear Signor Pantalone.

PAN. *(to himself)* Oh! Good, good!

CLA. *(still to Arlecchino)* If only I could stretch out and touch your fingers . . .

PAN. How nice.

CLA. . . . and stroke your forehead . . .

PAN. Charming.

CLA. . . . and place your head upon my bosom. . . .

PAN.   Lovely.

CLA.   Soon I shall cook all your meals with my own two hands . . .

PAN.   That'll save an extra servant.

CLA.   . . . and tuck you up each night cosily in bed. . . .

PAN.   And she'll be able to do all the laundry too!

CLA.   Oh, Pantalone, come quickly, come quickly. (*She leaves the window and retires.*)

   (Pantalone sits down exhausted with pleasure whilst Arlecchino mops his brow with relief. Pantalone calls for Arlecchino, who picks up the cloak and runs to answer his master's summons.)

Pantalone's house

PAN.   Arlecchino, I heard her very voice. . . . She was talking to me from over there.

ARL.   Oh! You didn't look out too, did you?

PAN.   No, I was too transported.

ARL.   Thank goodness!

PAN.   What did you say?

ARL.   I said thank goodness all is going well, Master. Now here's your cloak which Lady Clarice returns since she's very anxious that you don't catch a chill before the wedding. You must get yourself ready, sir, for very shortly we must go to the church. And, Master, I shall need some money to pay for the banquet.

PAN.   What banquet? There's only the old Doctor who'd want to come.

ARL.   But your Lady, sir! Don't forget her brother's the Duke of this noble city. You'll have at least half the Court at the wedding.

PAN.   Expensive!

ARL.   Think of your prestige, sir. Now three hundred pounds will just cover everything.

PAN.   Three hundred pounds?

ARL.   Yes, we musn't be niggly, I agree. Say three hundred and fifty. Now quickly please, sir, there's little time left.

PAN. (*handing over the money*)   Well, here you are, but order moderately for I'm getting a little low.

ARL.   Certainly, sir. (*aside*) Not as low as me!

   (Arlecchino exits and Pantalone retires. Arlecchino puts the money in his box. Colombina leaves her house. Arlecchino intercepts her.)

The Street

ARL.   Where to now, Colombina?

COL.   She's given me orders for the banquet.

ARL. Another banquet! Colombina—we shall shortly be able to retire. Who's on the list?

COL. Firstly, I must fetch the Leader of the Town Band.

ARL. She wants him now?

COL. Yes.

ARL. Then watch, Colombina, the Venetian master of disguises. Maestro Arlecchino himself in action!

(Arlecchino fetches from his box a short cloak, hat and trumpet. He dresses and blows a short blast. Colombina hides. Clarice appears at her window.)

ARL. Madame Clarice? I have the honour to be the leader of the Town Buglers—at your service.

CLA. Signor Pantalone and I are very shortly to be married. We shall need the richest musical accompaniment you can provide. I presume your men are all excellent musicians?

ARL. All good buglers, madam.

CLA. A sample of your fanfares, please.

(Arlecchino blows one excruciating note.)

CLA. Another, sir.

(The same note is blown.)

CLA. Your range appears a trifle limited, sir, and wasn't that out of tune?

ARL. Oh! rest assured, madam, it comes from a tune all right. I daren't play more for fear of the Union—strict rules you know—so much a blast and so on.

CLA. I understand, Will this cover your charge?

(She throws a bag of money out of the window.)

ARL. Fully, madam! We'll play something most appropriate and most artistic. (*Clarice withdraws from the window.*) Probably a requiem!! Now, Colombina, what next?

COL. She wanted the Master Pastry Cook.

ARL. That can be arranged. A trifling disguise for Arlecchino. It'd be a shame to waste good food on full stomachs and so . . . (*he runs to his box, deposits the money bag and clothes and dons those of a pastrycook*) . . . Voilà Monsieur Le Pâtissier! (*He calls to Clarice's window.*)

ARL. 'Allo, 'allo. (*Clarice looks out.*) Bonjour, madame, bonjour, bon appétit, je suis le pâtissier.

CLA. Pardon. M'sr. Le . . . Le . . . ?

ARL. Pâtissier, madame, pâtissier. Je fais la cuisine, bonbons, je falsifie les gâteaux, je cuis au four les biscuïts. Prenez deux pigeons, trois concombres, quatre topinambours, cinq châtaignes, six oignons frits, sept truffes, mêlez, marchez, lève-toi, asseyez—ooh! La

France Gastronomique! Ah! La belle dame sans merci, Le tour de France, comme on voit sur la branche—oui, oui—au mois de Mai —non, non—la rose en sa belle jeunesse——

CLA. Monsieur, monsieur, I'm sure you're an excellent cook, but I didn't catch all your remarks. Now if you would——

ARL. (*repeats all above twice as fast and finishes*)——Fifty pounds!

(Clarice tosses the money out of the window, Arlecchino blows a kiss, and Clarice withdraws.)

ARL. Did she ask for anyone else, Colombina?

COL. Only the Captain of the Dancing Girls.

ARL. The Capt——La! La!

(He shrugs, doffs his present disguise, and finds a veil and other suitable articles in his box. Music is heard. Clarice looks out again. Arlecchino dances.)

ARL. (*falsetto*) You like my dance, chérie? You wan' me dance for your 'usband with my girls? We dance for twenty-five poun's. Vairry cheap.

CLA. We have in mind something more edifying . . . a pavane or chaconne. There is ten pounds for you . . . to keep away from our wedding. Goodday, madame. (*Clarice withdraws.*)

ARL. We're made, Colombina! (*he strips off the veil, etc.*). One more part to play, one more disguise and then it's our turn—ours at last. Make sure she's ready, cover her, for she musn't see him or me, and fetch her out when you hear the music.

(Colombina runs into her house whilst Arlecchino stuffs various items from the box into his pocket. He then enters his house, Pantalone and Clarice appear in their respective houses.)

Pantalone's and Clarice's houses

ARL. Now, sir, the time draws near. On with your finery, sir.

COL. Madam, cover yourself well for it won't do to show your beauty freely to every ignorant bystander.

PAN. I'm as happy as a lark. I never thought an old buffer like me would win such a lady so cheaply—comparatively.

ARL. Nor did I! (*aside*) The old crow.

CLA. Oh! Colombina, don't you envy me—soon to marry my dear Pantalone?

COL. Oh! I expect I shall end by marrying Arlecchino.

CLA. What, that disreputable, shrivelled old man! How could you?

COL. (*aside*) Well they say love is blind!

(Music is heard.)

ARL. AND COL. Come—there's our cue.

PAN. AND CLA.   It's time.

ARL. AND COL.   For love.

PAN. AND CLA.   For marriage.

   (Pantalone and Clarice start to their doors, Arlecchino and Colombina wave to each other triumphantly.)

PAN.   Arlecchino, my dear fellow, give us your arm, you know I'm not safe without some support.

ARL.   Here I am, sir.

CLA.   Don't leave me, Colombina. I can't see at all with this veil.

COL.   That's a good thing (*aside*) Here I am, madam.

   (The two pairs circle the stage and meet in the middle.)

The Street

PAN.   Where's my dear Clarice?

CLA.   That's a strange voice, Colombina. Can this be my Pantalone?

COL.   Oh! yes, madam. His voice is quivering with emotion. Come join with him . . .

PAN.   I say, Arlecchino, is there anything wrong with my Clarice? She sounds . . . er . . .

ARL.   Muffled, sir! It's the veil of modesty she wears. Come join hand with her and hold still, for the rites and offices must begin. Here comes the Cardinal.

PAN. AND CLA.   Oh! the Cardinal. (*They kneel.*)

   (Arlecchino produces a collar and hat and places these on—as much for Colombina's benefit as anyone else.)

ARL.   Dear children . . . for such you are in spite of your . . . maturity. . . . I am here to make concrete your holy vows . . . may your married life be full of kindness to each other and generosity towards your servants. Be not prodigal—except to others, and restrain your tempers in all matters. And now I place my blessing upon you and pronounce you man and wife. Benedicte, ballico Belli, Veni, Vidi, Vici. Reflect and meditate until the bell sounds when you may embrace each other in piety . . . and moderation.

PAN. AND CLA.   Thank you, Cardinal.

   (They kiss Arlecchino's hand—he retires to the back and hides with Colombina.)

PAN.   Oh! my Clarice. How fortunate I am to be married to such a beautiful creature. When I think of that ugly old servant of yours, your beauty becomes an even greater prize.

CLA.   Oh! Colombina's not as bad as that. She hasn't my looks, I admit, but she's very bright for a servant girl.

16*

PAN.   Well, I only saw her once when she stood behind you, but that was
       enough. Dressed in those dirty black clothes. Disgusting, I won't
       have her in the house a day.

CLA.   Just as you say, Pantalone, but I won't tolerate having your rascally
       servant about the place. He really is too disgraceful.

PAN.   Arlecchino's sometimes cheeky, I agree, but hardly disgraceful, and
       it's such a pleasure to see his brightly coloured tunic each day.

CLA.   Tunic? I can only recall a shabby cloak with patches all over it. It
       smelt abominably . . . in fact, I'm not at all sure I can't smell it
       now. . . .

PAN.   This is very strange. Can I possibly be decei—— (*a bell sounds*) Ah!
       (*Clarice and Pantalone throw back their hoods and veils, and turn
       delightedly to gaze at each other. They recoil in mutual horror.*)

PAN. AND CLA.   Ugh!

PAN.   Are you Clarice?

CLA.   And you Pantalone?

PAN. AND CLA.   Horrible, horrible.   Arlecchino—Colombina—villains—
       thieves. (*They rush screaming to their respective houses.*)

COL. (*emerging*)   I think it's time for us to go.

ARL.   You're right, but think of it, Colombina—all this money—
       treasure for life. At last a plan has worked, we're free, no more
       disguises for me.

COL.   You're not forgetting anything, Arlecchino, dear?

ARL.   No, I don't think so.

COL.   We're to be married, dear.

ARL.   Oh! . . . indeed . . . no, of course I haven't forgotten.

COL.   Then come quickly. . . . I'll take the money . . . you carry the box.
   (*She takes the money from the box and exits—offstage she calls—*'Come
   on, Arlecchino.')

ARL.   Me! Arlecchino! Marriage! (*He shoulders the box.*) Arlecchino the
       perfect husband. This will need the biggest disguise of them all.
       (*He exits.*)

THE END

Bibliography

The following works have been of inestimable value in the preparation of this book:

ALBERT, Maurice. *Les Théâtres de la Foire (1660–1789)*. Paris. Hachette. 1900.

ATTINGER, Gustave. *L'Esprit de la Commedia dell'Arte dans le théâtre français*. Paris. Librairie Theatrale. 1950.

BARTON, Margaret. *David Garrick*. New York. The Macmillan Co. 1949.

BASCHET, Armand. *Les Comédiens italiens à la cour de France sous Charles IX, Henri III, Henri IV, et Louis XIII*. Paris. 1882.

BEARE, W. *The Roman Stage*. London. Methuen and Co., Ltd. 1950.

BEAUMONT, C. W. *A History of Harlequin*. London. C.W. Beaumont. 1926.

BERNARDIN, N. M. *La Comédie italienne en France et les Théâtres de la Foire et du Boulevard (1570–1791)*. Paris. 1902.

BLANCHARD, E. L. *The Life and Reminiscences of E. L. Blanchard*. London. Hutchinson and Co. 1891.

BROADBENT, R. J. *A History of Pantomime*. London. Simpkin, Marshall, Hamilton, and Kent. 1902.

CAMPARDON, Emile. *Les Spectacles de la Foire* (2 vols.). Paris. Berger-Levrault. 1877.

CELLER, Ludovic. *Décors, costumes, et mise en scène au XVIIe siècle (1615–1680)*. Paris. 1869.

CIBBER, Colley. *An Apology for the Life of Mr. Colley Cibber*. London. E. P. Dutton Co. 1914.

COURVILLE, Xavier de. *Luigi Riccoboni dit Lélio*. Paris. Droz. 1943.

CRAIG, Gordon. *A Living Theatre*. Florence. 1913.

—— "The Characters of the Commedia dell'Arte." *The Mask*. January 1912.

DAVIES, Thomas. *Memoirs of the Life of David Garrick* (2 vols.). London. 1808.

DESBOULMIERS, J. A. J. *Histoire anecdotique et raisonnée du théâtre italien* (7 vols.). Paris. 1769.

DICKENS, Charles. *Memoirs of Grimaldi*. Boston. C. E. Lauriat Co. 1923.

DISHER, M. Willson. *Clowns and Pantomimes*. London. Constable and Co. 1925.

DUCHARTRE, P. L. *La Comédie italienne*. Paris. Librairie de France. 1925.

DUFF, J. Wight. *A Literary History of Rome*. London. T. Fisher Unwin. 1909.

FIORENTINO, P. A. *Comédies et comédiens*. Paris. 1867.

FOSSARD (editor). *Recueil de plusieurs fragments des premières comédies italiennes qui ont été représentées en France sous le règne de Henri III, recueil dit de Fossard*. Paris. Duchartre. 1928.

FOURNEL, V. *Curiosités théâtrales anciennes et modernes.* Paris. 1859.

GHERARDI, Evaristo. *Le Théâtre italien de Gherardi* (6 vols.). Paris. Briasson. 1741.

GUEULLETTE, Thomas-Simon. *Traduction du scénario de J. Dominique.* Paris. 1760.

GOLDONI, Carlo. *Mémoires de Goldoni.* Trans. by John Black. New York. A. A. Knopf, Inc. 1926.

GOZZI, Carlo. *Memoirs.* Trans. by J. A. Symonds. London. 1890.

HAZLITT, William. *Criticisms and Dramatic Essays of the English Stage.* London. 1851.

LAVER, James. *Drama. Its Costume and Décor.* London. Studio Publications. 1951.

LEA, K. M. *Italian Popular Comedy* (2 vols.). Oxford. Clarendon Press. 1934.

MARTINELLI, Tristano. *Compositions de rhétorique de M. Don Arlequin présentées par P. L. Duchartre.* Paris. 1928.

MIC, Constant. *La Commedia dell' Arte.* Paris. 1927.

MOLAND, Louis. *Molière et la comédie italienne.* Paris. Didier et Cie. 1867.

NICOLL, Allardyce. *Masks, Mimes, and Miracles.* New York. Harcourt, Brace and Co. 1931.

—— *The Development of the Theatre.* New York. Harcourt, Brace and Co. 1937.

PLANCHE, J. R. *Recollections and Reflections.* London. 1901.

REMY, Tristan. *Les Clowns.* Paris. 1945.

RICCOBONI, Luigi. *Histoire du theâtre italien depuis la décadence de la comédie latine.* Paris. Delormel. 1728.

—— *De la Réformation du théâtre.* Paris. 1743.

—— *Le nouveau theâtre italien* (8 vols.). Paris. Briasson. 1733.

—— *Parodies du nouveau theâtre italien* (3 vols.). Ed. by Riccoboni. Paris. 1731.

ROUSSEAU, G. le. *A Chacoon for a Harlequin. With all the Postures, Attitudes, Motions of the Head and Arms and other Gestures proper to the Character.* London. 1730.

SAND, Maurice. *Masques et Bouffons* (2 vols.). Paris. 1860.

SITWELL, Sacheverell. *The Hunters and the Hunted.* New York. The Macmillan Co. 1948.

SPEAIGHT, George. *Juvenile Drama.* London. MacDonald and Co., Ltd. 1950.

STIRLING, Edward. *Old Drury Lane* (2 vols.). London. 1881.

TAYLOR, H. C. Chatfield. *Goldoni, A Biography.* London. 1914.

WEAVER, John. *A History of Mimes and Pantomimes.* London. 1728.

WILSON, A. E. *King Panto.* New York. E. P. Dutton Co. 1935.

—— *Christmas Pantomime.* London. George Allen and Unwin. 1934.

—— *The Story of Pantomime.* London. Home and Van Thal. 1949.

Index